QUEEN VICTORIA
AND
THE EUROPEAN EMPIRES

JOHN VAN DER KISTE

FONTHILL

Fonthill Media Language Policy

Fonthill Media publishes in the international English language market. One language edition is published worldwide. As there are minor differences in spelling and presentation, especially with regard to American English and British English, a policy is necessary to define which form of English to use. The Fonthill Policy is to use the form of English native to the author. John Van der Kiste was born and educated in England; therefore British English has been adopted in this publication.

Fonthill Media LTD.
Fonthill Media LLC
www.fonthill.media
books@fonthill.media

First published in hardback in the United Kingdom
and the United States of America 2016

This paperback edition published 2020

British Library Cataloguing in Publication Data:
A catalogue record for this book is available from the British Library

ISBN 978-1-78155-550-7 (hardback)
ISBN 978-1-78155-833-1 (paperback)

Typeset in 10.5pt on 13pt Sabon
Printed and bound in England

Foreword

Queen Victoria's various family and personal connections with the four empires—France, Germany, Austria, and Russia—and their emperors are the theme of this book. In the case of the German Empire, which did not exist until 1871, and in view of her close involvement with the Prussian royal family, who were elevated to imperial status at that date, I have chosen to trace her involvement from her earliest Prussian involvement in the 1840s onwards. The betrothal of her eldest daughter Victoria, Princess Royal, to the nephew of the King of Prussia in 1855 would ensure that, for most of her reign, the Anglo-German relationship was central to the family of the sovereign who was known as the 'Grandmother of Europe' by the time of her death. The marriage of a son to the daughter of one Tsar, and of a granddaughter to another, resulted in an affinity with imperial Russia. Though there would only be the loosest of family ties with the Habsburgs in Austria under Emperor Francis Joseph, and none with the Bonapartes in France under Emperor Napoleon III, the Queen's associations with both—though much closer in the case of the French rather than the Austrian—would also have some bearing on the British and European imperial network, such as it was.

I would like to acknowledge the hard work by my editor Joshua Greenland and, as ever, to my wife, Kim, for her support throughout and assistance with reading the proofs.

Prologue

On 8 February 1876, in her speech from the throne at the opening of the new session of parliament, Queen Victoria declared that at the time the direct government of the Indian Empire had been transferred to the crown, no formal addition was made to the title and styles of the British sovereign. That omission was about to be rectified, and a bill would shortly be presented.[1]

India had been under crown control since 1858, when the crown took over the government of the sub-continent from the old East India Company. Within a year or so, Benjamin Disraeli, at that time Chancellor of the Exchequer, was suggesting to her that she ought to associate her own name with that of her Indian subjects and modify her title accordingly. In elevating the British sovereign from Queen to Empress, he saw the significance of a gesture to link the monarchy with the empire further and bind India more closely to her mother country. It took some sixteen years for the idea to come to fruition. In January 1873, she explained to Sir Henry Ponsonby (her private secretary) that she was an Empress, and in normal conversation she was sometimes referred to as Empress of India: 'Why have I never officially assumed this title? I feel I ought to do so & wish to have preliminary enquiries made.'[2]

An enabling Royal Titles Bill was laid before parliament on 17 February by Disraeli, now Prime Minister, and it passed two months later, enabling Queen Victoria to assume the title Empress of India as of 1 May. A week earlier, she had noted in her journal that Disraeli stated the following:

[It is] not to be used in writs and other legal matters in England, or in ordinary transactions, but would be for commissions in the Army, as officers served in India as well as in England, also in all foreign treaties and communications with foreign Sovereigns. In these cases I should have to sign 'Victoria R. & I.'[3]

Family reasons had also helped to precipitate the move. In January 1871, her son-in-law, Crown Prince Frederick William of Prussia, who was married to her eldest daughter Victoria, had become an emperor-in-waiting with the proclamation of the German Empire, following Germany's victory over France in the Franco-Prussian War. Much as the Queen loved them both and was pleased for them, it rankled a little that one day her son-in-law would be an Emperor and her daughter an Empress while she would only be Queen, and it was perhaps inevitable that jealousy would colour her feelings to a degree. Although she kept her feelings to herself for much of the time, she confided in her granddaughter, Princess Victoria of Hesse and the Rhine, that they were 'not pleasant in Germany' and were too 'high and mighty there'.[4] The twenty-year-old princess, who was to become Princess Louis of Battenberg the following year, was one of her favourite granddaughters, a level-headed young woman whose discretion could be trusted.

Benjamin Disraeli had initially held the office of Prime Minister from February to December 1868, and again from February 1874 until April 1880. Soon after the beginning of his second term of office, the Queen's wish for 'preliminary enquiries' into an imperial title was granted. An astute judge of human nature, he was well aware as to why she placed such importance on the issue. His Foreign Secretary, Lord Derby, noted in his diary, in January 1876, that Disraeli had told him of the Queen's urgent desire to be declared Empress of Great Britain, Ireland, and India: 'The reason for it is that her daughter will have imperial rank, and she cannot bear to be in a lower position'.[5] Encouragement for an entirely different reason came from her cousin George, Duke of Cambridge, Commander-in-Chief of the Army, who warned her that Britain would soon be fighting Russia for mastery of the east. A British call of 'Hands off India' would carry considerably more weight if she too was able to declare an imperial title.[6]

The new imperial style was not a move that pleased the Queen's eldest son and heir, Albert Edward, Prince of Wales. By coincidence, he was in India at the time. He was annoyed that nobody thought fit to notify him personally, so that he knew nothing of his mother's new title until he read about it in the newspapers while travelling back to Europe. After making his irritation plain to Disraeli, the latter tried to mollify him by suggesting that he might also receive an addition to his titles. Assuming that there was an intention to give him the new designation of 'Imperial Highness', he immediately answered with a firm refusal of 'his consent to any change in his title', requesting that no such proposal should be made.[7] He was, however, eventually reconciled to the idea, and on his accession twenty-five years later he automatically assumed the title of Emperor of India, as did his son and two eldest grandsons when they later became king.

The result was that there were now four imperial heads of state in Europe, namely Queen (and Empress) Victoria; the German Emperor William; Emperor Francis Joseph of Austria; and Tsar Alexander II of Russia. Napoleon III had been emperor in France for almost twenty years, a reign cut short by his defeat in the Franco-Prussian War and the subsequent fall of the French Empire. Almost every other country in Europe was a kingdom, but Queen Victoria could not but feel pride in being able to join her fellow monarchs who were entitled to sign themselves 'R. & I.' If she had ever felt a slight sense of inferiority as a queen in welcoming emperors and empresses to England, she need do so for no longer.

Ironically, she only paid a state visit to one of these four empires during her long reign, and that was to the one with which she had no family connections—the Second French Empire, where she and Prince Albert were received in state in 1855. Twice she went to Berlin, in 1858 (while it was still the pre-imperial capital of the kingdom of Prussia) and in 1888, but on both occasions they were purely family visits to see her eldest daughter and son-in-law. After the death of Prince Albert in 1861, state visits would be a thing of the past for her. Although she continued to travel throughout Europe at intervals, her most regular destination, mostly in her later years, was the Riviera, where she often went on holiday in the spring. She never set foot inside the Austro-Hungarian Empire and only saw Emperor Francis Joseph briefly on four occasions, twice in Germany and twice in the south of France. Likewise, she never went as far afield as Russia. The two meetings she had with Tsar Alexander II, one before his accession to the throne and one after, both took place on English soil, as did her sole encounter with his son the Tsarevich, later Alexander III, on the only visit he ever made to England. Her closest imperial links were with the French sovereigns Emperor Napoleon and Empress Eugénie, both of whom became good friends despite her initial reservations about the former, and with the three German emperors, the second being her son-in-law and the third her eldest grandson.

Europe always would mark the farthest boundaries of her journeys overseas, her main reason being that she did not trust the sea. Suggestions that she should cross the Atlantic and see something of the United States of America were turned down on the grounds of age, while any thoughts of going to Australia were allegedly limited to threats to emigrate there if rude comments about her in the newspapers of 1870 did not cease. She briefly considered an expedition to India in the autumn of 1888, as she had planned to accompany her grandchildren, the small son and daughters of the Duke and Duchess of Connaught, when they went to be reunited with their parents, the Duke being on military service there at the time. Other family considerations put paid to the plan. Her eldest daughter, the recently widowed Empress Frederick, was coming to Windsor for a sorely needed respite from her unhappy life in Germany, and the Queen could not disappoint her.[8]

Being a constitutional monarch, her involvement with the political affairs of these empires was very slight. As Walter Bagehot wrote in *The English Constitution*, published in 1867, the sovereign had 'under a constitutional monarchy such as ours, three rights—the right to be consulted, the right to encourage, the right to warn'. Where the interests of England clashed with those of any of the European empires, she would on occasion do all three, with some firmness, sometimes wishing she could go further. 'Oh, if the Queen were a man, she would like to go & give those horrid Russians, whose word one cannot trust, such a beating!' she lamented to Disraeli at the time of the Russo-Turkish war in 1877.[9] For family and sentimental reasons, she might look more favourably on the German Empire than that of France or Austria, but she would rarely be well-disposed towards that of Russia. Not being an absolute monarch, her role was that of a queen who wished to be on good terms with other powers as far as was reasonably possible.

Contents

1

'The Wonderful Proceedings at Paris'

From the moment that Princess Alexandrina Victoria of Kent succeeded her uncle, King William IV, on the British throne in June 1837, taking the title Queen Victoria, it was inevitable that her personal relations with fellow monarchs in Europe would be close. Her uncle Leopold, who had been a parent to her in all but name since the loss of her real father Edward, Duke of Kent, when she was aged eight months, had been chosen as king of the newly independent Belgium in 1831. Having been a widower since 1817, with the unexpected death (through childbirth) of his first wife, Princess Charlotte, daughter of the English Prince Regent and future King George IV (otherwise he might himself have been Prince Consort to Queen Charlotte of Great Britain instead), he married Princess Louise-Marie of Orléans in 1832, eldest daughter of King Louis-Philippe, King of the French. A close link was thus immediately established between the three kingdoms.

Queen Victoria's first close encounter with imperial Europe would come two years later. In May 1839, a few days after her twentieth birthday, Grand Duke Alexander, Tsarevich of Russia, came to Windsor on a courtesy visit. As part of his preparation for the throne of the Romanovs to which he would succeed some fifteen years later, the twenty-one-year-old heir had undertaken a programme of visiting other European countries, which would give him some degree of experience of other courts as a monarch-in-waiting, and also further Russia's intentions of establishing friendly relations with the great powers. He and the Queen were distantly related, for her paternal grandmother, Queen Charlotte, consort of King George III, was an aunt of Queen Louise of Prussia, the Tsarevich's grandmother. There was an even closer Russian connection in that Tsar Alexander I, who was an ally of Britain in the war against Napoleon Bonaparte, had been one of her godparents, hence her first name Alexandrina. They got on very well together and particularly enjoyed horse rides in Windsor Great Park together every morning. At a state ball at Buckingham Palace, given in his honour on 27 May, she danced a number of quadrilles, but no waltzes as, because of their high station, neither were permitted to waltz with anybody else. Instead, she also danced a turn in a mazurka with him, and much to her excitement he whisked her round the floor.

In her journal she noted that she felt that she loved 'this amiable and dear young man, who [had] such a sweet smile'. Two days later, when he left Windsor and came to say goodbye to her, he told her how deeply grateful he was 'for all the kindness he met with, that he hoped to return again, and that he trusted that all this would only tend to strengthen the ties of friendship between England and Russia'. The two shook hands and kissed each other on the cheek. Victoria later wrote:

> I really felt more as if I was taking leave of a relation than of a stranger, I felt so sad to take leave of this dear amiable young man, whom I really think (talking jokingly) I was a little in love with, and certainly attached to; he is so frank, so really young and merry, has such a nice open countenance with a sweet smile, and such a manly fine figure and appearance.[1]

Before his arrival, she had admitted to Prime Minister Lord Melbourne that she had disliked the idea of the Grand Duke's coming to England. Now that he was leaving, she was sorry to see the last of him. The young, outgoing spinster Queen, who had had such a lonely childhood, largely starved of companionship with others of her own age, was making up for lost time. Many a good-looking young prince or grand duke was ready to set her pulse racing, particularly at a state ball, even though there could be no question of a romantic attachment between the Queen of England and the next Tsar of Russia. The Tsarevich had told his *aide-de-camp*, Colonel Simon Yurievich, that he felt he was in love with the young Queen and convinced that the feeling was mutual. Anxious to find out whether there was any evidence of this from a third party, Yurievich spoke to Baroness Lehzen, the Queen's former governess and confidante, who admitted that she had already spoken of her similar feelings for Alexander. It was rumoured that when Tsar Nicholas was informed of what he had little doubt was a temporary infatuation on both sides, he ordered his son to return home at once and that when he arrived back he told him that such a marriage would be impossible. If Grand Duke Alexander really appeared serious about becoming a British prince consort, his father would have spared no effort to talk him out of it, and, if he was bold enough to persist, he would have to renounce his place in the Russian succession. It all came to nothing, for the dutiful young man was well aware that his status as the Tsar's eldest son meant his destiny was sealed and he would never be able to consider marrying the Queen of a foreign country. An innocent little flirtation was permissible, but both parties would have to accept that it could never be anything more than that.

Queen Victoria had no problem in treating it as one of life's experiences to be enjoyed and then put to one side. Nevertheless, King Leopold shared the view of her ministers that it was time the twenty-year-old sovereign settled down with a suitable husband. In October 1839, partly at his behest, her Coburg cousins Princes Ernest and Albert were also invited to come and stay with her at Windsor. Within a few days, she and Albert fell deeply in love and became betrothed. On 10 February 1840 they were married, and the first of their nine children was born on 21 November that year. Victoria, Princess Royal, would one day follow in her mother's footsteps in becoming an Empress Victoria.

When Queen Victoria and Prince Albert visited the French royal family in the summer of 1843 and stayed with them at Chateau d'Eu, it was the first time that an English monarch had been to France since the meeting of King Henry VIII and King Francis I on the Field of the Cloth of Gold over three centuries earlier. Accompanied by Foreign Secretary Lord Aberdeen, they sailed on the royal yacht *Victoria and Albert*, with her cousin Lord Adolphus FitzClarence, one of the sons of King William IV, as captain. The visit lasted five days, from 2 to 7 September, and, although it was regarded largely as a private affair, it had been encouraged by the Prime Minister, Sir Robert Peel, in the interest of good relations between England and France. Business was mixed with pleasure, with the Queen and her husband attending two *fêtes champêtres* or garden parties and a military review, while Aberdeen and the French Minister of Foreign Affairs, François Guizot, took the opportunity to discuss affairs of state.

This encounter was widely reported in the European press of some significance as a friendly meeting between two monarchs of great powers that had been at war less than thirty years previously. Among those who regarded it with suspicion was Tsar Nicholas I of Russia. He had good reason for wishing to detach England from any alliance with the French, whose excellent relations with Egypt and Turkey did not correspond with his own designs on the area. Russian diplomats were equally keen to establish closer ties with England. In January 1844, Baron Bloomfield, British ambassador at St Petersburg, was present at a ball at the Winter Palace, St Petersburg. During a conversation with the Tsar, the latter referred warmly to the four months he had spent in England during the Regency era, adding that he was keen to return and make the acquaintance of Her Majesty The Queen this time. Coincidentally, at around the same time Count Philip Brunnow, Russian ambassador to the Court of St James, dined in London with Sir Robert Peel and Lord Aberdeen. During the course of the conversation, Peel remarked that he hoped the Tsar would be able to visit England before long.

On 24 May, four months later, the Russian Chancellor and Minister for Foreign Affairs, Count Karl Nesselrode, informed Bloomfield that His Imperial Majesty had left St Petersburg about twelve hours earlier and was on his way to London. Bloomfield was apparently taken aback, but it was evident that the visit had been carefully planned during the previous few weeks. Nevertheless, Queen Victoria and Prince Albert were seemingly 'somewhat taken by surprise' on 30 May, when informed that he was about to join them. King Frederick Augustus II of Saxony was already expected, and he arrived at Buckingham Palace on 1 June.

Tsar Nicholas arrived that same night and went to stay at Ashburnham House, the central London residence of Count Brunnow. The following day, he was conducted to Buckingham Palace by Prince Albert and officially received by Queen Victoria. After he had dined at the palace, he returned to Ashburnham, as he had chosen not to spend the night in the palace apartments that had been prepared for him. On 3 June, he was met at Slough station by Prince Albert and taken to Windsor Castle. Maybe he found the latter more to his liking than the palace, for he stayed for five days. It was, however, recorded that his first action on arriving at Windsor was to send to the stables for a bundle of straw on which to sleep that night. Moreover, he complained to the Queen of the custom of the court in not wearing uniform as, when he had to wear a frock coat, 'he felt as if he had lost a skin'.[2] Despite this, he was unfailingly gracious throughout his visit. When he went out for drives with the Queen, she seemed to be amused by his habit of ogling the more attractive ladies.

The Tsar was willing to admit that his object in visiting England was mainly political rather than personal. As he told the Queen, it was as well 'to see now and then with one's own eyes, as it did not always do to trust diplomatists only'. Face-to-face meetings were essential, he considered; they helped to create a feeling of friendship and interest, and 'more could be done in a single conversation to explain one's feelings, views, and motives than in a host of messages or letters'.[3]

While the Tsar avoided discussing political matters on the position of affairs in Europe with the Queen, he took regular opportunities of broaching such subjects with Peel, Aberdeen, the Duke of Wellington (at that time leader of the House of Lords), and Prince Albert. He seemed anxious to produce a good impression on the English statesmen, stating: 'I esteem England highly; but as to what the French say of me, I care not. I spit upon it'.[4] Nevertheless, his enthusiasm had to be restrained on occasion.

During a conversation with Peel, the Tsar was speaking so loudly that everybody outside could hear—it was a hot summer, so the windows of Peel's London house were wide open. The Prime Minister was obliged to tactfully ask him if he would come to the end of the room so that their discussions might remain private.

The Tsar was evidently unable to conceal his apprehension of the growing close relationship between England and France and the obvious friendship of their sovereigns. This, he knew, would affect most seriously any designs that he and his ministers might have for enlarging Russian territory at Turkish expense. For him to detach England from such an alliance would suit his purpose well. He was convinced that Turkey had fallen into a moribund state and would be unable to defend her borders, a fixed idea that would in time prove his undoing. With hindsight, there was a suspicion that he had come to England partly in the hope of securing the agreement of the government in some scheme of preconcerted action to meet the event of any catastrophe occurring in Turkey, and he may have convinced himself that England and France would never take their alliance to the point where they would thwart Russia's territorial ambitions. Some years later, Lord Malmesbury, a Conservative MP at the time and subsequently Foreign Secretary, alleged that during this visit a secret memorandum (recognising the Russian protectorate of the Greek Christians living in Turkey) was drawn up by the Tsar and signed by Peel, Wellington, and Aberdeen. This remained unsubstantiated, but it cannot be doubted that the matter was indeed on the Tsar's agenda. It is also probable at least that there was some agreement, perhaps verbal if not in writing, that, if the Turkish Empire was to cease to exist, he expected England and Russia to act together.[5]

While he scrupulously avoided any discussion with the Queen on political affairs in Europe, he took several opportunities of doing so with Peel, Aberdeen, and Prince Albert. He seemed uneasy about Anglo-French relations, which to him could be an impediment towards possibly enlarging Russian territory at the expense of Turkey, but Peel made it plain that England had no intention of altering her policy towards either territory.

After two visits to Ascot races with the Queen, the Prince, and the King of Saxony, and an evening at the opera, the Tsar left England on 9 June, with Prince Albert accompanying him as far as Woolwich. Two days later, the Queen reported back to King Leopold on what a success it had all been. She assured him that 'it was impossible to be better bred or more respectful than he was towards [her]'. She later wrote:

[Before he arrived] I was extremely against the visit, fearing the gene and bustle, and even at first, I did not feel at all to like it, but by living in the same house together quietly and unrestrainedly (and this Albert, and with great truth, says is the great advantage of these visits, that I not only see these great people but know them), I got to know the Emperor and he to know me. There is much about him which I cannot help liking, and I think his character is one which should be understood, and looked upon for once as it is.

She did not think him at all clever, thought his mind 'an uncivilised one', and that political and military concerns were the only things he seemed to take an interest in. However, 'he asked for nothing whatever, has merely expressed his great anxiety to be upon the best terms with us, but not to the exclusion of others, only let things remain as they are...'[6]

As usual, King Leopold received a full report from his niece on the visit containing her impressions of their fellow sovereign immediately afterwards. She said that it was 'a great event and a great compliment', and that everybody was very flattered at his being among them.

He is certainly a very striking man; still very handsome; his profile is beautiful, and his manners most dignified and graceful; extremely civil—quite alarmingly so, as he is so full of attentions and politesses. But the expression of the eyes is formidable, and unlike anything I ever saw before. He gives me and Albert the impression of a man who is not happy, and on whom the weight of his immense power and position weighs heavily and painfully; he seldom smiles, and when he does the expression is not a happy one. He is very easy to get on with. Really, it seems like a dream when I think that we breakfast and walk out with this greatest of all earthly Potentates...[7]

While she was aware that the news of this meeting might not be well received on the other side of the English Channel, she was confident that her relationship with King Louis-Philippe and his family was strong enough for them to understand. If the French really were annoyed with the idea of the Tsar being received in England, she said to 'let their dear King and their Princes come; they will be sure of a truly affectionate reception on our part'.[8]

As Queen Victoria and her contemporary sovereigns throughout Europe readily appreciated, it was as well for each to be on the best of terms with the other. Moreover, it was inevitable that there would always be a close relationship between her, Prince Albert, their ancestral home, and the various rulers in Germany and their families. The ruling British dynasty had been German ever since George Louis, Elector of Hanover and the closest living Protestant relative of Queen Anne, the last monarch of the house of Stuart, had succeeded to the throne as George I in 1714. Every British monarch since then had married a German princess, and six of Queen Victoria's nine children would likewise marry German husbands or wives.

In September 1846, Princess Augusta of Prussia, wife of Prince William, heir to his childless brother King Frederick William IV, came to stay at Windsor for a week. The Queen was most favourably impressed with her guest, a cultured and forward-looking woman who, in personality and interests, was greatly at odds with her military, philistine, narrow-minded husband and his family in Berlin.

After Augusta had returned to Berlin, the Queen wrote sympathetically to King Leopold that she had found her 'so clever, so amiable, so well informed, and so good; she seems to have some enemies, for there are whispers of her being false, but from all that I have seen of her—from her discretion, her friendship through thick and thin ... I cannot and will not believe it'. Her position, she continued, was a very difficult one:

> [She is] too enlightened and liberal for the Prussian Court not to have enemies; but I believe that she is a friend to us and to our family, and I do believe that I have a friend in her, who may be useful to us.[9]

Within less than a decade, a betrothal would have united the families of both women. Moreover, just twenty-five years later, the affinity would be between not merely the British and Prussian kingdoms, but between Britain and the new German Empire. The Queen and Prince Albert may have foreseen and, in a way, helped to pave the way for the birth of the young imperial power on the European mainland, although the outcome would not be quite as they had envisaged.

Within less than eighteen months, the tidal wave of what would be known to posterity as the year of revolutions began to roll across much of Europe. In February 1848, King Louis-Philippe, his early popularity tarnished by a severe economic crisis and subsequent unrest, abdicated in favour of his grandson Philippe, Comte de Paris. The National Assembly of France was prepared to accept him, but public opinion demanded otherwise, the monarchy was abolished and the Second Republic was proclaimed. Queen Victoria was appalled by the plight of the king and queen and their family, 'who are indeed most dreadfully to be pitied'. As a constitutional monarch, she recognized her limitations with regard to the state of their European neighbour. To King Leopold, she wrote:

> [You will] naturally understand that we cannot make cause commune with them and cannot take a hostile position opposite to the new state

of things in France; we leave them alone, but if a Government which has the approbation of the country be formed, we shall feel it necessary to recognise it, in order to pin them down to maintain peace and the existing Treaties, which is of great importance. It will not be pleasant for us to do this, but the public good and the peace of Europe go before one's feelings.[10]

King Louis-Philippe, clean-shaven, disguised in goggles and a cap, was smuggled across the Channel to England under the incognito of Mr Smith. He was later joined by Queen Marie-Amèlie, with their children and grandchildren, and they lived at Claremont, Surrey, where he died in August 1850. Meanwhile, a republic was proclaimed in France and Prince Louis Napoleon Bonaparte, nephew of Britain's (and much of Europe's) old adversary Napoleon Bonaparte, submitted his name as a presidential candidate. It seemed likely that he would be elected, partly on the strength of his name alone. Queen Victoria's Prime Minister, Lord John Russell, thought that he might turn out to be another Richard Cromwell-like character, who by his weakness would make a restoration of the French monarchy easier. She looked forward to his election, as did King Louis-Philippe, as they were sure that such a result would follow.

In December 1848, Napoleon was elected with over 74 per cent of the popular vote. Although she had been expecting it, she still considered it 'an extraordinary event, but valuable as a universal condemnation of the Republic since February. It will, however, perhaps be more difficult to get rid of him again than one at first may imagine'.[11]

The revolutionary tide had also reached Austria, at that time the only empire in central Europe. In the Hofburg Palace, the much-liked, but intellectually disabled and epileptic Emperor Ferdinand was asked to abdicate and his unambitious younger brother Archduke Francis Charles had no inclination to succeed to the throne. He renounced his place in the succession in favour of his eldest son, Archduke Francis, a youth of eighteen untainted by association with the events of recent months and who could thus serve as the symbol of a new era in the history of the Austrian empire. Adding the name of Joseph, after Joseph II, 'the reforming Emperor', to his own name, he was proclaimed Emperor Francis Joseph on 2 December 1848.

The Habsburgs, being Catholics, had no direct family ties with Queen Victoria and her family, although a daughter and a granddaughter of King Leopold would later marry the Emperor's brother and son respectively. However, the Queen and Prince Albert considered themselves broadly pro-Austrian. Albert's cousin Count Alexander von Mensdorff, a son of the elder sister of the late Duke Ernest of Saxe-Coburg Gotha, lived in

Vienna and both men enjoyed a lively correspondence for several years. Much as the Queen and her husband might deprecate the cruelty of the autocratic Austrian ruler—in theory Emperor Ferdinand, but in practice his Chancellor, Prince Clemens von Metternich—they were sympathetic to and broadly supportive of the monarchs of Habsburg dynasty as fellow sovereigns. They were alarmed by the Italians' quest for self-determination, which they were aware could result in the end of several central European thrones whose royal occupants were fully entitled to their support. In some case, this went beyond mere solidarity between hereditary heads of state, for in the German confederation and indeed throughout much of Europe there were few kings or grand dukes who were not related to Queen Victoria or Prince Albert, albeit distantly, by ties of blood or marriage.

Foreign Minister Henry John Temple, Viscount Palmerston, had in fact been one of the first statesmen in Europe to suggest that the Austrian succession should bypass the unenthusiastic Archduke Francis Charles in favour of his son. Nevertheless, his admiration for the Habsburgs and desire for a strong, united Austrian empire did not preclude his partisanship of the Italian rebels, who were intent on driving the Austrians out of the kingdom of Lombardy and Venetia—a constituent land of the Austrian empire that had been created in 1815 at the Congress of Vienna, with a population that yearned to become part of a greater, stronger Italy.

Palmerston strongly deprecated the role of Field Marshal Joseph Radetzky, whose army was engaged in bringing them to heel under the Austrian yoke, and was allegedly responsible for destroying the village of Castelnuovo with considerable loss of civilian life. In May, he drafted a despatch to Viscount Ponsonby, British ambassador at Vienna, severely censuring such action. The Queen persuaded him to withhold his message, but his unashamed self-defence made it plain that he would not be dissuaded from speaking his mind in future. When the Italians won a series of victories, Palmerston wrote to King Leopold to tell him that he could not but welcome the expulsion of the Austrians from Italy. He spoke too soon, for in July Radetzky won a decisive victory against the Sardinian army at the battle of Custozza and King Charles Albert of Sardinia had to agree to an armistice.

Later that year, Radetzky issued a proclamation declaring his government's intention to punish the ringleaders of the rebels in Lombardy and Venetia. Palmerston wrote to Ponsonby, asking him to urge the Austrian government to show clemency. Some two weeks later, by which time Francis Joseph had become Emperor, Felix von Schwarzenberg, the new Austrian Chancellor and Foreign Minister, took exception to Palmerston's missive. He announced that, contrary to the usual protocol, no Austrian archduke would be sent to the Court of St James to announce the accession of the new sovereign, as he was not prepared to expose a prince to contact 'with the devoted protector of the Emperor's rebellious subjects'. Although Queen Victoria and Prince Albert were annoyed with Palmerston's actions, they felt slighted by the pointed omission of an Austrian representative at such a time. All Prince Albert could do was ask King Leopold to express his and the Queen's respects to the court at Vienna and their annoyance at the actions of their 'heartless, obstinate and revengeful' minister. To him and to Queen Victoria, good relations with the young Emperor and his government were essential for the stability and peaceful co-existence of Europe.

As a protégé of King Leopold and Baron Christian Stockmar (the physician who became an unofficial mentor to the family), Prince Albert had been brought up to believe in a future for Prussian supremacy as the leader of a liberal German Empire. In this he was encouraged, if not aided partly by the liberal leanings of two of the Prussian royal family. The Hohenzollern dynasty had been noted largely for its military leanings in producing a succession of soldier kings, and the philistine Prince William, brother of the childless King Frederick William IV, was no exception. His wife, Princess Augusta, who came from the more liberal, enlightened court of Saxe-Weimar-Eisenach, was his exact opposite in temperament, personality, and interests. The elder child of this ill-matched and unhappily married couple, Prince Frederick William, had taken more in his political leanings after his mother.

All three, and the younger child, Princess Louise, were invited to London in 1851 to see the Great Exhibition in the Crystal Palace at Hyde Park, which opened on 1 May. This had been staged partly on the initiative of Prince Albert and, in spite of negative predictions from some quarters, it proved a great success for all involved. Prince Frederick William 'Fritz', then aged nineteen, had been particularly struck by the personality of the ten-year-old Princess Royal 'Vicky' as she escorted him around the different exhibits. An intelligent, even precocious little girl, she was very much her father's daughter with a thirst for knowledge and an ability to absorb information on a wide variety of subjects and interests.

The exhibition provided an opportunity not only for the first tentative step towards an Anglo-Prussian connection, but also for the first exchange of correspondence between Queen Victoria and Emperor Francis Joseph. Although the Austrian Empire did not send any representatives to London for the occasion, the Viennese Court, in the name of the young ruler, sent several exhibits, including a magnificent oak cabinet of intricate Gothic design. It was intended partly as a personal gift to the sovereign, and after the close of the exhibition in October it was installed in one of Prince Albert's workrooms at Buckingham Palace where it remained for many years, until presented by the Prince's grandson King George V to the University of Edinburgh many years later. In thanking the Emperor for this gift, Queen Victoria wrote that she hoped this expression of sincere friendship would 'one day be cemented by the personal acquaintance of [His] Majesty'.[12] Such a meeting would, however, not take place for another eleven years, while Prince Albert and the Emperor were never destined to come face to face.

Ironically, there was shortly to be another moment of tension that threatened to disturb good Anglo-Austrian relations later that year. In October 1851, a group of Hungarian and Polish refugees, led by Lajos Kossuth, came to England *en route* for America to express their thanks in person to Lord Palmerston for his moral support in their struggle against the Austrian and Russian governments during the uprising of 1848–9. On his arrival at Southampton, Kossuth was greeted with a reception and banquet by the mayor and corporation of the city, and a crowd of several thousand turned out to cheer him. In a series of public speeches in England, he bitterly denounced the absolutist governments of both empires.

Queen Victoria railed angrily against the 'stupid Kossuth fever', and her ministers were alarmed when *The Morning Post* officially announced the Hungarian patriot's intention of calling on Palmerston in order to express his thanks for the moral support he had given to refugees in Turkey. When Lord John Russell protested, Palmerston answered stoutly that he would not be dictated to as to whom he saw in his own house. After the Queen threatened to dismiss him from his post if he persisted, he capitulated. However, he got his own back later that week by receiving a deputation from the boroughs of Islington and Finsbury, congratulating him on his support for Kossuth in saving the oppressed Poles and Hungarians from the Austrian and Russian Emperors, who were denounced as 'odious and detestable assassins'. It had been a private meeting and, in Palmerston's speech of thanks, he made it clear that he could not be expected to endorse the language they had used about the Emperor and the Tsar. Even so, a reporter was present and a summary of what he had said appeared in the press. Once again, such annoyances did not augur well for relations between Queen Victoria and Emperor Francis Joseph.

In France, Louis Napoleon Bonaparte was prevented by the constitution and parliament from running for a second term as president. In December 1851, he seized power in a *coup d'état* and declared himself as holder of the office for life. 'I must write a line to ask what you say to the wonderful proceedings at Paris, which really seem like a *story* in a book or a play!' wrote Queen Victoria. 'What is to be the result of it all?'[13] 'Wonderful' was not always a word of praise in the Queen's vocabulary.

Although Prince Louis Napoleon was a colourful and somewhat unpredictable character, renowned for his ambition and deviousness, very few people had expected such an outcome. As Queen Victoria and Prince Albert had always been on good terms with the Orléans family and remained so with King Louis-Philippe's widow, Queen Marie-Amelie, after her husband's death in August 1850, they had their reservations about the man who had just replaced him as French head of state. It was her intention that the British government should follow 'a strict line of neutrality and passiveness' as regards the French republic, a move with which Russell was in full agreement. Neither was pleased when Palmerston, apparently believing that Napoleon had neatly forestalled an attempt at restoration by the Orleans dynasty, gave the *coup* his full approval. In a conversation with the French ambassador in London, Count Walewski, he assured him that the new president's assumption of power was welcomed by the British government. It was an impulsive move that led to Palmerston immediately being forced to resign as a minister. All the same, in January 1852, the Queen stated to King Leopold:

[We intend to] try and keep on the best of terms with the president, who is extremely sensitive and susceptible, but for whom, I must say, I have never had any personal hostility.[14]

During the next few months, it became apparent that Louis Napoleon's main objective was to restore the French Empire. As far as Queen Victoria was concerned, any monarchy would be better than a republic—a view she shared with most other crowned heads of the day. Most of them looked askance at the likelihood of his calling himself Napoleon III, in recognition of Napoleon Bonaparte and his son who had died in exile in 1832. This offended some European sovereigns, on the grounds that he was a mere adventurer who regarded the Bonapartes as a legitimate, established royal dynasty. Queen Victoria took a more pragmatic view. She advised Lord Malmesbury, who had succeeded Palmerston as Foreign Secretary, that it would hardly be worth offending France and her ruler by refusing to recognise it.

On 2 December 1852, Louis Napoleon was proclaimed Emperor Napoleon III, elected after an overwhelming majority in another plebiscite. The reaction of some of Europe's crowned heads was at best equivocal, but the Queen lost no time in accrediting her ambassador to Napoleon; she addressed him as 'my good brother, the Emperor of the French'.

For his part, the new Emperor was gratified at England being the first of the great powers to recognise him. Perhaps he had taken the lesson to heart that Napoleon Bonaparte had taken on England less than forty years earlier, and that in so doing had precipitated his downfall. Moreover, he had always been fond of England, London having been his home during several periods of exile, and he felt very much at home in English society. Nothing would please him better than to be on the best of terms with the country that had almost been a second home to him, as well as with its government and above all its sovereign.

If he could keep his title of emperor, it would be a worthwhile prize indeed. Of Europe's three empires, France was the most prosperous and the most centralised, comparing favourably with the ramshackle Austrian domains that comprised several different states speaking several different tongues, and with those of the vast, sprawling, and still largely undeveloped Russia.

However, as a bachelor of forty-four, he urgently needed to find a wife and secure the imperial succession. As it was unlikely that few, if any, of the most eligible unmarried princesses in Europe would consider marrying this middle-aged *parvenu* sovereign with what might be an uncertain hold on his throne, his choice would inevitably be limited. After short-lived negotiations for the hand of one from the Swedish house of Bernadotte, a more likely potential wife was found in the person of Princess Adelaide of Hohenlohe-Langenburg. Although not a member of a reigning house, she had a valuable royal connection as the daughter of Princess Feodora, elder half-sister of Queen Victoria. Such a marriage would not only provide him with a wife and heir, but also cement his connection with the British royal family, as well as Anglo-French friendship.

When Lord Malmesbury approached the Queen on the subject, she found herself in a difficult position. To reject the Emperor's scheme would lay her open to accusations of being unduly keen to show her support for the displaced Orléans dynasty, but to accept would suggest that she was risking the friendship of and alliances with the rest of Europe by associating herself with the new untested French regime. Lord Cowley, the British Ambassador in Paris, was convinced that the new French regime would collapse before long, gloomily convinced 'that all inside is rotten and that, with few exceptions, we are living in a society of adventurers'.[15]

While Queen Victoria might not have been quite so pessimistic, she was disinclined to support the marriage alliance, partly as the circumstances of his becoming emperor were no guarantee of stability, and also partly as she knew he had something of a reputation as a libertine. She feared that the young princess would be 'dazzled' if she heard of the offer, and could not but think of 'the sad fate of all the wives of the rulers of France since 1789'.[16] While a wild past did not necessarily preclude the possibility or even likelihood that as a married man he would mend his ways, such factors mattered greatly to the Queen and to Prince Albert, particularly in the case of a would-be wife who was twenty-seven years younger than him.

Fortunately for her, the matter was taken out of her hands. Princess Feodora was reluctant to consider the Emperor as a son-in-law, and she was saved from the possibility when she and everyone else learnt that he was paying court elsewhere, namely to a Spanish lady, Mademoiselle Eugénie de Montijo. On 22 January 1853, he announced their betrothal. They were married in a civil ceremony at the Tuileries on 29 January, and at a grander celebration at Notre Dame Cathedral the next day.

Later that year, another European Emperor was seriously considering his matrimonial future. In February 1853, Emperor Francis Joseph was attacked by János Libényi, a Hungarian tailor's apprentice, who set upon him while he was walking along a street in Vienna and stabbed him in the neck with a knife. He suffered from delayed shock and loss of blood and was confined to the Hofburg for three weeks while he convalesced from the wound. For some days, it was said that his life hung in the balance and, even in the first week of March, Queen Victoria learnt that 'though he may to all appearances seem well, he might die suddenly at any moment'.[17] There was a faintly comic element to the incident in that the knife used by Libényi was said to be one of Birmingham manufacture, stamped 'Palmer And Son'. Some people declared that the name was in fact 'Palmerston' and that the senior British politician who had voiced his support for the Hungarians had had the knives made on purpose.[18]

One result of this attempt on his life was that his mother, Archduchess Sophie, resolved to see him married as soon as possible so that he would be able to provide Austria with an heir to the throne. Queen Victoria and King Leopold hoped briefly that the latter's only daughter might be chosen as his bride. It was not to be, for in August he was betrothed to one of his Wittelsbach cousins, Princess Elizabeth of Bavaria. The Queen was rather disappointed as she 'had hoped for dear Charlotte'.[19] However, 'dear Charlotte' was also destined to become a Habsburg empress consort by marrying Francis Joseph's brother Maximilian, although her life would in some ways be no less tragic than that of her sister-in-law Elizabeth.

2

'Old Enmities and Rivalries were Wiped Out'

The failure of Emperor Napoleon to marry Queen Victoria's niece had forestalled one close connection between Britain and the new French Empire, but events further east would shortly bring about a closer alliance, this time on the field of battle.

The Turks had steadfastly refused to accept a Russian demand to protect and respect the rights of Christian minorities in the Ottoman Empire, with the French defending the rights of Catholics and the Russians those of the Eastern Orthodox Christians. The situation was exacerbated by the decline of the Ottoman Empire and the reluctance of a suspicious Britain and France to permit Russia to gain additional territory and power at Ottoman expense. While the churches settled their differences, Tsar Nicholas I and Emperor Napoleon refused to back down. When the Tsar issued an ultimatum that the Orthodox subjects of the Empire should be placed under his protection, Britain attempted to mediate and arranged a compromise that was accepted by the Tsar. The Ottomans demanded changes, but Nicholas refused and prepared for war.

Having obtained promises of support from France and Britain, the Turks officially declared war on Russia in September 1853. Events might not have taken such a turn had the Tsar not misjudged the situation by overestimating the importance of Lord Aberdeen, the British Prime Minister. He recalled the role that Aberdeen had played as a young diplomat in Allied negotiations at the end of the Napoleonic Wars, and considered him to be friendly towards the Eastern Powers and therefore no friend of France. On his visit to England in 1844, the Tsar had discussed political issues with Aberdeen as Foreign Secretary and had given every impression of being favourable to plans for Russian expansion at Turkey's expense. Convinced that while Aberdeen was in power he would never declare war on Russia, the Tsar was lulled into a sense of false security. Only too late did he realise his mistake.

Queen Victoria was equivocal about the outbreak of war. It did not seem so long ago that most of Europe had united to defeat the Emperor's uncle at the battle of Waterloo, and to the generations who could still recall those days, the idea of a military alliance with Britain's traditional foe seemed little short of astonishing. The elderly senior British commander at the Crimea, General Raglan, even kept on inadvertently referring to the Russians as 'the French' during the campaign. Moreover, Britain might find herself compromised after the war by close friendship with the unstable and Roman Catholic regime across the water. However, for better or worse, Britain and France were allies and solidarity had to be maintained. While she told Lord Aberdeen in September that 'she now rejoices the Fleets should be on their way to Constantinople', she still hoped that 'any outbreak may yet be averted'.[1] Aberdeen entirely agreed with her hopes that the conflict would not escalate. Ten days later, he answered that he was doing his best 'to keep open the possibility of peaceful communications'. He agreed that 'it may be very agreeable to humiliate the Emperor of Russia'; but, even so, he thought it was 'paying a little too dear for this pleasure, to check the progress and prosperity of this happy country, and to cover Europe with confusion, misery, and blood'.[2] Nevertheless, there would be much 'confusion, misery, and blood' ahead during the next couple of years before peace was restored.

As the personification of 'the enemy', in the eyes of most Britons, the Tsar was soon transformed into the embodiment of evil. The war was several months old when Lord Aberdeen provoked general dismay during a debate on the Eastern Question in the House of Lords on 19 June 1854. When Lord Lyndhurst, a former Lord Chancellor and now one of the most respected of elder statesmen, made a speech in which he denounced in ringing tones the aggressive policy and general untrustworthiness of Russia, Aberdeen came rather more gallantly to the defence of Russia than might have been considered appropriate. He alluded to the fact that Russia had not acquired a single inch of Turkish territory since the Treaty of Adrianople, which had concluded a war with Turkey in 1829 and emphasised that the only interference Russia had had with Turkey since then was to save the existence of the Ottoman Empire by sending Russian troops to protect her against the possibility of an Egyptian invasion. While he longed as much as his fellow lordships for a just and honourable peace, he pleaded that it was his intention 'not to wreak vengeance on an enemy for whom personally we can feel no hatred but to obtain with more security such a peace as we ought to desire'.[3]

Surprised and alarmed by what looked like a parliamentary olive branch towards their foes, Queen Victoria confessed in a letter to her Prime Minister that his speech had given her 'very great uneasiness'. While she knew him well enough to fully enter into his feelings and understand what he meant, she warned him that the public, 'particularly under strong excitement of patriotic feeling, is impatient and annoyed to hear at this moment the first Minister of the Crown enter into an impartial examination of the Emperor of Russia's character and conduct'. She stated:

> [His candour and courage in voicing opinions, even if opposed to popular feeling] are in this instance dangerous to him, and the Queen hopes that in the vindication of his own conduct to-day, which ought to be triumphant, as it wants in fact no vindication, he will not undertake the ungrateful and injurious task of vindicating the Emperor of Russia from any of the exaggerated charges brought against him and his policy at a time when there is enough in it to make us fight with all might against it.[4]

In the interests of good relations with Britain's ally, further personal contact between Queen, Emperor, and their consorts was vital. Prince Albert had major reservations about getting too close to Emperor Napoleon, a man whose moral compass was poor. Albert did not take lightly to dealing too closely with a man who smoked and gambled, had had two illegitimate children, and had lived openly with an English publican's daughter while President of France. It would suit his purpose better to send two other members of the family first, whose own morals, unlike his own, were not above reproach. The task of making the first approaches was therefore devolved on the Queen's cousin George, Duke of Cambridge, and his brother Ernest, Duke of Saxe-Coburg Gotha. Ernest was invited to stay at the Tuileries, a sojourn he greatly enjoyed. He reported that the Emperor, a consummate flatterer, had made glowing comments about the Queen and her family, and that the Empress was looking forward very much to meeting the royal children. He was closely followed by the Duke, who had been appointed to a senior command and spent a week in Paris on his way to the war. As a guest of Lord Cowley, he was treated to various military inspections and reviews, a reception at the Tuileries, and visits to the opera and the theatre. Both reported to Albert in glowing terms of the Emperor and Empress and their hospitality, and Prince Albert decided that he could make no objections to meeting Napoleon after all.

On 3 September 1854, he accepted an invitation to visit him at the military camp in Boulogne and sailed on the royal yacht *Victoria and Albert*.

The visit got off to a slightly unfortunate start as the escort of ships of war was nowhere to be seen and the royal yacht had to enter Boulogne harbour without an escort. Nevertheless, despite the initial reservations of the younger man, both got on very well. It proved hard work for Albert, for the Emperor was an early riser and tended to have him roused at 6.00 a.m. each day for a programme of inspections and military manoeuvres until late in the evening. As his bed was 'too short, the counterpane too heavy, the pillows of feathers and the heat frightful,' getting up early was perhaps not altogether unwelcome.[5] At other times, they had long discussions on politics and warfare, though, as a non-smoker, Albert found the clouds of cigar smoke tested his tolerance a little. Although the Prince had begun his visit with reservations, the Emperor succeeded in charming him, being ready to discuss anything frankly and also to listen to Albert's advice. On his last day in France, he admitted in his diary that 'upon the whole he has been greatly pleased'.[6]

After he left, the Emperor praised him warmly in a report to the ambassador in London, who forwarded it to the Queen. He said that in all his experience, 'he had never met with a person possessing such various and profound knowledge, or who communicated it with the same frankness. His Majesty added that he had never learned so much in a short time, and was grateful'.[7] A little flattery always went a long way with the Queen.

There was an ulterior motive. If there was one thing that Emperor Napoleon really needed to increase his prestige, it was to be invited to pay an official visit to England. When the Queen, responding to feelers for an invitation voiced by Foreign Secretary Lord Clarendon, suggested to the Emperor that mid-November would suit her well, he answered with supreme confidence that 'a better time would be later'. This irritated the Queen, who thought this betrayed a measure of arrogance in that he seemed to believe he was doing the Queen a favour by coming to England. She wrote to Clarendon that she 'would wish that no anxiety should be shown to obtain the visit, now that it is quite clear to the Emperor that he will be *le bienvenue* [welcome] at any time. His reception here ought to be a boon to him and not a boon to us'.[8]

Almost at once, the Emperor announced that he intended to visit the Crimea in order to take personal command of his armies. The British government, and in particular the Queen, did not relish the idea of this typically Bonaparte-like gesture. It would be rather demeaning if a Frenchman was to try and take command of the joint Anglo-French force, win a magnificent victory, and completely outshine the British war effort. French politicians were not pleased as to what might happen in France while he was away, as he probably would be for many months, while his senior commanders insisted that it was a soldier's war and his brief military training in Switzerland did not permit him the status of commander. Lord Clarendon was sent to France to try and divert him from his idea, but initially he would not be dissuaded.

There was only one sure way of distracting him, and perhaps the wily Emperor had seen it for himself—an invitation for him and the Empress to pay the state visit to England on which they were so keen. A return visit would inevitably follow, summer would be over and the Emperor would doubtless be prepared to give some ground on the scheme, especially as by that time the war would probably have reached in its closing stages. The Emperor accordingly advised Clarendon that for them to come to Windsor shortly after Easter would be most convenient, and a state visit was arranged to take place the following spring, from 16 to 21 April.

Meanwhile, there remained the slim possibility that Emperor Francis Joseph might bring the Austrian Empire into the Crimean War on the side of Britain and France. The Austrian ambassador in Paris, Count Hübner, warned the Emperor that, if their country was to remain neutral, Emperor Napoleon would regard his neutrality as tantamount to hostility. Francis Joseph was not convinced, but in order to show some solidarity he mobilised two army corps on the Russian frontier, with a view to his government taking additional measures later on. However, they stalled while the campaign continued in the Crimea, resulting in several victories for the British and French.

In August 1854, Austria, Britain, and France agreed jointly to curb Russian interest in the Balkans, and in December they signed a tripartite treaty by which it was understood that Austrian possessions in Italy would be guaranteed for the duration of the war. Austria did not join in the war against Russia because Russian forces had evacuated the regions around the Danube that they had occupied in May 1853. Nevertheless, the Habsburg Empire was now effectively isolated diplomatically. Having forfeited the respect of France and England and alienated Russia, Emperor Francis Joseph and his dominions now had the worst of both worlds. The Russian ambassador in Vienna, Alexander Gorchakov, warned Emperor Francis Joseph that he had so grossly offended Tsar Nicholas by his attitude that Austria would never enjoy an hour's peace as long as he remained on the throne.

By the end of 1854, dissatisfaction with the campaign at the Crimea was rife in England and, as reports of mismanagement of the conflict arose, parliament felt the need to take action. On 29 January 1855, an independent MP, John Arthur Roebuck, introduced a motion for the appointment of a select committee to enquire into the conduct of the war that was carried by a majority of 157. Treating this as a vote of no confidence in his government, which in the words of the Chancellor of the Exchequer, William Ewart Gladstone, 'fell with a whack', Aberdeen resigned and retired from active politics. Queen Victoria sent for Lord Derby as Conservative leader, but he told her that the country wanted Palmerston. Lord Lansdowne declined on the grounds of ill-health and old age and Lord Russell attempted to form a government, but could not find enough people to agree to serve under him. Having exhausted all other possibilities, she had no choice but to summon Palmerston, who eagerly accepted.

A few days later Tsar Nicholas fell ill and took to his bed in the Winter Palace, he died on 2 March. According to Sir Ralph Abercromby, British minister at The Hague, he had succumbed to an attack of influenza, although it was said that his heart had been broken by the heavy defeats and carnage wrought on his armies at the battles of Balaclava and Inkerman the previous autumn. Writing to Princess Augusta of Prussia, the Tsar's niece, Queen Victoria regretted that although he 'has died as our enemy, I have not forgotten former and more happy times, and no one has more than I regretted that he himself evoked this sad war'.[9]

Less charitable was *The Times,* which had barely a good word to say about the deceased, noting that 'it is impossible to doubt that the agonising sense of humiliation and remorse at the loss of all he had reason to prize has terminated his life'. Each successive month it went on 'has been marked by the steady progress of the Emperor of Russia down this declivity of bad faith, of aggression, of bloodshed, of defeat, of desolation, and at last of death, which terminates the appalling history'.[10]

Queen Victoria always remained on the best of terms with the exiled Orléans family at Claremont. In widowhood, Queen Marie Amelie was always a welcome visitor at Windsor and it may have been a little on Queen Victoria's conscience that one of her appearances was not long before the eagerly, if nervously, anticipated coming of Emperor Napoleon and Empress Eugénie to England. On 16 April 1855, they set sail from Calais on board the *Pélican*, a first-class mail streamer, accompanied by another vessel, the *Pétrel*, on which the Empress's hairdresser M. Félix travelled, together with her wardrobe and jewel boxes. It was a foggy crossing and the Empress was violently sick on board. They landed at Dover to be met by Prince Albert, with whom they took the royal train to London before driving across the city in an open carriage with an escort from the Household Cavalry to Windsor, where Queen Victoria was waiting. The Empress had had the foresight to wear a tartan dress, which was much admired.

Throughout her life, the Queen always had a dread of meeting strangers and she was quite nervous at the prospect. During Napoleon's exile in

England, the Queen had briefly met him in Fulham in 1848, at an official breakfast to mark the erection of baths and wash-houses. However, coming face to face with him as one head of state to another would be a very different matter. The preparations for the visit had been in hand for several weeks, with not only a full programme to be arranged, but also rooms to be decorated and, as a personal touch, fourteen of the Emperor's horses were to be brought over to the stables for the duration of the visit. The streets of Windsor had been decorated to welcome the French party and the entire court, officers of state, and household assembled at the grand hall, while the Yeomen of the Guard lined the walls and formed a guard of honour on the grand staircase. As the trumpets from the band, drawn up in the quadrangle, played the anthem of the Second Empire, 'Partant pour la Syrie', the carriages drew up at the entrance and the Queen, followed by members of her family, came out to greet their guests.

Two slight mishaps threatened to mar the start of the occasion. The Empress's hairdresser had not arrived at Windsor, but was at Charing Cross, threatening to kill himself if somebody did not take him to Paddington at once. He was eventually fetched, but arrived too late to be of assistance to his mistress that evening. Moreover, she was told that her dressing case and the trunk containing her dresses was also missing. One of her ladies came to the rescue by lending her a simple dress and placed chrysanthemums, taken from a vase, in her hair.

At dinner that evening, the Queen fell under the Emperor's spell at once. They 'got on extremely well', she recorded, 'and my great agitation seemed to go off very early; the Emperor is so very quiet: his voice is low and soft, and *il ne fait pas des phrases*'.[11] Writing to King Leopold the next day about her guests, she commented on the 'great fascination in the quiet, frank manner' of the Emperor, 'and [the Empress] is very pleasing, very grateful, and very unaffected, but very delicate'.[12] For both women, it would be the start of a friendship that endured for over forty years. When Queen Victoria raised the rather contentious subject of the Emperor's planned journey to the Crimea, the Empress explained that her husband needed to repair the damage done to the French imperial image by his unpredictable and undependable first cousin, Prince Napoleon. Generally known by his nickname of 'Plon-Plon', he was the son of Napoleon Bonaparte's youngest brother Jerome, ex-King of Westphalia, and had recently made his own brief expedition to the Crimea, from which he had returned a figure of ridicule. The Emperor, she stressed, would cut a more dignified figure if he was to go himself.

Even the ever-sceptical Prince Albert fell under the spell of Empress Eugénie. The Queen noted how much he liked and admired her, which delighted her, 'as it is so seldom that I see him do so with any woman'.[13]

Throughout their fifteen years of married life, he had been completely impervious to attractive ladies-in-waiting at court, and she might have been slightly relieved to observe that even this most faithful and steadfast of husbands did have an eye for feminine grace and beauty in others after all.

The state visit was divided into two parts, with four days spent at Windsor and three in London. At the former, a military review was held in the great park, and the Emperor was invested with the Order of the Garter. After they came out of the throne room together at the end of the ceremony, he was heard to remark to her with a smile, '*Enfin je suis gentilhomme*' ('At last I am a gentleman').[14] One spectator remarked that never before had he seen such a look of triumph on somebody's face. After a ball one evening, she noted her astonishment at the irony of the circumstances in which the two heads of state found themselves:

> Really to think that I, the granddaughter of George III, should dance with the Emperor Napoleon, nephew to our great enemy, now my nearest and most intimate ally, in the Waterloo Room too—and this ally, only six years ago, an exile, poor, comparatively little known, living in this country, seems incredible.[15]

Immediately after the Emperor and Empress had arrived at Buckingham Palace, they were obliged to leave for a state luncheon at the guildhall. Crowds lined the route, with British detectives and French secret police mingling discreetly in the event of any threats on the illustrious lives in their midst.

This was followed by a diplomatic *levée* at the French embassy, and in the evening a command performance of *Fidelio* at Covent Garden. The Queen noted that they 'literally drove through a sea of human beings, cheering and pressing near the carriage' through richly illuminated streets.[16] Rather astutely, the Emperor pointed out to the Queen that the initials of the royal couples, Napoleon, Eugénie, Victoria, and Albert, spelt 'NEVA', the river on which St Petersburg, the capital of Russia and therefore their enemy capital, was situated. Their reception at the opera was equally enthusiastic. It was, however, noticed that the Queen seated herself without taking her eyes off the audience, whereas Eugénie, who had not been born royal, looked round to make sure there was a chair in place behind her before she sat down.

The following day, which was also the Emperor's forty-seventh birthday, they drove to see the Crystal Palace at Sydenham. As the public had been excluded from the building on this occasion, they were able to walk around undisturbed, although by the time they had finished luncheon, the building was again opened to the public and they had to pass out through a crowd of at least 30,000 people cheering them. It was an ordeal that the Queen found somewhat unnerving, both for her own sake and that of the Emperor, whom she was anxious to protect from any attempts on his life. The ever-present if remote threat of assassination of European emperors and kings on journeys abroad was rarely far from their minds, and, as events later in the nineteenth century would prove, not without reason.

The last event on the programme was a concert at the palace with 400 guests invited—a day after this was the last of their visit. Although it consisted mostly of operatic arias, which the Queen enjoyed, as with the case at *Fidelio* two days earlier, she and the Emperor spent most of the time talking throughout the performance. She had already noticed that he was not very interested in music. By the following morning, they found themselves at a sad leaving party outside the palace, as the Empress flung herself into the Queen's arms and begged them to come and spend a return visit at Paris as soon as they were able. 'It went off so beautifully', the Queen noted, 'not a hitch nor *contretemps*, fine weather, everything smiling. The nation enthusiastic, and happy in the firm and intimate alliance of two great countries, whose enmity would prevent peace for their country'.[17] A few days later, she wrote a lengthy memorandum on the visit and her impressions of her guests. Her admiration for Napoleon knew few bounds:

[He is] a very extraordinary man, with great qualities there can be no doubt—I might almost say a mysterious man. He is evidently possessed of indomitable courage, unflinching firmness of purpose, self-reliance, perseverance, and great secrecy … and at the same time he is endowed with wonderful self-control, great calmness, even gentleness and with a power of fascination, the effect of which upon all those who become more intimately acquainted with him is most sensibly felt.[18]

She was convinced that while their personal friendship endured, Britain and France would remain on the best of relations, and it would surely not be lost on him that she was the only European sovereign who had yet treated him as 'one of them'. At the same time, she would consider it her duty to make sure he stayed 'on the right course', and protect him 'from 'changeableness' and the fickleness of his servants and fellow countrymen.

Emperor Napoleon had barely returned to France before he was planning a return visit from the Queen and Prince Albert. Much to their relief, he wrote to say that he had decided not to go to the Crimea after all. Though he did not admit as much, there was a general feeling that if the unthinkable was to occur and there were any military reverses in the war, he might not have a throne in France to return to after all.

Palmerston was sure that the gentle pressure he had been put under while he was in England had been successful in changing his plans, and he wrote to the Queen congratulating her upon the Emperor's decision 'to give up his intended journey to the Crimea, which could only have led to embarrassments of many kinds'.[19] Moreover, that summer there would be an *Exposition Universelle* in Paris, and this provided the perfect excuse for an invitation to the sovereign and her consort who had so far proved his strongest allies. A date was accordingly set for a ten-day stay in August 1855.

On 18 August, the royal party, including the two eldest children, Victoria, Princess Royal, and Albert Edward, Prince of Wales, set sail on board the royal yacht *Victoria and Albert*. As they sailed in to Boulogne, the Emperor was there to meet them and they drove through the decorated streets of Paris, with their flags, banners, Venetian masts, and similar finery, to the Chateau St Cloud. It was the first time that a British sovereign had set foot in the French capital since King Henry VI had been crowned King of France in the Cathedral of Notre Dame in 1431. Here, Queen Victoria and Empress Eugénie were reunited, the Empress being careful to take care of herself as it had been announced in June that she was *enceinte*. As she had already had at least two miscarriages, she was under instructions to take the utmost care of herself. After they had embraced each other, the Queen was introduced to Plon-Plon's sister, Princess Mathilde. As she was separated from her husband, Count Anatoli Demidoff, and now living openly with another man, the sculptor Emilien de Nieuwerkerque, there had been some speculation as to how the sovereign would receive her, but she embraced her warmly nonetheless.

Napoleon proved himself the perfect host just as much as he had been the perfect guest four months earlier. He had ensured that the suite of rooms prepared for Queen Victoria and Prince Albert, formerly the apartments of King Louis XVI and Queen Marie-Antoinette, had been redecorated in white and gold and that the Queen's room had been designed to resemble her own at Buckingham Palace as far as possible. Even the legs had been sawed off a valuable table so that it would not be too high for the particularly short Queen. On being asked how she liked her rooms, she told the Emperor without hesitation that she was charmed to find she had 'such a home feeling'. It compared favourably, she had to admit ruefully, with her earlier experience of the French Court: 'I must say we are both much struck with the difference between this and the poor King's [Louis-Philippe] time, when the noise, confusion and bustle were great'.[20]

During the next few days, the itinerary drawn up for the royal party included three visits to the *Exposition Universelle* at the Palais des Beaux Arts and one to the Louvre. Lord Clarendon, who was obliged to walk behind the Queen, was astonished at her energy, complaining afterwards that 'no Royal Person ever yet known or to be known in history comes up to her in indefatigability'.[21] Even the Emperor was seen to be flagging a little by the end. One member of the French entourage, who was very fat and evidently suffering in his tightly fitting uniform, whispered in Clarendon's ear that he would give absolutely anything, even the *Venus de Milo*, for a glass of lemonade. After a brief rest, while the Queen wrote a report in her journal, they attended a state ball in the evening, where she was dancing with energy that amazed those who watched her and she did not retire until after midnight. For a few evenings, she was once again almost the carefree, young, unmarried sovereign who had astonished her courtiers at home by relishing such functions that would continue into the small hours.

Much as Her Majesty enjoyed herself and lavished praise on almost everything she saw and experienced, she failed to warm to the charmless Plon-Plon. Aware that few things would cement his position more firmly than a marriage alliance with a member of her family, the Emperor had tentatively proposed a match between him and her cousin, Princess Mary of Cambridge (later to become the Duchess of Teck and mother of the princess who would become Queen Mary), but the Queen refused to hear of it. His reputation had been bad enough in her eyes, but now she had actually come face to face with him, she disliked him even more. He had none of the Emperor's ease of manner and, after he had escorted her round the exposition, she complained that he was ungracious, 'gruff and contradictory'. For the sake of appearances, she was obliged to confer on him the Order of the Bath, but she did so with reluctance, thinking his manner 'rude and disagreeable in the highest degree. *Il me fait peur*, and has a diabolical expression'.[22] However, Princess Mathilde was on her best behaviour and put herself out to be particularly kind to the royal children. In private, Empress Eugénie admitted to the Queen that Plon-Plon and Mathilde were 'a difficulty and a disadvantage to them'. Much to everyone's amusement, the more forthright Lord Clarendon referred to them as 'the assassin and the cook'.[23]

On a subsequent afternoon, the royal party went to visit the coffin of Napoleon Bonaparte, which had been brought back from St Helena by King Louis-Philippe and placed in the side-chapel beneath the dome of the Hotel des Invalides. A crypt was still being constructed where it had been decided that the remains would rest in perpetuity. The coffin was covered with a velvet pall, with his hat and sword at the foot, while around the chapel stood veterans from the First Empire, holding flaming torches. The party, which included Queen Victoria, Prince Albert, their two eldest children, Prince Napoleon, and Princess Mathilde, stood for several minutes in silence, then the Queen told the Prince of Wales to kneel before the tomb of the Great Napoleon. As he did so, a clap of thunder burst overhead and crashed around the chapel walls, as flashes of lightning whitened the glare of the torches, then an organ burst into a rendition of *God Save the Queen*. When they walked out afterwards through the driving rain into their carriage, the Queen observed, as she wrote later in her journal, that it was as if 'old enmities and rivalries were wiped out, and the seal of heaven placed upon that bond of amity which is now happily established between two great and powerful nations! May Heaven bless and prosper it!'[24]

On the following day, they went for a carriage drive through the Forêt de St Germain, a visit to the hunt at La Mouette, and finally a grand ball at the Salle des Glaces at Versailles. Once again, the Queen amazed everybody by her tireless energy and she noted in her journal that they did not get back to their rooms afterwards until 2.30 a.m., 'much delighted— the children in ecstasies—and past three before we got to bed'.[25]

Emotional partings and goodbyes took place on 27 August. As the carriage arrived, the Queen found it particularly hard 'to take leave of the dear Empress, which [she] did with great sorrow, as she is such a dear, sweet, engaging, and distinguishing being, a fairylike *Erscheinung* [vision], unlike anyone [she] ever saw'.[26] Even the ever-sceptical Prince Albert, who was generally so reluctant to place his trust in anyone, had been gradually won over by the Emperor. As for the royal children, they were captivated. The Princess Royal, then aged fourteen, had become a devoted admirer of the Empress, while the thirteen-year-old Prince of Wales had become deeply attached to the Emperor. As they were taking a short stroll together one day, he remarked casually to him that he would like to be his son. Although the destiny of the Princess Royal and that of her family was to be linked to a certain extent with that of the Emperor and his family some fifteen years later and her views would change, the Prince of Wales always remained a fervent admirer of France and particularly of the city of Paris.

As Queen Victoria and her family returned to England, she and Prince Albert had every faith in the Anglo-French alliance. Yet, only a month later, they were to make an even more lasting connection with Germany, their ancestral home. The result would come to fruition in the creation of another European empire.

Over the last four years, 'the Prussian marriage' had gradually taken hold in the minds of the elders. Anglo-Prussian relationships had been sullied a little by the Crimean war, as Prussia had been a tacit supporter, though not actually a firm ally, of Russia. The capture of Sebastopol in September 1855 brought the end of the Crimean war in sight. A few days earlier, Queen Victoria, Prince Albert, and their children had gone to stay at Balmoral, their home in the Scottish Highlands, and the news was celebrated with a bonfire on the hills nearby. On 14 September, a rather nervous Prince Frederick William of Prussia joined them, accompanied by his *aide-de-camp*, General Helmuth von Moltke. The aide was immediately impressed by the homely atmosphere that met his eyes. It was hard to believe, he wrote to his wife, that the woman whom he called the most powerful monarch in the world could leave court life behind: 'it is just plain family life here.... Nobody would guess that the Court of one of the most powerful estates resides here, and that from these mountains the fate of the world is decided'.[27]

To Prince Frederick William, the change in the Princess Royal since he had first met her some four years earlier was immediately evident. She and the Prince sat next to each other at dinner that first evening, chatting in French and German. She found it impossible to keep her eyes off this handsome young suitor. Her parents had already agreed between themselves that if the two young people had not shown any signs of being attracted to each other, they would do nothing to force the issue. While they tried not to look too interested, they were secretly overjoyed that matters appeared to be turning out as they had hoped if not actually planned.

The next day, Prince Albert took Prince Frederick William out deer-stalking, got soaked to the skin, and took to his bed with an attack of rheumatism. When the young prince and princess found themselves alone together for a moment, she took his hand and squeezed it tightly. After a night of little sleep, following breakfast the next morning he plucked up the courage to ask her parents for a quiet word. In the Queen's words, he wanted 'to belong to our Family; that this had long been his wish, that he had the entire concurrence and approval not only of his parents but of the King—and that finding Vicky so *allierliebst* [lovely], he could delay no longer in making this proposal'.[28]

She agreed at once, on the understanding that her daughter was to know nothing about it until after her confirmation at Easter the following year. If possible, he ought to come to England then, attend the ceremony, and propose to her immediately afterwards. In strict confidence, Prince Albert notified Lord Palmerston, now Prime Minister, and Lord Clarendon, and wrote to Baron Stockmar that 'Fritz had laid his proposal before us'. Yet, having taken the first step along the road to betrothal, the prince found it difficult to wait any longer and, on 25 September, he asked the Queen if he might have her permission to present his intended with a bracelet. She agreed, saying that something had to be told her and he ought to tell her himself.

Four days later, the family went for a ride up the heather-covered slopes of Craig-na-Ban. The Prince and Princess lagged behind and he picked her a sprig of white heather as an emblem of good luck, telling her as he did so that he hoped she would come and stay with him in Prussia—always.

When they reached the carriage where everyone else was waiting, he gave the Queen a meaningful nod to imply that all had gone according to plan. Back at the castle, a half-remorseful daughter threw herself into her parents' arms, weeping tears of joy as she told them everything. Four days later, they all took their sorrowful leave of Prince Frederick William as he returned home. After he had gone, Prince Albert wrote to him that 'from the moment you declared your love and embraced her, the child in her vanished'.[29]

The betrothal was not officially announced at home or to foreign courts until the following spring. Nevertheless, Prince Frederick William had barely left on his journey home before *The Times* was remarking acidly on his appearance in Scotland, for the sole purpose of 'improving his acquaintance with the Princess Royal'. It was understood that 'a kind of preliminary understanding was entered into' at the time of their first meeting at the great exhibition, and that such a marriage had long been planned. Drawing attention to King Frederick William's sympathies with Russia during the Crimean War, at what had been a critical juncture for Britain, it concluded that an alliance with Prussia would be tantamount to one with Russia. If the Prince was called up to join the Russian army, his wife would be placed in a situation where loyalty to her husband would be treason to her country, and if Prussia was to lapse into the status of a petty power, she would be sent back to England as an exile: 'For our part, we wish the daughter of our Royal House some better fate'. It ended with an unequivocal statement that the people of England had 'no wish to improve its acquaintance with any Prince of the house of Hohenzollern'.[30] Prince Albert was deeply wounded by such comments, remarking that *The Times*, 'our sulky grandmother [was] deeply offended that its permission was not first asked'.[31] He had little doubt that the future would belong to Prince Frederick William, who had been second in line to the throne since his birth. His father William, Prince of Prussia, would succeed his childless and now ailing brother, but William was already aged fifty-eight and his reign, when it came, was thought unlikely to be a long one.

In Berlin, the rest of the Prussian royal family were divided in their views, but there was scant enthusiasm for an English bride for their future King. King Frederick William IV was not ashamed to admit to his associates that his nephew had gone to meet Queen Victoria's family and propose to her eldest daughter, but he was almost alone in defending the enterprise. Prince William refrained from expressing a view one way or the other, although he was broadly supportive of his son's intentions, while Princess Augusta had her reservations. On a political and personal level, she had more in common with the English royal family, especially the liberal-minded, art and music-loving Prince Albert, than with her military minded philistine Hohenzollern in-laws. However, as the wife in a loveless marriage who had no influence at all over a husband whom she respected but found it hard to like, she was a little jealous that her son should be about to make a genuine love-match with a princess who seemed so precocious, too clever by half, if Queen Victoria's endless letters of praise about her were to be believed. If nothing else, she could at least take some consolation in the fact that a British princess would bring Prussia and the Hohenzollerns considerable prestige, and that her son was not going to marry another haughty Romanov grand duchess, a family she particularly disliked.

Prince Frederick William had been prepared for an indifferent reception from some quarters to the impending news, but he was irritated that some of the family were so angry because he held such unashamedly Anglophile views:

> One can feel their curiosity, uncertainty, etc., only they are always letting off random shots in the form of sarcastic, barbed reference with pretty unkind comment! The unhappy party is seething with anger at not having been informed and consulted in advance, and is now trying to get revenge by incredibly petty cackling that sheds a most revealing light.

Thankfully, his friends, particularly from university days, were more gracious in their comments: 'Expressing joy about the probable purpose of my journey to England [sic]. This warms my heart, and without more or much enquiry such indications suffice to give me real happiness'.[32]

Meanwhile, Prince Albert assured his future son-in-law that the Princess Royal was being kept hard at work and her education was being maintained. Father and daughter had a period of study together every evening between 6.00 p.m. and 7.00 p.m.:

> I put her through a kind of general catechising, and in order to give precision to her ideas, I make her work out certain subjects by herself, and bring me the results to be revised. Thus she is now engaged in writing a short Compendium of Roman History.[33]

The betrothal was made public and officially announced to the European courts in April 1856, a month after the Princess's confirmation, which Prince Frederick William was unable to attend because of his army commitments. A few days previously, the Queen had advised the government at home and Lord Palmerston had been instrumental in helping to persuade parliament to provide a dowry and allowance for the Princess Royal. When Gladstone had suggested that it was clearly an arranged marriage, she contradicted him strongly.

The Chancellor, she wrote, was probably unaware that the choice of the Princess, while 'made with the sanction and approval of her parents, has been one entirely of her own heart'. Now she was confirmed, she was 'old enough to know her own feelings and wishes, though she may not be old enough to consummate the marriage and leave her parents' roof'.[34]

Now at last it could be discussed openly by those who had already foreseen the news. General Leopold von Gerlach, an adjutant to King Frederick William IV, asked Otto von Bismarck, at that time Prussian envoy to the Diet of the German Confederation in Frankfurt, for his view of 'the English marriage'. Bismarck declared that he did not like the English part of it, but the bride-to-be was said to be a lady of intelligence and feeling. If she was able to 'leave the Englishwoman at home and become a Prussian, then she may be a blessing to the country'. If she remained 'the least bit English, then [he could see the] Court surrounded by English influence. What will it be like when the first lady in the land is an Englishwoman?'[35]

With hindsight many years later, the journalist Charles Lowe, a correspondent in Berlin for *The Times* between 1878 and 1891, a period that covered the height of Bismarck's powers as Imperial Chancellor (and who was a lifelong admirer of Bismarck), considered that the Princess's remarkable qualities had made her ill-equipped for her life as Crown Princess and so briefly Empress. Had she been 'less gifted by nature', he wrote, 'and less perfected by education, which had made her the darling and the intellectual image of her father, she would have achieved far greater success at the Court of Berlin'.[36]

Meanwhile, Britain was fully committed to her military campaign in the Crimea. In France, Emperor Napoleon, aware that France had sent far more soldiers to the battlefront than Britain and suffered much heavier casualties, knew that his empire could not afford the drain on her finances for much longer and he was anxious to end hostilities. The Congress of Paris, which met in February 1856, was called largely on his initiative and peace was signed at the end of March. Among its guarantees was a pledge by the great powers to maintain the integrity of the Ottoman Empire and guarantee the independence of Turkey, to restore Russia and Turkey to their pre-war boundaries, to neutralise the Black Sea so that no warships were permitted to enter, and to open the Danube River for shipping to all nations.

Nevertheless, within a few months, the Anglo-French alliance would be placed under some strain. Napoleon appointed his illegitimate half-brother, the Duc de Morny, son of his mother, Queen Hortense, to the post of ambassador to St Petersburg. The British government suspected that he was planning an alliance with Russia and that both Emperors were planning to meet in person. This suggested that the Anglo-French understanding could be under threat. Queen Victoria wrote in some alarm to Empress Eugénie, who was able to reassure her that there was nothing to fear. Lord Clarendon likewise put her mind at rest by reporting that the Emperor was as faithful to the alliance as ever, believing that all his personal interests as well as those of France were fully bound up with England.

The Queen was further discomfited when she heard of his liaison with the nineteen-year-old Countess de Castiglione, one of several mistresses, whose mere presence he was aware would not make life easy for the Empress. On 16 March, after a protracted labour, she had given birth to the long-awaited son and heir, who was christened Napoleon Eugene Louis Jean Joseph in June, known as Louis within the family and given the title of Prince Imperial. She took several weeks to recover from the birth and was solemnly warned by the doctors that another child would kill her. She should never sleep with her husband again and it was probably this which encouraged him to seek mistresses.

Although Queen Victoria's faith in the Emperor of the French was slightly shaken, the initial reports she received of Tsar Alexander II of Russia did not fill her with confidence either. The dashing young grand duke and Tsarevich whom she had entertained on his visit some seventeen years earlier, according to Earl Granville, was (not surprisingly) 'thinner and graver than when he was in England'. His manner, he said, was 'singularly gentle and pleasing', but he did not give the impression 'of having much strength either of intellect or of character', and neither did he have 'the talent of surrounding himself with able men'.[37]

Anglo-French relations were not improved when the Queen received a request from Plon-Plon, who was planning a visit to Manchester, and as he was coming to England he felt he needed to pay his respects to the Queen as well. She was initially inclined to refuse, until Lord Cowley pointed out that he was second in line to the French throne and, with the Prince Imperial a none too healthy babe in arms, it was still possible that he may yet succeed. However, the visit in the summer of 1857 proved much more of a success than anybody had dared to hope. He visited Osborne House while they were in residence, stayed there a few days, and the Queen and Prince Consort (created thus a few weeks earlier) were delighted to find how pleasant to them he was.

Nevertheless, the Queen's admiration for Emperor Napoleon was beginning to wane. She was well aware of his mistresses, and as a devoted friend of Empress Eugénie, now not only a wife but the mother of his son, she felt that as a husband he was behaving unforgivably. In addition, she distrusted what she felt to be his increasingly pro-Russian stance and also his obsession with building a French navy, which might one day be used against England. The upstart Emperor of five years ago, who had been so quick to forge an alliance with Britain, was now the most powerful ruler in Europe, and his adherence to the British alliance could no longer be taken for granted.

Napoleon was not ready to relinquish the British alliance. After the Empress made him aware of the deteriorating relations between both countries, he became eager to suggest another visit to England himself. A more informal stay for the Emperor and Empress at Osborne was accordingly arranged to take place from 6 to 10 August 1857. There was no formal entertaining and they amused themselves walking and driving around the estate, sailing up the Solent, visiting Carisbrooke Castle, and driving to Ryde. This time, the Queen and the Prince were closer to the Empress, whom they thought had matured greatly, and was probably more trustworthy than her husband. She thought that the Empress was 'very well informed and read', and was convinced that the Emperor would do well to follow her advice as she understood all the major questions of the day and was much more serious than people gave her credit for.

Like the Queen and the Prince Consort, the Empress did not favour the idea of a Franco-Russian rapprochement. 'She is full of spirit and good sense', the Queen noted, 'so kind and amiable, very accomplished and well informed'. The Emperor was his usual diplomatic self. Before they left, he told the Queen that it was just as well they could not stay any longer 'or [they] would finish up by totally forgetting France'.[38] He and his advisers had long talks with Prince Albert, Palmerston, and Clarendon, after which the latter commented that a very black cloud had hung over the alliance on his arrival, but it was now completely dispelled. Even so, Clarendon was well aware that the Prince did not trust the Emperor.

Napoleon may well have been aware that he had slipped somewhat in the ever-critical Prince Consort's estimation, if not that of the Queen as well. As ever, his thank-you letter to the Queen could not be faulted; he told her 'that after passing a few days in Your Majesty's society, one becomes better; just as when one has learned to appreciate the various knowledge and the exalted judgment of the Prince, one goes away from him more advanced in one's ideas, and more disposed to do good'.[39]

This royal friendship would be tested severely in the days ahead. On the night of 14 January 1858, Queen Victoria was shocked to learn that there had been three bombs thrown at the carriage of the Emperor and Empress in Paris as they were driving in state to the opera. They had escaped serious injury, sustaining only slight cuts on their faces from splintering glass, but eight people had been killed and 142 wounded. As the Empress, her dress spotted with blood, fearlessly opened the carriage door, she faced one of the would-be assassins and the police pounced on him. When the theatre manager offered her his arm, she told him calmly that she would get out alone as they had more courage than their attackers. Unlike Napoleon, who looked ashen with shock immediately afterwards, she appeared totally composed.

The Queen immediately telegraphed her congratulations on their miraculous escape. Once investigations began and arrests were made, it was established that the conspirators had hatched their plot in London and their bombs were made in Birmingham. The ringleader, Felice Orsini, a member of the Carbonari revolutionary group, had travelled to France with a British passport under an assumed English name.

Convinced that the Emperor was the main obstacle to Italian independence, he resolved to kill him so that the French would rise in revolt, allowing the Italians to exploit the situation to advantage by rebelling themselves. France was furious, and the Duc de Morny led those who angrily asserted that England was granting political asylum to the Empire's bitterest foes and giving refuge to 'a nest of vipers'. In France, Orsini and his right-hand-man, Colonel Guiseppe Pieri, were tried and sentenced to death. Orsini defended himself so eloquently that the Empress tried to save him from the guillotine. She was aware that he would be less of a threat to the peace of the empire if he was still alive than he would be as a martyr who had given his life for the cause in which he believed.

Queen Victoria was annoyed by the criticism and 'offensive insinuations against this country', while Napoleon asked for an assurance that political refugees in England would be treated with more severity in future. In order to demonstrate how seriously the British regarded the issue, Lord Palmerston introduced a Conspiracy to Murder Bill, which would increase the penalties for intended crime as well as for those that had already been committed. Declaring that it was basically an attempt to appease the French, if not actually craven surrender to bullying on the other side of the Channel, parliament refused to pass it and the government was obliged to resign. Dr Bernard, a French refugee living in London who had been arrested for complicity in Orsini's conspiracy, was tried and acquitted by an English jury, despite the judge's belief that he was guilty.

Queen Victoria was furious, railing at 'the cowardice of the Jury and the shameful behaviour of the public'.[40] For a while, there was an escalation of ill-feeling between both countries, and even rumours of war with France. Despite the outcry in Paris, the Empress refused to join in the anti-British clamour. Nevertheless, she wrote to Lord Cowley, telling him that it was not the fear of seeing her husband and son struck down in her arms that concerned her, so much as a feeling that the acquittal of Bernard suggested that he had the moral support of the British judiciary. It did not bode well for relations between the two great powers that had been so harmonious only two or three years earlier.

'The Sad and Distressing State of Germany'

Escalating tensions between Britain and France were far from the Queen's mind; she had more pressing family matters to attend. The wedding of her eldest daughter Victoria, Princess Royal, and Prince Frederick William of Prussia had been arranged for January 1858. As the groom would one day be King of Prussia, the court at Berlin had expected the ceremony to take place there, but the Queen would not hear of the idea. Lord Clarendon was instructed to tell Lord Bloomfield 'not to entertain the possibility of such a question'. She insisted that they had never had the shadow of a doubt on the part of Prince Frederick William as to where the marriage should take place, and 'whatever may be the usual practice of Prussian Princes, it is not every day that one marries the eldest daughter of the Queen of England'.[1]

Prince Frederick William landed at Dover on 23 January and went straight to Buckingham Palace, where the court had moved from Windsor a week earlier to receive all the guests. Two days later, the wedding took place at St James's Palace, where the Queen and Prince Albert had been married almost eighteen years earlier. Having been promoted that morning to the rank of Major-General of the Prussian First Infantry Regiment of Guards, he arrived at the chapel in his new uniform. The bride was wearing a dress of white silk trimmed with Honiton lace, trembling and very pale as she entered the chapel on her father's arm. Returning to Buckingham Palace after the ceremony, the young couple appeared on the balcony, both with and without their parents, and after a wedding breakfast they left by train for a two-day honeymoon at Windsor.

On the next day, the diarist Charles Greville noted that everything had proceeded very well, 'and it is rather ludicrous to contrast the vehement articles with which the Press teemed (*The Times* in particular) against the alliance two years ago with the popularity of it and the enthusiasm displayed now'.[2] A week later, on 2 February, amid tearful family farewells, they crossed the North Sea on the royal yacht *Victoria and Albert* for Antwerp, *en route* for Berlin.

Queen Victoria, the Prince Consort, and King Leopold of the Belgians all looked forward fondly to the day when King Frederick William would succeed his father Prince William, at present heir to the throne of Prussia, and the kingdom would take her place at the head of a liberal German Empire. The Princess had been well schooled in politics by her father, and she was expected to play her part in supporting and encouraging her progressively minded husband in his role as future heir and ultimately sovereign. Lengthy letters from her parents followed her several times a week, full of advice and demands, sometimes conflicting, which did nothing to smooth her way in an environment where she was extremely homesick and had to tread carefully in order not to offend her in-laws. About ten days after her arrival in Berlin, the Prince Consort reminded her in one of his long letters of her place: 'That of your husband's wife, and of your mother's daughter. You will desire nothing else, but you will also forego nothing of that which you owe to your husband and to your mother'.[3] It evidently never occurred to him that advising her thus was placing her in a position of divided loyalties, for her in-laws would certainly not have considered her allegiance to the interests of the Hohenzollerns and her mother's family as one and the same thing.

Queen Victoria was just as forthright as her husband in reminding her daughter of her duty 'as my daughter and Princess Royal' by ordering her to follow English practices in her own personal life, regardless of whether they would cause any resentment at Berlin.[4] Princess Frederick William, who would come to be known slightingly by her adopted country as *die Engländerin*, was often blamed for being tactless and insufferably superior, but she was torn between conflicting loyalties, which made it impossible for her to be a faithful English princess and daughter to her parents and a good, selfless, subservient Prussian princess at the same time. She had always had a special relationship with her father and respected his judgment implicitly. It may never have occurred to her, or to Queen Victoria, that the Prince Consort had not lived in Germany since he was a young man, and that even if he had Coburg and Berlin were two very different places. He had absolutely no experience or even close acquaintance with the narrow-minded Prussian court and the views of such men as Bismarck, who was by no means untypical of his generation. His judgment was sorely at fault, and neither he nor his daughter appreciated that he was not doing either of them any favours by his attitude.

A cultured, well-read young woman, the Princess relished the company of intellectuals and artists, as her mother-in-law had done, regardless of whether they were commoners or not. Princess Augusta had not made herself liked by doing so, and *die Engländerin* would find the same to her cost, although she was the determined kind of person who was not prepared to sacrifice her principles merely for the sake of courting popularity. Princess Victoria would not hesitate to complain about the lack of baths and lavatories, dirty floors, threadbare carpets, or ill-fitting windows in the Berlin palaces, or even the absence of libraries and museums in the city. With persistence, she went a long way towards achieving what she wanted, but her demands for modernisation did not go down well with the Prussian establishment, who strongly resented the very thought of this young girl who gave the impression that she knew better than they did.

In addition, it was asserted that she ruthlessly dominated her husband and would do so throughout their life together. Prince Frederick William was a quiet, easy-going personality who was not only more liberally minded in politics and interested in the arts than most of his contemporaries—characteristics he had inherited from his enlightened mother, definitely not his philistine father—but also prone to moods of depression and lack of self-confidence, in an age when such traits were barely understood. She suffered from what was at the time an unrecognised physical condition, her symptoms including severe chronic pains, fevers, and unexplained rashes, which played havoc with her patience and sometimes confined her to bed for days at a time. Recent research suggests that she had inherited porphyria, a more severe form of which had blighted the life of her great-grandfather King George III, and which she would pass on with devastating effect to her eldest daughter Princess Charlotte and the latter's only child Princess Feodora. It was all too easy for her detractors to perpetuate the picture of a ruthless, domineering foreign princess, controlled by her parents across the North Sea, with a weak-willed husband who was putty in her hands. While there may be a grain of truth in such a portrait, it was soon exaggerated out of proportion. Princess Frederick William was a determined young woman who appeared to be on a mission to shake up a quasi-medieval environment, and as such she was widely feared by too many of those around her, some of whom had the power to blacken her good name and did not hesitate to use it.

The repercussions of the attempt on the lives of the Emperor and Empress in France had soon died away. In August 1858, Napoleon invited the Queen and Prince Albert to the Cherbourg Fêtes, a week of celebration designed to mark among other things the inauguration of a large new dock. Queen Victoria accepted the invitation with mixed feelings, but King Leopold advised her to ignore the criticism of France at home, do what she could to remain on good terms with the Emperor and his country, and, instead of worrying about increased French naval activity, concentrate on persuading her ministers to build up the English fleet if necessary.

The visit took place in an atmosphere that was very different to that of their sojourn in Paris three years earlier. The meetings between both royal couples were polite, but rather distant. It all got off to a bad start when the Queen pointedly refused to kiss Madame Walewska, one of the party, as she knew all about the Emperor's close relationships with her. As a result, the Walewskis boycotted the official dinner of welcome given on board the Emperor's yacht *La Bretagne*. At the dinner, the Emperor unbent and talked to her in his usual frank manner, 'but he was not in good spirits, and seemed sensitive about all that has been said of him in England and elsewhere'.[5] Afterwards, he rose to propose the Queen's health and made a speech about the Anglo-French alliance, with a few well-chosen phrases about how 'hostile passions, aided by certain untoward incidents', would do nothing to alter the friendship or the desire of both nations to remain on peaceful terms.[6] Prince Albert, who had always been a reluctant public speaker, was obliged to reply with a few cautious phrases:

> [The Queen is] doubly happy to have the opportunity, by her presence here at this time, of joining with you in the endeavour to knit as closely as possible the bonds of friendship between the two nations.[7]

The evening concluded with the party going on deck to watch a magnificent display of fireworks, for which no effort had been spared. The night sky blazed with cascades of colour, below which every ship in the bay was brilliantly illuminated, with the *Victoria and Albert* picked out sharply in red, white, and blue.

Next morning, the Emperor and Empress came on board the yacht to take their leave, with the customary mutual expressions of how they both hoped to see each other before long again. Nevertheless, Queen Victoria and the Prince Consort had been disturbed to see for themselves the extent of newly built fortifications in the town and returned with determination to do something about what they considered the lack of British coastal defences. Perhaps they ignored the point that, if Napoleon had invited them to see his new vessels and inspect the fortifications, it implied that he had nothing to hide and he would hardly have been so accommodating if he had intended to use them against Britain. Afterwards, the Prince Consort wrote with some feeling to the Duchess of Kent to tell her that the visit was 'safely over', that the Emperor looked 'preoccupied and sad', and the Empress 'out of health'. The French marine's war preparations, he thought, were 'immense', while those of the British were 'despicable'.

The British ministers might use fine phrases, but they were doing nothing, stating that his 'blood boils within [him]'.[8]

They might have been relieved to know that, although the French emperor did have war in mind, it was not going to be directed against Britain. In December 1858, Lord Malmesbury assured the Queen that His Imperial Majesty was contemplating nothing of the sort. Little did they know that the Emperor was secretly coming to an arrangement with King Victor Emmanuel of Sardinia, by which their combined armies would drive the Austrians out of northern Italy, to be followed by a campaign that would be followed by the conversion of Italy into a confederation. The arrangement would be cemented by a Franco-Italian alliance with Plon-Plon marrying King Victor Emmanuel's daughter Princess Clotilde, a rather naïve adolescent of sixteen, twenty years younger than her husband-to-be.

Queen Victoria made her apprehension clear in a letter to King Leopold:

[I hope there is] no real desire for war in the Emperor's mind; we have also explained to him strongly how entirely he would alienate us from him if there was any attempt to disturb standing and binding treaties.[9]

By a month later, her views had hardened:

[I believe that if Austria is] strong and well prepared, and Germany strong and well inclined towards us (as Prussia certainly is), France will not be so eager to attempt what I firmly believe would end in the Emperor's downfall![10]

Yet King Leopold's suspicions that Napoleon was determined on the war in Italy proved correct. In the spring he marched his armies into northern Italy. After his victory over the Austrian army at the Battle of Magenta on 4 June, the Prussian forces mobilised and were on their way to come and fight alongside their Austrian ally when Napoleon opened peace negotiations, concluded at the Treaty of Villafranca on 11 July. It was proposed that most of Lombardy should be transferred from Austria to France, which would immediately cede them to Sardinia, and that the rulers of central Italy who had been expelled by revolution shortly after they beginning of the war should be reinstated.

The end of the war had brought Anglo-French relations to a low ebb. Queen Victoria expressed her relief 'that this horrid blood-shed is over—and that we had nothing to do with it!'[11] The Prince Consort was relieved that Prussia had not been put in an awkward decision, but he held no brief for either of the empires involved. To his brother, Ernest, he inveighed against 'the immorality of the Napoleon and Sardinia conspiracy' against Austria, but it left him with no respect for the Habsburg dominions either.

> The boasting of the Austrians and the miserable impotence of their enormous army has raised contempt against the Austrian power. If they had defeated the French they would have been applauded by the English, as everybody would have been applauded by the English, as everybody would have been happy to see them sustain a new defeat.... As it is, they are no use for anything, but to put the whole of Europe in difficulties.[12]

Nevertheless both countries still had a common cause in a casual war in the Far East. In 1859, their combined fleet had been attacked by the Chinese, and a few months later a combined Anglo-French force advanced on Peking, destroying the Summer Palace. Once more, Queen Victoria and Emperor Napoleon found common ground in congratulating each other on the success of the expedition.

However strained the relations between both countries might have been, nothing disturbed the friendship between Queen Victoria and Empress Eugénie. In November 1860, the Queen was advised that the Empress had privately come to England a couple of days earlier, having decided that she desperately needed to get away from Paris for a while. The reasons were obscure, but it seemed that she was in shock following the untimely death on 16 September of her sister Paca, Duchess of Alba, after a long illness, which her husband had briefly withheld from her while they were together on a visit to Algeria, and possible anger with her husband over his continued infidelities. She arrived in London on 14 November, drove with her suite to Claridge's Hotel, and spent a couple of days in London, where she went shopping on foot in the morning and paid a visit to the Crystal Palace in the afternoon. Although it was strictly a private visit, she was recognised and cheered wherever she went, and was seen to be genuinely moved and pleased at such a reception.

She and her suite then travelled up to Scotland in a jolting, unheated train, swathed in cloaks and rugs and equipped with foot warmers. They stayed there for a couple of weeks, during which she took the incognito of Comtesse de Pierrefonds. While there, she consulted a doctor at Edinburgh and then went to join her friend the Duchess of Hamilton at Hamilton Place near Glasgow. Shortly after returning to London at the beginning of December, she paid a private visit to Windsor, at which the sympathetic Queen found her 'thin and pale and unusually melancholy'. It was a sad contrast, she noted, to that glorious visit of five years earlier.

That same month, the Queen had direct contact, albeit of a fleeting nature, with the other European empress. Elizabeth, the consort of

Emperor Francis Joseph, had recently suffered some kind of physical and mental breakdown, probably relating to a venereal infection she had contracted from her husband after his seeking pleasure from elsewhere. For her it was the last straw in a series of problems that had been building up and making her life a misery, in particular the plight of her sister, the former Queen Maria Sophia of Naples whose husband had just lost his throne, and a conflict of personalities at the Court of Vienna between her and her well-meaning, but domineering mother-in-law, Archduchess Sophie. She insisted that she had to go as far away from Austria as possible for an indefinite period. Her choice fell on the island of Madeira, about which she had received such favourable impressions from her brother-in-law, Archduke Maximilian. Moreover, it was sufficiently remote from the likelihood of visits from neighbouring royalties and Austrian officials, and she realised that if she went there she would almost certainly be left completely in peace.

When the Emperor tried to make her delay her departure on the grounds that there was no imperial yacht ready or capable of such a journey in winter, she applied to Queen Victoria to lend her a suitable vessel. Alarmed to hear of her plight, the sympathetic Queen generously placed the *Victoria and Albert* at her disposal, as the only really fast and comfortable means of transport. With the loan of the yacht went an invitation for Empress Elizabeth to come and visit her in England on the way, but this was the last thing the notoriously shy young woman had in mind. Through the British ambassador, Lord Bloomfield, she declined this on the grounds of ill-health and the fact that she was travelling incognito.

A fortnight later, the Queen had what she called 'a most affectionate letter from the Empress herself' written from on board, in which she said she was 'delighted with everything and hoping to visit [her] on her way back'.[13] Yet the Empress probably had no intention of doing any such thing, and in May 1861 she was reunited with Emperor Francis Joseph in the Adriatic Sea on her return home.

Meanwhile in Berlin, a new age was dawning, with the failing health of King Frederick William IV. Having been left incapacitated and partially paralysed after a stroke in 1857, he was increasingly helpless, living a twilight existence. When Prince and Princess Frederick William visited him at Sans Souci Palace in June 1860, they were horrified by the sight of him, a 'human ruin' lying in a bath chair, his left hand, arm, and both legs tied up, unable to speak or direct his eyes to look at anyone, showing no signs of consciousness except for looking up feebly to his right. By Christmas he was evidently dying. Shortly after midnight on New Year's Day in 1861, they were summoned by telegram to join the rest of the family at his bedside, and twenty-four hours later he breathed his last.

With the accession of his brother William to the throne, Frederick William was now Crown Prince. Few doubted that before long he would be king. He and his wife now had two children, William and Charlotte. William had suffered badly at birth during a difficult delivery, leaving him with a deformed left hand and arm that refused to respond to treatment.

King Frederick William IV had added a codicil to his last will and testament, urging his successors to the throne to refuse to take the oath to uphold the Prussian constitution. The Prince Consort was shocked that the late monarch should have 'tried to provoke a breach of faith even after his death' and even more by those at court in Berlin who attempted to put pressure on King William to comply with this out of respect for his late brother.[14] To his relief, the new sovereign rejected their advice, saying he felt it was his duty to conform to the constitution, albeit with reluctance, on the grounds that it would be dangerous for him to oppose it.

For the Prince Consort, King William's accession was the time to make another attempt to write and influence him with his ideas. A free, united, outspoken Germany alone could win respect abroad, he told the Crown Princess, while 'a reactionary tendency in Berlin would play havoc with everything'.[15] He had probably taken some further encouragement from the sudden death of Gerlach, one of the old ultra-conservative guard whom he had regarded as a malign influence on the late king. Gerlach caught a chill at the late king's funeral, held at Potsdam on a day of bitter cold, snow, and frost, with a temperature of 17 degrees below freezing point, and succumbed to pneumonia within a few days. However, King William was annoyed by what he regarded as the Prince Consort's interference. He destroyed the letters without reading them, and scolded his son and daughter-in-law for encouraging him to continue pestering him with his unsolicited ideas and advice.

Nevertheless, in February, the King was flattered and honoured to be made a Knight of the Garter by Queen Victoria, and an emissary was despatched to the court of Berlin to carry out the investiture the following month. In writing to the Prince Consort to thank him and the Queen, he concluded his letter by saying how he shared his hope 'that this event may prove a new bond of friendship between us and our respective countries'.[16] King William was more than happy to remain on the best of terms with England, although allowing the Prince Consort to try and dictate Prussian policy was a different matter entirely.

The Crown Prince fully supported his father's plans to strengthen Prussian military reforms. When newly created regiments in the army were presented with their colours at the beginning of the year, he was proud and delighted to be able to command the assembled troops. Even so, he was dismayed by the King's perception of the political situation and apparent intention to let the conservatives hold sway. He wrote to the

Prince Consort that 'Papa can unfortunately not free himself from those black thoughts which see revolution everywhere and frequently ascribes levelling intentions to our ministers'.[17]

Prince Albert was reluctant to give up hope, but he was particularly dismayed by his failure so far in attempting to influence the new sovereign. When the King made it evident that, as a military man, he was more interested in his army, which was to him the source of Prussia's strength, than in nationalist aspirations, he was even more dispirited. At the same time, the new sovereign's unwillingness to take a leading role on behalf of Prussia in German affairs was also a disappointment to Crown Prince Frederick William and the liberals. Loath to give up, three months later the Prince Consort maintained that Prussia must become 'the moral leader of Germany before it can raise itself as a power in Europe'. This could only come about, he insisted, by adopting 'a bold, confident, truly German and completely liberal policy that corresponds to the needs of our time and the needs of the German nation, which will in turn make it impossible for any of the other German states to adopt any alternative course'.[18] Much, he knew, would depend on whether the King would keep liberal ministers in power and, if so, how much he would listen to them. It was generally assumed by those closest to him that he would have many more years ahead of him as an observer of the political scene, regardless of any influence he might or might not have on the future direction of German affairs.

Fortunately, his son-in-law proved more amenable to his guiding hand, although they were not always in perfect agreement. When Prince Frederick William spoke of his desire to see Prussia deliver 'one hearty blow' in the field of foreign policy to rally the smaller German states behind them, Prince Albert counselled caution. This could not be achieved through sudden decisions, he warned, but only through a 'long, self-confident, logical, courageous, truly German and thoroughly liberal policy'.[19] The elder man still cherished the dream of Prussia leading and merging into Germany at the same time by liberalism and assuming the moral high ground. It was a noble mission, but a dream that—given the direction of Prussian policy and the predominantly soldier-class of Hohenzollern princes and, just over a year later, the appointment of 'a certain strong man'—bore little relation to reality.

The year 1861 was a one of double bereavement for Queen Victoria. On 16 March, she lost her mother the Duchess of Kent, aged seventy-four, after a short illness. Her grief at the loss of the parent from whom she had been briefly estranged at the start of her reign probably had the unfortunate effect of blinding her to a progressive deterioration in the health of the Prince Consort, who was by now increasingly overworked and ageing beyond his forty-two years. During the summer, the Crown Prince and Princess and their family came to stay at Osborne, where he wrapped his little grandson William in a towel and gently swung him in it. When he came to write his childhood memoirs in exile more than sixty years later, William noted that this was one of his earliest memories, as he was only aged two and a half at the time. It was the second and last occasion that he ever saw the grandfather who had entertained such high hopes for him.

After Queen Victoria and the Prince Consort returned from what would be their last happy annual holiday at Balmoral together, it was to be an autumn filled with one worry after another. The Crown Princess of Prussia became seriously ill in October after a severe chill developed into bronchitis, and she took to her bed. At one stage, her doctor warned the Queen that her life could be in danger. No sooner had she recovered than the Queen's eight-year-old youngest son, Prince Leopold—a delicate child who suffered from haemophilia (the bleeding disease)—was sent to the south of France for the good of his health under the care of Sir Edward Bowater, a royal groom and former equerry. The elderly Bowater was far from well himself and, after taken ill, died soon after he and his young charge reached Cannes. At around the same time, King Pedro of Portugal and two of his brothers, second cousins of Queen Victoria and Prince Albert, were taken ill with typhoid fever and died within seven weeks of each other.

All these anxieties and bereavements coincided with news from Baron Stockmar, who had written from Coburg to tell him that, according to rumours circulating throughout Europe, the Prince of Wales had had an affair with an actress while he was at military camp in Ireland. Most fathers of the day would have dismissed such an occurrence as perhaps worthy of a gentle reprimand, but the father of the heir to the throne took it very much to heart. He travelled to Cambridge to see his son in order to find out the truth of the matter and forgive him in person, and by the time he returned to Windsor he felt utterly wretched. The man who had admitted to his wife that he did 'not cling to life', and was sure that if he had a severe illness, he would 'give up at once' and not 'struggle for life', took to his bed and did not get up again.[20] When his second daughter, Princess Alice, who was helping to nurse him, said she had told her elder sister Vicky in Berlin that he was very ill, he corrected her sadly, 'You should have told her I was dying.'

On 14 December, ironically the same day that claimed the life of Bowater in France, Prince Albert passed away. The official diagnosis was typhoid fever, although, in view of his declining health over the previous couple of years, it has been suggested that the more probable cause was renal failure or stomach cancer.[21]

Queen Victoria had been buoyed up by false hopes from some of the doctors, who perhaps shrank from preparing her for the worst. Up until the last day, she seemed to think or let herself be persuaded that her husband would pull through after all. Only in the last few hours did she realise that she was on the point of losing him for ever. Six days after the initial paroxysms of grief, when some feared that she might lose her reason, she managed to put pen to paper and write to various members of the family, particularly King Leopold and the Crown Princess of Prussia, that her life as a happy one was now over. She wrote:

[If I must live on, henceforth it will be] for our poor fatherless children— for my unhappy country, which had lost all in losing him—and in only doing what I know and feel he would wish, for he is near me—his spirit will guide and inspire me![22]

The Crown Prince and Princess of Prussia had also lost the Prince Consort at a crucial time. Although King William was a soldier through and through and not expected to show more than token sympathy to the liberals or more progressive elements in Prussia, there had been hopes at the beginning of his reign that he would allow forward-looking elements to have some influence on the government. Crown Prince and Princess Frederick William and Queen Augusta all shared this optimism to an extent, as did the Prince Consort. With the latter's death, King William, who had always been slightly in awe of him, felt free to do what he wanted, now free of the possibility of reproach from regular letters from England, which he had thrown into the fire unread, but which still made him feel uncomfortable.

During much of 1862, a Prussian political crisis was in the making. Early in the year, the moderates in the ministry insisted that, as extra funds had recently been fraudulently diverted towards expenditure for the army, all government expenditure should be strictly accounted for in future. The King panicked and dissolved the *Landtag* in March, blaming his ministers for not having exerted sufficient influence on the December elections and thus making possible such a large Liberal vote. He became increasingly headstrong and intolerant of any other views. The Crown Prince was increasingly concerned, writing to his wife that he felt more sorry than ever for his father 'whom [he] found so internally collapsed and excited that he was quite incapable of accepting as correct any opinion other than his own'.[23]

Further elections in May increased the progressive vote, frustrating the King's determination to introduce a military budget that the *Landtag* intended to reject. He would not yield, declaring that he would rather rule without a military budget, but his ministers rejected this on the grounds that he would be placing the crown in violation of the constitution. His most staunch ally, Minister of War Albrecht von Roon, advised him to summon Otto von Bismarck, Ambassador to France, as head of government in order to strengthen the powers of the crown. The King hesitated to do so, on the grounds that Bismarck would demand to have unrestricted control of foreign affairs. At first, he declared he would sooner step down from the throne in favour of his son. After watching what she called 'the alarming state of affairs at Berlin' from afar and discussing it with Lord John Russell, now Foreign Secretary, Queen Victoria believed that it would be better if the King abdicated.[24]

Over the weeks, it was apparent that King and ministry had reached deadlock. He refused to concede on his reforms, particularly his insistence on extending the two-year army service. In September, he sent for the Crown Prince and told him tearfully that he felt he had no alternative but to renounce his crown. Horrified, the latter tried to persuade him to think again, while the Crown Princess believed that they owed it to Prussia and to themselves to assume the mantle of his father and accept the crown. The Crown Prince was loath to see such a thing happen, and he warned his father firmly about the immeasurable damage that abdication would do to crown, country and dynasty, merely because of a parliamentary resolution. To the Crown Princess, he wrote how he was appalled by the idea of the 'maleficent, wicked step of abdicating which threatened dynasty, house and crown'.[25] He may have had at the back of his mind that once the matter of the military reforms was settled, the *Landtag* and his father between them could just as easily rescind any instrument of abdication and restore him to the throne.

Neither of them were aware that, as they were deliberating, Bismarck was on his way from France to Prussia. On his return to Berlin, he told the King that there were two alternatives open to them—royal government or the supremacy of parliament. Thus reassured, King William immediately appointed him Minister President and Foreign Minister.

Almost at once, it became apparent to the Crown Prince, Princess, and gradually Queen Victoria that Prussia would be setting on a very different political direction. Within a few weeks, Bismarck had closed the chambers and proceeded to levy the taxes without parliamentary sanction. In a speech, he proclaimed that the great questions of the time would not be solved by speeches and majority decisions, but by blood and iron. The King protested that he felt honour-bound to preserve the constitution, but at the same time declared that he was also required to maintain intact the rights of the crown.

In May 1863, the King and his Minister-President dissolved parliament after the opposition claimed their right to free speech without interruption from the government ministers. Before beginning a tour of military inspection in East Prussia, the Crown Prince, fearful of what might happen next, wrote to his father begging him not to infringe the constitution, in return for him keeping his promise not to oppose his views openly. The King replied that his son's promise had proved a hollow one and now he had a chance to redeem himself by keeping aloof from the progressive party and allying himself with conservative opinion. A decree was about to be published, empowering the suppression of newspapers and periodicals 'for persisting in an attitude endangering the commonweal'. This was plainly an infringement of the constitution, which guaranteed freedom of the press; in condemnation of such a measure, the Crown Prince answered that he considered this to be not merely illegal but also contrary to state and dynastic interests. He did not receive a reply.

Two days later, at a reception at Danzig town hall after a military parade by the garrison, the Crown Prince delivered a speech that he had drafted himself, in which he said he regretted the conflict between government and constitution. He explained that he had been absent and had taken 'no part in the deliberations which led to these ordinances'.[26]

Reaction from the immediate family was swift. Queen Victoria unequivocally applauded the action of her son-in-law, encouraging him to stand firm: 'he must not shrink from separating himself from all his father's unhappy acts!'[27] King William was furious, writing him a letter 'treating him quite like a little child', charging him with disobedience, ordering him to retract his words at once, and telling him firmly that 'if he said one other word of the kind he would instantly recall him and take his place in the Army and the Council from him'.[28] Bitterly upset by his father's unforgiving attitude and filled with remorse, the Crown Prince offered to withdraw completely from public life and even briefly considered what would have amounted to self-imposed exile in England, but the King merely ordered him to continue his tour of inspection and refrain from making any further speeches. His brother, Prince Charles, and the veteran commander General Friedrich von Wrangel had angrily insisted that he ought to make an example of his errant heir by having him confined in a fortress, but Bismarck advised them that it would not do to advance the cause of the liberals by making a martyr of their royal spokesman. He recommended instead that the King should 'deal gently with the young man Absalom'. As it was, the Minister-President's long-lasting distrust of the Crown Prince and Princess would prove to be punishment enough.

In the summer of 1863, Emperor Francis Joseph called a conference at Frankfurt, at which the German sovereigns could discuss the constitution and future of the federation. King William of Prussia wanted to attend, but Bismarck, who had no intention of allowing him to appear subservient to Austria, persuaded him not to go, largely on the rather hollow excuse that his invitation had arrived so late that it was an insult. The proceedings opened without him on 17 August. Queen Victoria had planned to visit Coburg, in order to see the widow of her old friend and mentor, Stockmar, who had died the previous month. Crown Prince and Princess Frederick William went to see the Queen and asked her to try and persuade King William to attend Frankfurt, but when the King paid her a courtesy call he refused to listen. Without him, it could not reach any binding agreements and in his summing up, the Emperor of Austria could only hope—without much optimism—that there might be a similar reunion at the earliest possible date at which Prussia would be represented.

The Queen then cordially invited the Emperor to meet her at Schloss Rosenau, which as the birthplace of the Prince Consort held special memories for the family. As he had had to forego similar social calls on her two previous visits to Germany, he could hardly refuse, but he made it clear that it would be purely '*la visite de politesse*'. This first meeting of both sovereigns took place on 3 September and lasted about three hours, with Ernest, Duke of Saxe-Coburg, her brother-in-law, the only other person present. The Emperor, she thought, was 'very quiet, simple and unaffected, not talkative, but very dignified'. She was convinced that he agreed with her that it was necessary that Prussia and Austria should be 'put upon a feeling of equality' in Germany. Austria was prepared to be friendly and he deeply regretted King William's non-appearance at Frankfurt, for which he laid all blame at the door of Bismarck.[29] In replying to her mother, the Crown Princess wrote that her father-in-law the King was anxious for an understanding between both, but she believed that Austria had not behaved well towards Prussia and that there was a strong feeling of resentment against her.[30]

At around this time, Queen Victoria was involved, albeit in a minor role, with another imperial episode. Mexico had been a Spanish colony until 1821 and a republic since 1824, torn by civil war that led to the arrival of French troops who were brought in on the pretext of unpaid debts. By 1861, they had apparently succeeded in routing the troops of President Benito Juarez and Napoleon intended to establish an empire there under French patronage, with the continued presence of his army as a guarantee of security. Emperor Francis Joseph's brother, Archduke Maximilian, who was married to King Leopold's daughter Princess Charlotte, was named as a potential Emperor of Mexico.

The idea appealed to him as a role that would bring him independence from his elder brother, and even more to the ambitious Charlotte who was thrilled at the prospect of becoming an Empress. His mother, Archduchess Sophie, was convinced that it would be a hazardous venture, a view shared by Emperor Francis Joseph, to whom Napoleon was 'that arch-rogue'. He let it be known that his brother's acceptance of the Mexican crown was out of the question unless offered by the Mexican people themselves and guaranteed by the maritime powers. Lord Palmerston and Lord John Russell, at the time Prime Minister and Foreign Secretary respectively, both believed that Maximilian was 'far too good for Mexico'. Instead, they believed he would do better to become King of Greece, now that the unpopular and childless King Otto had been deposed and the Greeks' first choice for their new sovereign, Queen Victoria's second son Prince Alfred, had been overwhelmingly elected, but was ruled ineligible to accept the crown under the terms of a London Protocol of 1830.

With the unequivocal support of Emperor Francis Joseph, Archduke Maximilian rejected the Greek throne, thinking it undignified to consent to it after it had been hawked around in such a fashion. After much hesitation, in October 1863, he agreed to become Emperor of Mexico. The Queen was dismayed that he had done so, sharing her government's view that they could do nothing for him and Charlotte beyond wishing them well. Like her government, she regarded it as a foolhardy enterprise and doomed to almost certain failure. On 9 April 1864, Maximilian and Emperor Francis Joseph signed a 'family pact', by which the former renounced for himself and his issue all rights of succession and inheritance in Austria. As they embraced each other with tears streaming down their cheeks, it was as if they had a presentiment that they would never see each other again. That same day, Queen Victoria wrote to Crown Princess Frederick William, commenting sadly that Maximilian and Charlotte had had much annoyance about 'this wretched Mexico', which she feared would 'end badly for them. It really grieves [the Queen] deeply'.[31]

Bismarck had presciently pointed out that their Royal Highnesses, the Crown Prince and Princess, needed to realise that 'in ruling Houses the nearest of kin may yet be aliens'.[32] Queen Victoria's family were indeed about to experience the first of what would be many a bitter division of family loyalties. In November 1863, King Frederik VII of Denmark died and was succeeded by Prince Christian of Schleswig-Holstein-Sonderburg-Glucksburg, who took the title King Christian IX. The duchies of Schleswig and Holstein, situated geographically between Denmark and Germany, but belonging to the German Confederation, had been placed under Danish rule by the London Protocol of 1852. Holstein boasted a large German population, and it was inevitable that, on King Frederik's death, demands by one if not both duchies for recognition or self-government would come to a head.

The Crown Prince, Crown Princess, and Queen Augusta all supported the claims to the duchies of Frederick, who was nominally their duke. They were at one with Queen Victoria, whose niece, Princess Adelaide of Hohenlohe-Langenburg—the same princess whose hand Emperor Napoleon had briefly sought in marriage—was married to Frederick. The Prince and Princess of Wales, son-in-law and daughter of King Christian IX, were naturally passionate in their defence of Denmark's continued claim to the disputed territories. The Crown Prince and Princess were staying in England for a few days in November 1863, and the atmosphere was made difficult by furious family arguments on the issue, until at length the harassed Queen Victoria took the advice of King Leopold of the Belgians and forbade any further mention of the subject in her presence.

Suspicions were rife that Bismarck would lay claim to Schleswig and Holstein in order to amalgamate them and add to the strength of Prussia. In January 1864, without consulting the other German states, he sent King Christian an ultimatum to evacuate and renounce all claim to the duchies within twenty-four hours or else war would be declared. On 1 February, Prussia and her German allies marched into Schleswig, with the Crown Prince as a reluctant second-in-command under the elderly General Wrangel. A conflict in which the Danes were hopelessly outnumbered ended with German victory in June and peace was concluded at the Treaty of Vienna in July. Towards the end of the year, Denmark renounced her claims to Schleswig and Holstein in favour of Prussia and Austria, and the claims of Frederick of Holstein were ignored.

Emperor Francis Joseph shared the disquiet about the partitioning of the duchies, and a few months later he suggested that they should be handed to Duke Frederick after all. The matter was referred to the Diet at Frankfurt, where representatives endorsed the claim of the Augustenburg family. However, by the early months of 1866, it was evident that Bismarck's plan had been for Prussia to annex the duchies and that, in order to resolve the issue, a new war between Austria and Prussia would be only a matter of time. King William did not want to fight his neighbour and ally and he asked the Crown Prince to write to Queen Victoria, saying he would accept any offer of mediation her government might be prepared to make.

In May, the Queen informed her son-in-law that she had tried her hardest to intercede with King William and all her pleading and warning was having no effect. As Foreign Secretary, Lord Clarendon was well aware that Bismarck wielded more power than his sovereign. He insisted that the British government was powerless to do anything and it was up to the Queen to use whatever influence she possessed if she so wished.

The pacifist liberal majority in the *Landtag* suggested calling a European conference to settle the dispute, but the Queen insisted that neither she nor her government would take part in any proceedings that would allow Prussia to annex the duchies, and the idea collapsed.

In June, the federal army, comprising troops from Austria, Hanover, Saxony, Bavaria, Württemberg, and Hesse, was mobilised, while Coburg remained neutral. Bismarck interpreted this as a declaration of war and, after a few small skirmishes, the full armies of both sides met on a plain near the town of Königgrätz, Bohemia, on 3 July. After several hours of fierce fighting with heavy casualties on both sides, in the face of a determined advance from the Prussian forces, the Austrian commander ordered his troops to retreat. For the Prussians, it was a decisive victory that effectively brought an end to what would be known to posterity as the Seven Weeks' War.

An armistice was called two weeks later. Hesse was one of the few German states allowed to retain its independence, although she was forced to pay considerable financial reparations to Prussia. It retained its autonomy largely as much of it was situated south of the River Main, a line beyond which Prussia refrained from expanding her territory as it would be considered unduly provocative to France. Hanover, the ancestral home of the British monarchy, was less fortunate. The blind King George V, who had fled with his family to Austria, was deposed, although he never renounced his rights to the throne before his death in exile in Paris in 1878.

In England, the royal family were shocked by this wanton assimilation of their ancestral home. Prince George, Duke of Cambridge, wrote to Queen Victoria:

> It certainly never entered my head that I should live to see the day when the King of Hanover was to be driven from his Kingdom by his neighbour the King of Prussia, nor would I have believed that my old friends of the Hanoverian Army would have to lay down their arms, after making a most gallant resistance.[33]

The Queen answered the following day that she fully agreed with him:

> Respecting the sad and distressing state of Germany, and the extraordinary and unheard-of conduct of Prussia towards Hanover and Saxony. But I fear I can do but little respecting Hanover, beyond expressing my deep interest in its integrity and well-doing.[34]

In September, the Prussian government formally annexed the Kingdom of Hanover. Queen Victoria felt powerless to do anything but protest; she asked the Crown Princess to tell the Crown Prince that she was writing him a long letter to show the King, requesting that the former sovereign and his wife should be treated with kindness and generosity. If there was anything she could do 'to facilitate this painful negotiation' she was ready to do so, as none of them could forget that the unfortunate former sovereign was the head of their family in the male line, and there would be very strong feeling in England against the King of Prussia 'if poor King George and his family, after being despoiled of their own lawful possessions, were left in poverty and in a position not befitting to their rank and near relationship to [her] family'. King William, she added, formerly used to be so generous 'and ought to be the more so now when everything is in his power'.[35] Her entreaties fell on deaf ears.

During the next few years, Queen Victoria's children were sharply divided in their attitudes to France and to Emperor Napoleon himself. The German Crown Princess, who as a young unmarried Princess Royal had been devoted to Empress Eugénie, but was now firmly committed to the cause of Prussia, even if she was no friend or admirer of the Minister-President, Otto von Bismarck, had revised her opinions. Much as she liked the Emperor and Empress as people, and could not forget their kindness to her in happier times, she shared the view of her late father that the Emperor and the 'decadent' French Empire had plans on Germany. The Prince of Wales, now married to Princess Alexandra of Denmark, would never be less than consistent in his admiration for everything and everyone French. His tastes were shared by his brothers, Alfred and Arthur, who had visited Paris and thoroughly enjoyed the experience. Their sister, Alice, married to Prince Louis of Hesse and the Rhine, had become German by marriage, but Hesse was a smaller, less powerful rival to Prussia and she, too, became an occasional and very enthusiastic visitor to Paris.

Queen Victoria's sympathies with Prussia—and, from 1867 onwards, the Prussian-led German Confederation—were stronger than any she had with the increasingly liberal French Empire, of which she had once seemed such a staunch supporter. While she wanted to be on amicable terms with France, she was insistent that, if hostilities should break out between both countries, she would rather Britain sided with Germany. As early as 1862, she was starting to refer to Paris as 'that Sodom and Gomorrah'. When the Prince of Wales was due to travel back through France after returning to Europe from a tour of the Holy Land, she gave orders to his entourage that he could only spend one day in Paris and on no account was he to stay there overnight. The 'wicked city' was too full of temptation for a young man who was so easily led astray, as his one-night stand at the Curragh military camp a year earlier had proved beyond all doubt. After the Prince of Wales married Princess Alexandra of Denmark in 1863 and was planning another expedition to Paris, she grudgingly gave her consent on the condition that they did so incognito. Moreover, she insisted that they stayed at a hotel and did not lodge with the Emperor and Empress. Perhaps fortunately for the Prince, his young wife rapidly became just as enamoured with Paris as he was; although, within a few years, rheumatic fever, deafness, and a preference for staying at home with their growing family would result in his visiting France increasingly on his own, without her by his side.

In April 1867, the *Exposition Universelle* opened in Paris, on the Champ de Mars, the great military parade ground of Paris. Planned by Emperor Napoleon three years earlier as a celebration of the economic success of the era, it proved to be the zenith of the Second Empire. Queen Victoria was not persuaded to attend, but she was represented by the Prince of Wales and the Duke of Edinburgh, both of whom never needed an excuse to visit Paris, while other guests included Tsar Alexander II of Russia, King William of Prussia, and Bismarck. The former had a narrow escape from assassination one day as he was returning in the Emperor's carriage from a military review, when a Polish exile fired at him from close range.

Ironically, the glory of the exhibition was to be marred by one piece of unwelcome tragic news, which a few people had seen coming, but still shocked the public once fully known. Those who had predicted that the Mexican empire would end in tears were about to be proved all too correct. Once Maximilian and Carlota were established in their court in Mexico City, they began to realise too late that, despite all they had been led to believe, French troops were not in control of the country. Resentment at a Habsburg Archduke being sent to rule the country ran high and, after the end of the American Civil War, pressure on Napoleon to withdraw his troops and financial support intensified and he was obliged to withdraw his interests. Carlota returned to Europe on a desperate mission to beg him for help, but to no avail. He could offer her nothing, and the strain and effort of her mission had cost her her reason. After the remaining French military presence left Mexican soil in February 1867, Maximilian placed himself at the head of imperialist troops, but three months later they deserted him and transferred their allegiance to General Juarez. He surrendered, was court-martialled, sentenced to death for treason, and alongside two officers who had remained loyal with him to the end he was executed by a firing squad on 19 June. Opposition parties in France were quick to pay ironic tributes to the man they derided as 'the Archdupe'.

On 1 July, a telegram in cypher reached Paris, just as a prize-giving ceremony was about to take place at the exposition in the *Palais d'Industrie*. On reading the message, Napoleon burst into tears, but quickly pulled himself together and broke the news to Eugénie. The presentations took place as planned, but her self-control gradually gave way and, on her return to the Tuileries, she was carried half-fainting to her bed.

Next day Queen Victoria heard from a telegram sent from an Austrian ship from Vera Cruz to Sir Thomas Biddulph, her Keeper of the Privy Purse, announcing the fate of Maximilian, adding that it 'seemed uncertain'. A further wire from the Austrian Minister at Washington two days later confirmed the sad news. The Queen was deeply grieved for 'poor dear unhappy Charlotte bereft of her reason', but perhaps not altogether surprised. To her it was 'a shocking end to their luckless undertaking, which [she] did all [she] could to prevent, and which dearest Albert was so much against'.[36]

Ironically, it had happened at a convenient time for Her Majesty. She had been due to review the troops at Hyde Park on 5 July, in a ceremony that would be made 'as imposing as possible' by the presence of her cousin the Duke of Cambridge, Commander-in-Chief of the Army. Lord Derby, her Prime Minister, was keen to persuade her not to take John Brown, the Royal Highland attendant, whose association with her had already given rise to adverse comment and even salacious gossip at home and abroad, but she refused to 'be dictated to'. The deadlock between monarch and head of government was only resolved when it was deemed prudent to cancel the review as a mark of respect to the memory of the late Emperor.

Later that month, she read in the papers 'with a horror not to be expressed' of full details of the death of Emperor Maximilian. She wrote forthwith to her ministers that she trusted the British Mission would be recalled from Mexico at once, and that all relations with the administration of President Juarez would be severed: 'It would be an eternal disgrace to us were we to entertain any diplomatic relations with such a bloodstained Government as that of the monster Juarez and his adherents'.[37]

His execution also resulted in an alteration to plans for Empress Eugénie to spend three days with Queen Victoria at Osborne. She had planned to attend a naval review at Spithead, but as the imperial court was in a month's mourning for the execution of Emperor Maximilian of Mexico, the visit was changed to a private one. Eugénie had been among those who most fervently championed the scheme that had ended so quickly in disaster. She could not but refer with a sense of guilt to 'poor Max's murder' and the precarious state of mental health of his widow Empress Carlota. The one saving grace was that her father, King Leopold, had died in December 1865, some eighteen months before the execution of Maximilian, and had not lived long enough to witness their ignominious fate.

With regard to her partisanship of Prussia, the Queen had to choose her words with care. Her sympathies were strongly with the recently created Prussian-controlled North German Confederation. Had the Prince Consort still been alive, she knew he would never have ceased to champion the cause of Germany. Her two eldest daughters had both married into Germany and, in the event of a Franco-German war, it was inevitable as to which powers she would support. The best she could do was to urge the Empress to bring what influence she could on the Emperor—which, she doubtless knew, would only be very slight—to maintain peace between both countries and, if possible, avoid any further arming on the part of France, lest the whole of Europe should be suddenly plunged into war. It was ironic that the Queen should find herself championing the autocratic and militaristic Prussia of Bismarck, the man who had declared that the great questions of the day would be settled by iron and blood, than the France in which Emperor Napoleon III was gradually introducing and granting liberal reforms to his government.

By this time, there was a feeling that the greatest days of Napoleon's empire were behind them. Some felt that France's position as a world power had been shaken by the Prussian victory at Königgrätz, which had confirmed Prussia as the most powerful military state in Europe. The ignominious end of the Mexican empire was a further blow to French prestige and the Emperor and Empress were no longer as popular in their own country. Ominous parallels were drawn between Queen Marie Antoinette, 'the Austrian', and the Empress, 'the Spaniard'. It was believed that, in some of her darker moments, Empress Eugénie feared that she might possibly end up suffering the same fate as the ill-starred Queen had done some seventy years earlier.

Queen and Empress were destined to meet again before long, in August 1868, and once again in less happy circumstances. Queen Victoria was passing through Paris on her way to Lucerne, Switzerland, for a short holiday. Having travelled from Cherbourg, she arrived in Paris on the morning of 5 August 1868, incognito as the Countess of Kent. It was an alias that deceived no one, although it emphasised to the world outside that she was travelling as a private citizen. It had been arranged that the Empress would come up from Fontainebleau to the Elysée Palace, next to the British Embassy in Paris, to pay a short courtesy call on the Queen. She visited the embassy for a little less than an hour in the afternoon and, of this, precisely ten minutes was spent in the company of Queen Victoria.

Once the latter had left Paris, there were indignant comments in the French press on the grounds that she had done so without returning the Empress's call and therefore insulted France. She should, it was maintained, have waited until the Empress had returned to the Elysée and visited her there. An explanation from the Empress that she had begged the Queen not to tire herself satisfied nobody. The press insisted that the Queen was being aloof and that the slight proved beyond doubt that she still favoured the exiled house of Orléans over and above that of the reigning Bonapartes.

In her defence, the Queen claimed that she had found the heat overpowering. It was, however, well-known that since the death of the Prince Consort she hated appearing anywhere in public, either at home or abroad. Lord Cowley noted on a visit to the Empress a few days later that she seemed rather annoyed and at one stage she even asked Queen Sophie of the Netherlands why, if the Queen found public life so unbearable, did she not abdicate.[38]

In order to avoid further controversy, it was suggested that, when the Queen returned from Switzerland and was due to reach Paris on her way home in September 1868, it would be best for all if the Emperor and Empress were to leave Paris for Biarritz before her arrival. Although they were still at Paris, the Queen spent a day at the British Embassy and then drove out briefly to the Palace of St Cloud. As her carriage turned into the quadrangle and stopped at the main entrance, she did not alight, but looked through the door and up the great staircase, where she saw a vast painting of her ceremonial arrival at the very same place thirteen years earlier. At once she was struck by the extraordinary contrast between circumstances in happier days and the changed situation now.

Empress Eugénie was once again displeased at this strange lack of courtesy from her old friend. Disraeli was told that at first she 'was inclined to pass the matter over, but her Ministers and everybody round her kept telling her that she had been badly treated so that at last she began to believe it herself and the French Court was very sore about the matter'.[39]

4

'Such Meekness, Dignity and Patience'

By this time, Emperor Napoleon was suffering from increasing ill-health, and increasingly prone to poor judgment. He was suffering from pains in the bladder and severe discomfort, and it was noticed by the Empress and others close to him that he was liable to procrastinate, evade, and not be reliable when it came to making decisions. Lord Lyons, British ambassador in Paris, was told by others that he was increasingly weary of his position. Any crisis in which France might become involved could have severe consequences.

The road to the end of the French Empire began in March 1870. It was the month in which Queen Victoria received a confidential letter from her son-in-law, the Crown Prince of Prussia, asking her what her reaction would be to the acceptance of the Spanish crown by one of his relations, Prince Leopold of Hohenzollern-Sigmaringen. The great powers of Europe had been actively seeking a sovereign for Spain since the childless Queen Isabella II had been deposed in 1868. After consulting Lord Clarendon, she answered that it was a matter for the Prince himself to decide and it was not for the British sovereign or her government to express a view. Her letter was duly passed to King William of Prussia and to his Chancellor, Bismarck, who interpreted the reply as an assurance that Britain would not interfere if Prussia was to place a Hohenzollern on the Spanish throne. This was all part of his strategy, in trying to bring all the German states into the Prussian fold, which would thus secure German unification.

Aware that the French would never tolerate a Hohenzollern on the Spanish throne, Bismarck saw that to provoke a war with France in which Germany would surely emerge triumphant would give him all he needed. In July 1870, news of Prince Leopold's acceptance of the Spanish throne broke. The furious French government demanded that King William of Prussia should order Prince Leopold to withdraw forthwith. The King refused to comply, saying that if the Prince wished to withdraw of his own free will he was entitled to do so. Persuaded by several other European crowned heads, he withdrew his candidature. With this, Emperor Napoleon was content. However, others in France, including the Empress, demanded that Prussia must give a guarantee that the question of Prince Leopold's candidature would never be raised again, King William refused. Declaring that they had been insulted before all the world, the French declared war on 19 July.

Throughout the crisis, Queen Victoria had been increasingly anxious. She foresaw that, if such a war was to break out and France was to be defeated, it would almost certainly mean the unification of Germany under Prussian leadership and also the end of the French Empire and the downfall of Napoleon. If France was to be victorious, the lives of two sons-in-law, the Crown Prince of Prussia and Prince Louis of Hesse, would be in jeopardy on the battlefield. She agreed with the verdict of *The Times* that the French attack on Prussia was nothing short of a great national crime and would lead to an unjust, but premeditated war. Bismarck had ensured that the sympathies of the world would be with Prussia, a move he reinforced when, with immaculate timing, he released another document. In 1866, Napoleon had been attempting to obtain some form of compensation from Bismarck for French neutrality during the Austro-Prussian War and had proposed a secret treaty between Bismarck and himself, but which Prussia might at some unspecified date in the future, help France to annex Belgium. The French ambassador had made a copy of the draft treaty in his handwriting and given it to Bismarck. The latter had assured Napoleon that he agreed with it, and put it away safely for future reference. Now, when France declared war on Prussia, Bismarck instructed the Prussian ambassador in London to show it to Gladstone, the Prime Minister. The text was accordingly released to *The Times*. Gladstone, Queen Victoria, and the general public were all appalled.

As ever, the British royal family was divided. The Queen claimed that the war had been provoked by German aggression. Her eldest daughters were equally committed to the German cause, as was the third sister, Princess Helena, who had married Prince Christian of Schleswig-Holstein in 1866. The latter particularly wanted to go to Germany so he could serve in the army, but, as Queen Victoria's son-in-law, it was thought better that he should not 'as it might lead to difficulties and complications'.[1]

The Prince of Wales and Alfred, Duke of Edinburgh, were just as unequivocally pro-French. When he attended a dinner party at the French Embassy on the evening before war was declared, the Prince of Wales was alleged to have remarked to Austrian Ambassador Rudolf, Count Apponyi, his hopes that the Austrian army might join the French in order to defeat

Prussia and that the latter would be taught a lesson at last. Before long, the story was being reported to Berlin by the Prussian Ambassador in London, Count Albrecht von Bernstorff, a man whom Queen Victoria called 'a shocking mischief maker'. All the same, the German Crown Princess and her family reacted with horror. Although the Prince of Wales denied saying any such thing, he refrained from expressing any support for Germany. When the Crown Princess addressed an emotional appeal to the Queen for England to assist Prussia and Germany, he told their mother that nobody 'could express feelings more touchingly or simply' than his elder sister, but he felt it only right to ask her to consider how the Danes must have felt when they heard that the armies of Prussia and Austria were engaged in conflict against them: 'Everybody must confess that that campaign was a war of aggression'.[2] Despite this, he conceded that the French were 'quite in the wrong, and, as all our relations are in Germany, it is not likely that [he would] go against them'. Bernstorff, he added, was 'an ill-conditioned man,' and he longed for the day when he was removed from London.[3]

Nevertheless, Queen Victoria and her government were resolute in remaining neutral during the conflict. On the morning of 28 July, Napoleon, accompanied by the fourteen-year-old Prince Imperial, left St Cloud. Despite ill-health, he intended to take personal command of his army, while he left the Empress behind in Paris to act as regent. A fortnight later, in constant pain and taking regular doses of laudanum, he had no choice but to hand over supreme command of the army to Marshal François Bazaine.

Any predictions that the French forces would prove superior were very soon proved wrong. The campaign went against them almost immediately, with one defeat in battle after another. Earl Granville blamed French defeat on poor government and corruption, though a more careful view suggested that the army was suffering from indifferent organisation and uninspired leadership from incompetent generals and, above all, an ailing Emperor. On 3 September, one of the two French armies capitulated at Sedan. Having been told that the French position was hopeless, the Emperor authorised General Emmanuel de Wimpffen to negotiate terms of surrender and said he would personally write to King William of Prussia in order to confirm his decision. The following day, he was escorted by a guard of honour to the Belgian frontier, spending two nights in Belgium, and was then held as a captive at Wihelmshöhe, near Cassel.

In England, Queen Victoria was deeply moved by their fate, and thought it remarkable if not shameful that a French Republic was proclaimed in Paris with not one vote in the chambers cast on behalf of the imperial cause. On 9 September, she received a telegram informing her that Empress Eugénie had landed at Hastings and had been reunited with the Prince Imperial. A couple of days later, she was given a more detailed account of the Empress's escape. An Englishman, Sir John Burgoyne, High Sheriff of Bedfordshire, had been aboard his yacht in Deauville Harbour on the afternoon of 6 September, having sailed from England to fetch his wife who was on holiday, when he was visited by two unknown men, who asked to be shown over the vessel. A little later, one of them, who turned out to be her dentist, Dr Evans, drew him to one side and revealed that the Empress was in hiding in the resort. She and one of her ladies-in-waiting had sought refuge in his house after they had escaped from the Tuileries two days before, without any luggage, and was anxious to escape from France at all costs. He therefore drove her to Deauville and was now asking whether Burgoyne would be prepared to take her to England that evening. The latter hesitated, partly because it was a stormy night and partly because he did not want the danger of being involved in any political escapades at such a time. At length, he agreed after consulting with his wife. Just after midnight, Dr Evans brought the Empress and her lady, Madame Lebreton, on board. The Empress was very upset at first, but Burgoyne assured her that she would have nothing to fear and that she would be safe in the hands of an English gentleman. Although the overnight seas proved rough, as had been expected, a few hours later they landed at Ryde and she was able to join her son.

At once, the Queen wrote to her, commiserating and saying that she thought frequently of her at this time of terrible trial. She remembered past times and the hospitality that she and the Emperor had shown her and her family. When the Prince of Wales was told, he offered her Chiswick House as a home, a kind, but impulsive gesture that immediately caused uproar. Even the Queen thought it was a 'presumptuous indiscretion'. Lord Granville considered it indiscreet in the extreme, especially since she was still technically Regent of France and Britain was about to offer official recognition of the new Republican government in France. Perhaps fortunately for everyone, the Empress declined the offer. She assured him that Camden Place in Chislehurst, in which she had just established herself, would provide her with the tranquillity and calm that she was seeking. A modest country house, close to a Catholic church and only half an hour's train journey from London, it would suit her needs very well.

At the end of November, the Queen and thirteen-year-old Princess Beatrice came to see her. They found her dressed completely in black, looking 'very thin and pale, but still very handsome', with 'an expression of deep sadness in her face, and she frequently had tears in her eyes'.[4] The visit lasted about half an hour, with the Empress giving them a full report of her last few nightmarish days in France. She had remained in the Tuileries as long as she could, but once the mob had invaded the chambers, with a threatening crowd outside calling for her dethronement, she escaped, throwing herself into a passing cab and eventually finding refuge with her dentist. After she and Beatrice left, the Queen considered that the sad visit had 'seemed like a strange dream'. She found it astonishing, and poignant, that the Emperor and Empress who had entertained them in such splendour not so many years before should now be fugitives, reduced to such desperate measures for their survival.

Six days later, the Empress and her son returned the Queen's visit. A still visibly upset Empress spoke intimately of her last meeting with the Emperor on French soil and their reconciliation after a period of coolness, the prospects for peace in France that would undoubtedly be difficult while there was no official government, and finally a short visit in a closed carriage to the mausoleum at Frogmore, where the Prince Consort had been laid to rest. 'What a fearful contrast to her visit here in '55!' the Queen observed afterwards. 'Then all was state and pomp, wild excitement and enthusiasm—and now? How strange that I should have seen these two Revolutions, in '48, and '70!'[5]

The Franco-Prussian War had resulted in the death of one European empire and the birth of another. In January 1871, the German Empire was proclaimed in the Salle des Glaces at Versailles, although it proved to be an anything but glorious ceremony. The Crown Prince had tried to impress on his father that the elevation of three German princes to the rank of King by Napoleon Bonaparte some sixty years earlier had made it necessary for him to accept the rank of Emperor in order to assert his superiority. Even so, King William remained as touchy and glum as ever as he muttered goodbye to 'the old Prussia'. Not for the first time, he threatened to abdicate and hand over the reins to his son. To him, the new empire was a betrayal of Prussia's time-honoured noble traditions, as he snapped that his son supported the new state of affairs wholeheartedly: 'Whereas I don't give a fig for it and stick to nothing but Prussia'.[6] He was even denied his choice of title, which he had wanted to be 'Emperor of Germany'. The Crown Prince and Bismarck had preferred and advised 'German Emperor', or 'Emperor in Germany', which emphasised the merging of Prussia into something greater and would be more acceptable to the other German princes.

Now that peace had come, King—shortly to be Emperor—William was anxious to justify his status to Queen Victoria as the victor. In a lengthy letter written that same week, probably drafted by Bismarck, he thanked her for her 'lively sympathy with the unexpected and glorious successes of the war', which she had asked the Crown Prince to pass on to him. He deeply regretted all that she had told him about the change of popular feeling in England, which had been very much on the side of Germany at the outbreak of war six months earlier, as well as English neutrality, which he thought 'so contrary to our hopes and expectations'. Nobody, he said, regretted more than he did 'the signs of ill-feeling which are arising between England and Germany, for the two countries are in all respects destined to go hand in hand'.[7] It was, however, the beginning of a road that would culminate in two world wars. The more far-seeing Napoleon realised at the time that the result of Prussia's victory was that eventually Europe would need to crush Prussia.[8]

That same month, Crown Princess Frederick William sent a large parcel from Berlin to her mother at Windsor. It contained a screen that had formerly had pride of place in the Empress Eugénie's boudoir at St Cloud. When the French shells set fire to the building, the Prussian soldiers tried to save the valuable items before they were completely engulfed by the flames. One man managed to rescue the screen with only a few minutes to spare, and one of the generals obtained permission to pass it on to the Crown Princess. It put her in a difficult position, for although St Cloud had not been the private property of the Emperor and Empress but of the state, she did not consider it a trophy of war and knew that in all conscience she could not keep it for herself. Moreover, she had no desire to have anything in her possession that had belonged to the woman who was always such a generous friend to her in happier times. She asked the Queen whether she could pass the screen to the Empress when the opportunity arose. It would be impossible for her to offer it as a present while France and Germany were still at war and she considered it nothing more and nothing less than restoring a piece of property to its rightful owner.[9]

This placed the Queen in a difficult position and she consulted Lord Granville. After consideration, he advised that it would be difficult for Her Majesty to receive as a present something that had been taken from the palace of an allied state, and there was 'something awkward in restoring, to the Empress here, that which belongs to the State in France'. The Empress might refuse the offer, 'and the French entourage might make much of this proof of plunder'.[10] Sir Henry Ponsonby, her private secretary, endorsed this advice, suggesting to her that the parcel 'should not remain here longer than necessary'. Once newspaper correspondents began to interview people who were involved in the war, the story was bound to get out 'and ill-natured distortions of a well-meaning act might rouse the angry feeling in England against the Crown Prince, and attempt to associate it with [Her] Majesty's name'.[11] The screen was accordingly packed up on arrival and returned to the Crown Princess, who later sent it to the former Emperor and Empress once they were settled in England.

The end of the Franco-Prussian War meant that Emperor Napoleon could be released from Wilhelmshöhe, where he had been held in captivity for the last few months. On 20 March, he arrived in England to join the Empress at Camden. There had been some discussion between them by letter as to where they would live, and whether to stay in England, once he was freed. He had thought of living in Switzerland, while she had suggested Trieste. They did not wish to live in a less stable state abroad, where they might prove an embarrassment to individuals and governments. Any doubts that the English might not be happy to have him within their midst were dispelled as soon as he landed at Dover, where he was given a rapturous welcome, cheered, applauded, and pelted with flowers.

A week after his arrival at Camden, the Queen invited him to Windsor. It was, as expected, again a sad contrast with happier times, as she watched him alight painfully from his carriage, now looking elderly, stout, and grey, his moustaches no longer waxed as they had once been. He looked depressed and had tears in his eyes, but he pulled himself together as he told her what a long time it was since they had last met. As they sat talking in the audience room, they spoke about his captivity. He had no word of complaint against his German captors whom he said had treated him well throughout, and he expressed his renewed admiration of England. His angriest words were reserved for 'the dreadful and disgraceful state of France, and how all that had passed during the last few months had greatly lowered the French character, the officers breaking their parole included'.[12]

Once the Queen had returned this visit to Camden Place a few days later, she was greatly struck by the Emperor's stoicism. While the Empress was fierce in her condemnation of those whom she felt had betrayed the Empire, he never complained about those who had misled or deserted him. When the Empress begged him to defend himself against slanders circulating about him, he replied calmly that it was the prerogative of a sovereign to shoulder 'the responsibilities incurred by those who had served him or betrayed him'.[13] His presence, it was noted, seemed to have a soothing effect on everybody around him.

Once again, Queen Victoria was warming to the relaxed and gentlemanly manner of the man who had so charmed her when he had been at the height of his powers. It was gradually becoming apparent to her that he was not responsible for the Franco-Prussian War, as so many people had assumed. When the German Crown Prince and Princess came to stay with her at Osborne in July, the former was able to reveal to her the part Bismarck had played in provoking France and therefore bringing about the war. The German Chancellor, he told her, was 'no doubt energetic and clever, but bad, unprincipled, and all-powerful', as well as Emperor in all but name. He thought that they were living on a volcano and it would not surprise him if one day Bismarck tried to make war on England.[14]

The Queen went out of her way to treat Napoleon and Eugénie as if they were still fellow sovereigns. They were particularly touched on the occasion of her state drive to St Paul's Cathedral in February 1872, when she was attending a service to give thanks for the Prince of Wales's recovery from what had been an almost fatal attack of typhoid two months previously and she invited them to view the procession from the privacy of Buckingham Palace. She regularly visited them at Camden Place and on one occasion they were very gratified when she assured them that she no longer had any desire to visit Paris, now that they were no longer there. She was also particularly taken with Louis, the Prince Imperial, admiring his high spirits and excellent manners. Many years later, the Empress told the diplomat and historian Maurice Paléologue, who was a boy of twelve at the fall of the empire, that she was always conscious how much they owed to the Queen.

> You would never believe all the delicate attentions she lavished upon us in those first cruel days of our exile. She always treated us as sovereigns, just as in the days when we were allies of England; one day she said to me: 'you no longer have the sovereignty of power; but you have a still higher sovereignty, that of misfortune'. Her visits to Chislehurst did us so much good.[15]

Despite everything that had happened, Napoleon had not given up all hope of regaining his throne. During the Siege of Paris, which lasted from the beginning of April to the third week of May, the city was in a pitiful state. Napoleon and Eugénie were appalled to hear of hostages being shot in batches by the communards, and the violent deaths of the archbishop, alongside several dozen monks and priests. The Palace of St Cloud was not the only landmark to go up in flames and the destruction by firebombers of the Tuileries, the Palais Royal, and the Hôtel de Ville were soon added to the sorry lost, while the Louvre was saved just in time. A mob billeted themselves in the orphanage founded by the Empress and many of the children were raped.

Queen Victoria was perhaps fortunately unaware that Napoleon was working on a plan to try and save the country he loved. He had not been settled at Camden long before he had decided on what he intended to be triumphant and bloodless march on Paris. With the aid of Bonapartist agents and sympathisers, in March 1873, he would leave England in secret, join Plon-Plon in Switzerland, and go to Lyons. There they would be assisted by a commander of the garrison who was known to be loyal to their cause and from there they would set out to their capital. However, as time went by, it looked increasingly as if he was living on borrowed time. After he had been in almost continuous pain for several months, in December 1872, the Queen's physician, Sir William Gull, and an assistant were summoned to Camden Place to examine him. A large stone in his bladder was diagnosed and an operation to crush and remove as many fragments as possible took place on 2 January. A second was performed four days later, but it left the Emperor severely weakened. He lost ground steadily and, on the morning of 9 January, the day on which a third operation had been scheduled to take place, a priest was summoned to administer the last sacraments. Twenty minutes later, muttering to his doctor, 'We weren't cowards at Sedan, were we, Conneau?' he passed away. Eugénie whispered, '*C'est impossible!*', then flung herself across the bed in tears. A telegram was despatched by his secretary, Franceschini Piétri, to Queen Victoria.

The Queen had been kept informed of the state of his health on a regular basis and, although she had been well aware of the severity of his illness, she was shocked when she received the news. She noted:

> Had a great regard for the Emperor who was so amiable and kind, and had borne his terrific misfortunes with such meekness, dignity, and patience. He had been such a faithful ally to England, and I could [not] but think of the wonderful position he had.

It seemed 'too tragic and sad' that he should die like this from the results of an operation.[16]

Sitting down to send her condolences to the Empress, she assured her that she would never forget the Emperor's kindness to her, the memory of the days they had spent together in France and England, which would never fade, signing it, 'Your Imperial Majesty's affectionate sister, Victoria R.'. As she handed the letter with an equerry and then spent the rest of the afternoon despatching and receiving telegrams, she was touched that the German imperial family seemed especially concerned about the fate of the man whom they had vanquished as an enemy only two years earlier.

Her immediate dilemma was whether she should attend the Emperor's funeral or not. She decided that, whatever her personal feelings, as a reigning monarch she could not risk offending the French Republic by doing so. The Prince of Wales, whose commitment to the family's cause had never been in any doubt, was adamant that he would go. The Queen was in two minds, initially inclined to let him attend and then, after consultation with Lord Granville and others, feeling he ought to stay away, lest he should become involved with any Bonapartist demonstrations staged by supporters who were intending to be present and who might take the opportunity of turning the occasion into a public protest against the Third Republic and against Germany. A number of these had already gone to Camden and she believed it would be best if he stayed clear of them. She suggested that, as it could be political dynamite for the heir to the throne to be there, it might be better if one of his younger brothers, such as Alfred, Duke of Edinburgh, or their brother-in-law, Prince Christian of Schleswig-Holstein, went in his place. However, he pressed his point, saying that if he was not permitted to be present then no lesser royal representative should attend: 'One cannot be wrong in showing respect to fallen greatness'.[17] Having been secretly in sympathy with her eldest son all along, she conceded that he was right. She refrained from commenting on his intention to invite some of the most prominent Bonapartists to stay at Sandringham, a move that led to Gladstone writing with irritation to Granville of the contrast between the heir's 'real good nature and sympathy' and his 'total want of political judgment, either inherited or acquired'.[18]

On 14 January, the Prince, his brother, and brother-in-law were all present at the lying-in-state and the funeral at St Mary's Church, Chislehurst, on the following day. The Empress was too overcome to attend and the Prince Imperial walked behind the hearse at the head of the *cortège*. The Prince of Wales experienced one moment of awkwardness when a deputation, assuming him to be openly sympathetic to the Bonapartist movement, offered to present him with an address and he politely declined to receive it. The demonstration that the Queen had feared he might find himself drawn into did not take place until he had left Chislehurst. As he had gone, the deputation turned to the Prince Imperial instead. As they waved a large tricolour, they ran across the lawns of Camden Place, shouting, '*Vive l'Empereur!*' The young man looked at them apprehensively before running for the safety of the house.

A few days later, the Queen paid a visit to Chislehurst, accompanied as ever by Princess Beatrice. First they went to St Mary's, where the Emperor had been buried and where they intended to lay wreaths on his coffin. They then drove to Camden Place, where they met the Empress and the Prince Imperial. The Queen and Empress both embraced and then, taking the Queen's arm, the Empress led her upstairs to her little boudoir. She told the Queen all about the Emperor's last days, his suffering over the last few months, and how even carriage drives had been absolute agony for him. On the morning of his death, she said she had been preparing to drive to Woolwich to see the Prince Imperial when the doctors stopped her, as the Emperor was having '*une petite crise*'. She hurried to the sickroom at once and, as a doctor rushed past her calling for a priest, she realised that this was the end.

Adding further to her distress was the behaviour of the hated Plon-Plon. Thinking that he would be able to wrest his position as head of the

Bonapartes from a woman and a minor, he invited himself over to Camden Place, where he rummaged around for and then found the Emperor's last will and testament, which he had drawn up while still Emperor. Plon-Plon was astounded to find that he had been left in control of everything. After accusing her angrily of having destroyed a second will, he stormed out of the house. A couple of days later, he contacted her to say he was prepared to resume their friendship on two conditions: that he be given absolute control of the Imperial Party, and that he be given sole guardianship of the Prince Imperial. She was astounded at his impertinence and sent him away empty-handed.

The next time Queen Victoria met the Empress, she showed her the Emperor's apartments at Camden Place, two small rooms, a study, and a bedroom, at the back of the house, exactly as he had left them. For the next twenty-eight years, the exiled Empress would always be assured of the Queen and her family's steady support and companionship.

Another of Queen Victoria's major family concerns at this time was the marital future of the Duke of Edinburgh. Like his elder brother the Prince of Wales, he was fond of good living and the opposite sex, and the Queen hoped that he would renounce his life of frivolity and settle down once he was married. As he was now in his late twenties, he needed a suitable wife. Fortunately, although his mother was unaware, he had already met the woman who was to become his wife. On a family visit to Jugenheim, Germany, in the summer of 1868, he had met Grand Duchess Marie for the first time. The only surviving daughter of Tsar Alexander II, she was aged fifteen at the time. Her elder sister Alexandra had died at the age of seven, and the Tsar and Tsarina were deeply attached to the one remaining daughter whom they had also nearly lost to illness at about the same age. Marie evidently made a deep impression on the seafaring bachelor prince and at some stage he told Queen Victoria that he intended to marry her.

The Crimean War was still well within everyone's living memory and the Queen also had grave reservations about accepting a Romanov Grand Duchess into her family, partly for religious reasons and partly as she thought the family were 'false and arrogant'. Some fifteen years earlier, shortly after the newly married Princess Royal in Berlin was offered a decoration by the court of St Petersburg, the Queen was not in the least impressed. 'So you have got the order of St Catherine,' she wrote rather ungraciously. 'You can wear it with the others if you like.'[19]

When Tsar Alexander II realised that the Duke of Edinburgh and his daughter were evidently serious about each other, he wrote to the Queen in August 1871, stressing that he and the Tsarina had no intention of opposing a union between their families, although stating: 'We have made it a principle never to impose our will upon our children as regards their marriages'.[20] However, the choice of suitable brides for Prince Alfred was dwindling. A shy taciturn man of twenty-nine, there was more to him than the carefree bachelor that his mother was sometimes too keen to portray him as. He was a hard-working, if hard-drinking naval officer and an enthusiastic amateur violinist, although he lacked the geniality of his more popular elder brother and the ability to make friends readily.

The Tsarina was not keen on the idea, and felt that her daughter would never be happy in England. At one stage, Queen Victoria was pressing for a speedy resolution or else for abandoning the scheme altogether. She thought that her second daughter Alice, who had become increasingly fond of the Russians since her marriage, had 'pushed' her brother and mother into the idea, '& without the slightest real ground for hoping that he w[ou]ld succeed'. As she had also heard that Grand Duchess Marie was very 'indulged and spoilt', it would surely be better to terminate the idea at once.[21] Yet, the two young people persevered and before long they had won over the reluctant Tsar and Tsarina. Alexander II had objected mainly as his daughter would be living so far away from her parents, but he would agree to the marriage if there was 'a willingness in case such a marriage took place, to pay visits during the first years of the marriage' to them, either in Russia or in Germany.

By coincidence, in June 1873, the Tsarevich and Tsarevna, later Tsar Alexander III and Empress Marie Feodorovna, were on the point of paying a visit to England, taking their two eldest boys, Grand Dukes Nicholas and George. It would be the only time Alexander set foot on British soil. The Prince and Princess of Wales (the latter being Marie's elder sister) entertained them at their London home, Marlborough House. Queen Victoria met them briefly at Windsor when the Prince and Princess brought them over, as she noted in her journal: 'Bertie & Alix arrived with the Cesarevitch & Minny looking very dear & nice, quite unaltered, & as simple as ever. He is very tall & big, good natured & unaffected.'[22] In the years to come, she would not readily speak of the man destined to become Tsar Alexander III as 'good natured'.

Though the Tsar and Tsarina were reluctant to part with their daughter, they had to accept the inevitable. If not strongly opposed to the match, Queen Victoria remained steadfastly unenthusiastic. At the same time, she was writing to Sir Henry Ponsonby that the young Grand Duchess had 'been very much spoilt and indulged, in every whim & fancy & accustomed to every possible luxury'. Moreover, she objected strongly to 'the falseness of the Russians, this want of principle & a different religion'. If her son was so determined to take a Romanov bride, it would be far better for him to go and live in Russia 'than bring a discontented spoilt wife to England or Coburg'.[23]

After a short period of courtship, Alfred and Marie were betrothed in July 1873. A 'greatly astonished' Queen Victoria was not long in demanding that one of her parents would have to bring her to England to meet her before the wedding took place. The Tsar denounced her privately as a 'silly old fool', ungallantly forgetting that she was thirteen months younger than him, while the Tsarina offered to meet her halfway at Cologne, a suggestion the Queen dismissed as 'simply impertinent'. This, however, was one request from Queen Victoria that would remain unfulfilled.

Having originally opposed the betrothal, the Tsar now accepted it with good grace. Alfred and Marie were married in the chapel of the Winter Palace on 23 January 1874. It was a double ceremony, the first service being performed by the Metropolitans of St Petersburg, Moscow and Kiev, according to the rites of the Orthodox Church. The second ceremony was conducted according to the rites of the Church of England. Queen Victoria was not present—it being the only wedding among her children that she did not attend—but she sent the Prince and Princess of Wales to represent her and Arthur Stanley, Dean of Westminster, to perform the English ceremony.

After a short honeymoon, the bride and groom left Russia, travelling across Europe and arriving at Windsor early in March. Queen Victoria's first impressions of her new daughter-in-law were that she was 'most pleasingly natural, unaffected and civil', even if she was not pretty or graceful and held herself badly, but these good impressions did not last long. The Tsar and Tsarina had informed the Queen that they wished their daughter to be known as Her Imperial Highness, 'as in all civilised countries'. Thoroughly offended as she was not yet imperial herself, the Queen retorted that she did not mind whether her daughter-in-law was known as Imperial or not, as long as Royal came first.

An equally trivial dispute about her official title followed. Which was to come first, Duchess of Edinburgh or Grand Duchess of Russia? Out of her depth, as she was still not yet an empress—an omission, as far as she was concerned, which would shortly be made good—the Queen asked Sir Henry Ponsonby, who was amused by so much fuss about what he thought an extremely trivial business, quoting Dr Johnson to his wife Mary: 'Who comes first, a louse or a flea?' Marie sought revenge in mischievously flaunting the magnificent jewellery from her father at her first drawing room in England. The Queen, whose own jewels were modest by comparison, looked at them coldly, 'shrugging her shoulders like a bird whose plumage has been ruffled, her mouth drawn down at the corners, in an expression which those who knew her had learned to

dread'.[24] Her daughters could barely conceal their jealousy at the sight
of their affluent sister-in-law's finery. It was only about fifteen years since
the Queen had told her eldest daughter somewhat loftily that 'our princes
never admitted the Grand Dukes of Russia having precedence over them'.[25]
She was determined that the Duchess of Edinburgh should not assume she
was better than the family she had married into, simply because she had
inherited more valuable treasures than them.

Marie was very disappointed with life in England, where she thought the
food was abominable, late hours very tiring, London 'an impossible place
where people seemed mad with pleasure', and she found visits to Osborne
and Windsor tedious beyond belief. Though she spoke perfect English, she
disliked the language intensely and much preferred to converse in French,
which had long traditionally been the second language at the court of St
Petersburg. With her imperious manner towards servants and defiance of
English convention by smoking cigarettes in public, thought to be most
unladylike, she was deeply unpopular.

Every autumn, her husband invited a houseful of guests to their country
house, Eastwell Park, and they would have large shooting parties. Marie
dreaded these occasions, complaining that after a day with their guns the
men would return very sleepy and in no mood for mentally stimulating
conversation. A cultured woman, she once remarked that she preferred
the company of politicians, diplomats, and artists to that of soldiers,
sailors, and sportsmen. It was ironic that, notwithstanding his artistic and
scientific interests, the Duke of Edinburgh was first and foremost a sailor
and sportsman. Well might she lament to their eldest daughter, another
Marie, subsequently Queen of Roumania, that 'Papa considers sport
sacred above all'.

In May 1874, Tsar Alexander II paid what was intended to be a purely
family visit to England, accompanied by one of his younger sons, Grand
Duke Alexis. Although not a state occasion, it was inevitable that his
arrival in London would be turned into an event of some importance.
The comic weekly magazine *Punch* welcomed him with a full-page
cartoon and a short list of 'Things the Czar won't do', including 'Burst
into tears at the sight of the Crimean War Memorial in Waterloo Place,
and renew the Treaty of Paris on the spot, out of consideration for the
feeling of the neighbourhood', and 'Understand what an "immense
draw" he will be at the Crystal Palace on the 16th [May], along with the
fireworks'.[26]

The visit began a little inauspiciously on 13 May, when the imperial
yacht, expected at Gravesend shortly before midday, ran aground
off Dover. A luncheon party and then a dinner at Windsor had to be
cancelled because of the delays as he did not arrive by train until 10 p.m.

However, the rest of the week went very successfully, with a programme including dinner with the Prince of Wales at Marlborough House; a guildhall banquet with the Lord Mayor of London and corporation, where speeches were made extolling peace and Anglo-Russian friendship; a visit to the Royal Arsenal at Woolwich, with an inspection of the Royal Artillery and lunch at the Mess afterwards; and a grand review at Aldershot, where he rode on horseback and saluted British troops that had just returned from the Ashanti War. Between his schedules of public engagements, he found time to visit Empress Eugénie at Chislehurst. She had been very kind and attentive to him after the attempt on his life at Paris at the exhibition in 1867, and now she had fallen on hard times he was eager to repay the compliment.

He was delighted to see his daughter again and while he was in England she rarely left his side. A state concert was staged at the Royal Albert Hall, with a programme chosen by the Duke of Edinburgh containing selections from Russian Church Orthodox polyphony in honour of the Tsar. Many of the audience attended less to listen to the performers than to come and gape at His Imperial Majesty, and the Albert Hall had accordingly raised their prices that evening. Marie had written scathingly of the venue in one of her first letters home, telling him that when he paid his visit to England he would be required to attend concerts there. Much as she loved music herself, she urged him to try and leave early if possible, as every concert lasted for several hours. He evidently took her advice and did not attend the first half of the concert.

To his suite, when the time came to return to Russia, he expressed himself satisfied with his visit to England, especially the large, curious, but good-humoured crowds that had been kept in order with ease by unarmed police. It might not have surprised him had there been another attempt on his life there, but his eight days in the country were relatively free of anti-Russian demonstrations. However, the Queen had been disturbed by the change in the man whom she had welcomed thirty-five years earlier as a dashing young imperial heir; she thought he was 'very kind but [was] terribly altered, so thin, and his face [looked] so old, sad, and careworn'.[27] For both sovereigns, the meeting brought back mixed memories. At the state banquet in St George's Hall, he recalled his visit so many years before and that of his father in 1844. Tsar Nicholas I, he told her, had been very attached to England, but 'tout a malheureusement changé' when the Crimean War broke out. She had been poorly served, he went on, alluding to the bellicose Lord Palmerston. When she deeply regretted that there had been misunderstandings in the past, he added graciously that he saw no reason why their countries should not now be on the best of terms. After that, his emotions got the better of him, as he thanked her for her kindness to his daughter. The Queen gently put her hand out across the Tsar and took that of the Duchess of Edinburgh, 'she herself being nearly upset'.

After he had taken his leave and was on his way back to Russia, the Queen wrote to him of her great pleasure in having seen him again after so many years and her gladness at his assurance of his hopes that England and Russia would henceforth remain on friendly and cordial terms: 'You cannot desire this more earnestly than I do both on account of the great national interests involved and for the sake of the daughter whom I have learnt to consider as my own'.[28] Equally graciously, the Tsar thanked her for all the proofs of friendship she had shown him and his daughter. Yet such fine words and formal expressions of mutual gratitude could do no more than temporarily bridge the gulf between two powerful nations, which, notwithstanding one recent solitary dynastic marriage alliance, still had good reason to distrust one another.

Empress Elizabeth of Austria, although declining to visit England in 1861 on her return from Madeira to Europe, was still interested in coming to see the country, but it would have to be on her own terms. What persuaded her more than anything else was the recommendation of her sister Maria, the former Queen of Naples, who had assured her firstly that England was the one country where royalties were allowed to live in peace if they so wished and secondly that the hunting was excellent. The latter had been confirmed to her by the Prince of Wales, when they met briefly at the Vienna Exhibition of 1873, and by now she could no longer wait to see for herself.

At the end of July 1874, she took her youngest child, the six-year-old Archduchess Valerie, to the Isle of Wight. It was a strange choice, for Queen Victoria was staying at Osborne House at the time and the Empress was not noted for responding with enthusiasm to social obligations when on holiday. Nevertheless, the island was thought to be more secluded than mainland Britain, and had its 'bracing and salubrious resorts'. They went ostensibly on medical advice, for court doctors had prescribed sea-baths for mother and daughter. However, she felt the need to get away from Vienna, where the atmosphere was uncomfortable with talk of political intrigues, some of which she was being blamed for and accused of trying to influence the Emperor unduly.

On 28 July, the 'Countess and Fraulein von Hohenembs', the Empress and her daughter, left Vienna and travelled to England via Strasbourg and Le Havre. Accompanied by two maids and a large suite, including chaplains, doctors, governesses, nurses, and others, as well as horses, carriages, grooms, and trainers, they descended on the island on 2 August. Count Ferdinand von Beust, Austrian Ambassador to London, had rented Steephill Castle, near Ventnor, for them. Although she enjoyed the seclusion, she was well aware that it would be impossible to evade Queen Victoria for long. She and her suite were barely installed before Queen Victoria announced her intention to come and call. The Queen was pleasantly surprised to find the Empress was more normal than gossip might have led her to believe. She had half-expected an unbalanced neurotic who was liable to drift off and sit staring out of the window or lock herself away in fits of weeping at a moment's notice. Instead, she found an apparently fit and healthy young woman, full of enthusiasm for the joys of bathing and walking and the splendours of the island scenery, as proud of her small daughter as any other mother.

Subsequent letters afterwards from both suggested that it was not a comfortable meeting for either. Queen Victoria wrote to the German Crown Princess that Empress Elizabeth had insisted on coming over to see her, but they were all disappointed by her appearance and she could not call her 'a great beauty'. She had 'a beautiful complexion, a splendid figure, and pretty, small eyes and not a very pretty nose'. The Princess of Wales, who was also much admired for her beauty, was in her opinion much prettier.[29] At the same time, the Empress was writing to her husband that the Queen had been very kind, 'and said nothing that is not amiable, but she is not sympathetic to me'.[30] She had found the Queen a little unnerving and Valerie was terrified of her, telling her mother afterwards that she had never seen such a stout lady.

On the following day, the Empress met the German Crown Princess at a hotel in Sandown. Crown Princess Frederick William was one of the few royalties whom she regarded as a genuine friend, a sympathetic woman who knew only too well how it felt to live at an imperial court at which intelligence and individuality were deeply resented by diehards who maintained that women, especially princesses and archduchesses, should have no interests outside the three Ks (*Kinder, Küche, Kirche*, or children, kitchen, and church). The Crown Princess respected her desire not to see anybody else, or show herself anywhere, while she was in England. 'All the same I like her very much and she is very kind to me', she reported to her mother.[31]

The Empress wrote to Emperor Francis Joseph that she had been very polite, 'at which everybody seemed quite astonished'. Now she had done her duty, though, she was sure everybody understood that she wanted to be quiet and nobody had any wish to intrude.[32] She had reckoned without Queen Victoria, who sent her an invitation to dinner. When this was gently refused, the Queen sent another, which was also declined. The Queen concluded that the Empress might be beautiful, but evidently lacking in any sense of duty where royal obligations were concerned. She then left to spend a few days in London, where she was happy to pay visits to two other branches of the royal family. One was the Tecks, where she called upon Francis, Duke of Teck at White Lodge, Richmond, whom she remembered from his days in the army in Austria. She was also briefly a guest at Clarence House, where the recently married Duchess of Edinburgh was at home awaiting the birth of her first child. From London, she went north to Melton and Belvoir castle, estates of the Duke of Rutland, attending the first cub-hunt of the season, rising at dawn and spending all day in the saddle. After sleeping at Melton that night and visiting the stables, she felt that before long she would have to arrange to spend a complete hunting season there. It was with sadness that she said goodbye to Leicestershire, returned to Ventnor, and in September made the journey back to a Vienna, which increasingly bored her.

In March 1876, she kept her word by returning to England for a full hunting season, renting Easton Neston in Northamptonshire for six weeks. Queen Victoria was not pleased at the prospect of 'that singular dear Lady ... really coming over here to hunt!!! [She thought] it very unbecoming as well as dangerous'.[33] This time the Empress was under strict instructions from Emperor Francis Joseph that she was to pay her respects properly to Queen Victoria, and there must be no repetition of her behaviour on the Isle of Wight eighteen months earlier. She therefore stopped in London on her way to Northamptonshire, only for the Queen to send word that she was too busy to receive the Empress at present, but looked forward to doing so at some later date. 'Imagine if I were so ill-bred,' the Empress complained to her husband, evidently forgetting her own refusals.[34] After a few enjoyable days of hunting, she sent word to the Queen that she would visit her at Windsor on Sunday 12 March. It was obvious that she intended to stay for the shortest time possible, as she declined an invitation to spend a night at the castle, and allowed several conflicting messages to be sent as to whether she would stay for luncheon or not. She was doubtless aware that neither the Queen nor the court approved of Sunday visiting.

During divine service at Windsor, which began at midday, the Bishop of Peterborough, William Magee, was informed that Her Majesty commanded him on no account to preach a long sermon. It was to no avail. He was about to mount the pulpit when a page entered the church, walked up to her, and whispered that the Empress of Austria's arrival was imminent. Angry at her routine being interrupted thus, the Queen stumped down crossly to the chapel door to receive her. There was a flurry of presentations and introductions, by which time it was snowing heavily, and the Empress seized on this as a perfect excuse for not staying to luncheon. The visit thus lasted about three quarters of an hour. However, divine retribution came when the train bearing her and her suite back to London that day broke down in the snow, and she had to order the stationmaster to bring her luncheon and a bottle of claret in her carriage. The next day, hunting was impossible because of the snow, but as if to draw attention to her indiscretion she paid a full and formal visit to Ferdinand de Rothschild at Leighton House, and they rode over to inspect his stud at Mentmore. Queen Victoria was not impressed by such tactless behaviour.

5

'Poor Dear Empress!'

Within two years of Tsar Alexander II's visit to England, Anglo-Russian relations deteriorated sharply. The British government feared that Russia planned to occupy Constantinople. The Tsar was at pains to stress that he had no personal intention of doing so and could not understand why there could not be 'a perfect and cordial understanding' between their countries. As was to be expected, he had a firm ally and defender in the shape of his son-in-law, the Duke of Edinburgh, who was anxious to ensure Queen Victoria that he was deeply hurt at all the unpleasant and untrue statements about him in the British press.[1]

Nevertheless, the Tsar found himself at odds with several members of his family, especially the Tsarina, who were strongly in favour of Russia's holy mission to stake a claim to Constantinople as Russia's rightful capital, and if necessary wage war with Turkey in pursuit of that objective. The devout Tsarina saw it as a religious crusade, as it would surely prevent persecution of the Balkan Christians and re-establish Constantinople as the greatest city in Christendom, while the Tsarevich saw it as a golden opportunity to open the Dardanelles to Russian ships. Most of the royal family thought the responsibility lay with Russia for driving the Turks to such desperate measures, by fomenting discord among other Balkan territories for her own ends. On the other hand, the Princess of Wales took the side of Russia, not only on account of her family connections, but also as Turkey was the hereditary enemy of Greece and therefore of her brother King George as well.

A conference of the great powers opened in Constantinople in December 1876 to January 1877, agreeing on a series of political reforms in Bosnia and in the Ottoman territories with a predominantly Bulgarian population. The agreed decisions of the six great powers were formally handed over to the Ottoman government, which accordingly submitted objections and alternative reform proposals that were rejected by the great powers. Proceedings broke up when the government announced the definitive refusal of the Ottoman Empire to accept the conference decisions.

In April 1877, the great powers delivered a protocol to the Sultan of Turkey demanding autonomy for Bosnia, Herzegovina, and Bulgaria, which was rejected. When Turkey refused to consider Russia's proposal for simultaneous demobilisation and a plan for peace with guarantees for the liberty of the Balkan peoples, the Tsar reluctantly declared war on Turkey.

Unlike his father, Tsar Alexander II was more a man of peace and a reluctant war leader. Anxious for good relations with the other powers, he was particularly concerned by the attitudes of foreign governments towards Russia. He particularly valued good relations with Britain, partly as his daughter was now a British Duchess by marriage. Britain was still officially neutral, but openly pro-Turkish in her sympathies and anti-Russian in tone, and he was anxious to try and avoid the possibility of a small localised conflict in the Balkans that threatened the interests of the other European powers and could engulf the whole continent in war. It was a risk that the Russian ruling classes and the army, unlike him, were prepared to take.

It was also an acutely difficult situation for his son-in-law as well. As *The Times* had observed when the Duke of Edinburgh was granted an honorary appointment in the Russian navy as the Tsar's son-in-law, he would be 'in a singular position' if war was suddenly to break out. With such a volatile situation, the prospect of a second Anglo-Russian conflict within a little more than two decades came very close. At the time, he was stationed with the Mediterranean Fleet, based in Malta. After Russia's declaration of war on Turkey, the fleet sailed eastwards through the Dardanelles to the Sea of Marmora, dropping anchor within sight of Constantinople in order to be on hand to protect lives and property of British subjects in the area. The Duke and Prince Louis of Battenberg, who he had engaged as an unofficial flag-lieutenant, were unhappy at being so close to the war, one that cut across family loyalties as bitterly as Prussia's campaigns had done in the previous decade. Louis had even closer relations on the battlefield, for his younger brother Alexander ('Sandro') was *aide-de-camp* to the Russian Commander-in-Chief, the Tsar's brother Grand Duke Nicholas.

By February 1878, the tide was running in Russia's favour and the fleet proceeded through the Dardanelles, when a Russian victory placed them within striking distance of Constantinople. Within a few days, the Turks were forced to surrender and sue for peace, signed at the Treaty of San Stefano in March and brought considerable Russian gains. Foremost among these was the creation of a large Bulgarian state supposed to be independent, which would initially be garrisoned by Russian troops. The nomination for ruler of Bulgaria was none other than Prince Louis's younger brother, Prince Alexander of Battenberg. Negotiations began between Russia and the great powers to persuade the former to moderate her demands. At this time, the Mediterranean Fleet was in the Sea of Marmora and it was at this time that a well-intentioned, but tactless act by the Duke of Edinburgh was to have considerable repercussions.

When Louis heard that Alexander was in Constantinople, he was determined to see him and the Duke granted him permission to go ashore. The brothers were overjoyed to see each other safe and sound, and Louis invited Sandro on board the Duke's ship HMS *Sultan*. Later, they went on to the flagship and then on to *Temeraire*, a modern battleship equipped with several new devices. As Alexander was an officer, he had to be accorded certain privileges, such as watching a demonstration of fleet exercises, and dined on board the flagship. The brothers later went ashore and visited Russian army headquarters, where they were received cordially by Grand Duke Nicholas, younger brother of the Tsar and commander of the Russian army of the Danube, and shown around the camp where several Turkish officers were imprisoned and captured armaments kept.

When informed of their activities, the British Ambassador at Constantinople, Sir Austen Layard, was aghast, fearing that peace negotiations would be jeopardised by the entertaining of a Russian officer on board a British ship and made party to top confidential information. In order to prevent the Queen and Admiralty from hearing vague rumours from unofficial sources, he cabled to London. A furious Queen Victoria wrote angrily to the Duke of Edinburgh that it was hard to believe even he was capable of such indiscretion. The best that could be said in his defence was that he was guilty of extreme thoughtlessness, but as a captain in command of a ship, and as son of the sovereign, at a time when the two nations might soon be at war, was much too serious to be passed over. He had undoubtedly injured the prospects of both Louis and himself.

Only a few weeks earlier, the question of the Duke's promotion from captain to rear-admiral had been discussed. The Queen was anxious that the Duke of Edinburgh should not return home too quickly, for she regarded him as a bad influence on his younger brother Arthur. As the *Sultan* was due to come back to England for servicing, her captain was bound to return with her. In the light of this incident, it was imperative that the Duke should be posted elsewhere without delay and perhaps even forfeit his leave. To have a prince whose behaviour was seen as perilously close to treason arriving home was out of the question. At Darmstadt,

Alice, Grand Duchess of Hesse, had heard from various sources that he could not show his face there after such openly pro-Russian behaviour and even his favourite sister, Princess Christian of Schleswig-Holstein, Helena, had written to say how ashamed she was of him.

Louis was promptly transferred to a ship at Malta. He and his parents were so upset that he seriously considered having to leave the Royal Navy altogether. The Tsarina, who was no admirer of Queen Victoria, wrote angrily to her brother Prince Alexander of Hesse, the father of Louis and Alexander:

> That crazy old hag [the Queen], made him the pretext for persecuting Alfred, and more especially Louis. I was so indignant that at first my one idea was that he should leave the English service. But perhaps it would be a rash thing to do if there really is danger of war. But just because the danger threatens, I should be heartily glad for Alfred and Louis both to be out of it, wouldn't you?[2]

Distressed by the animosity between England and Russia, and now this new incident, Prince Alexander of Hesse agreed that in the circumstances Louis ought to resign from the service unless an apology was forthcoming. At length, the Queen was persuaded to believe that no harm had been done. Prince Alexander of Battenberg had confirmed that no Russian had accompanied him on board and that he had merely accepted a family invitation. It became apparent that Layard's telegram had been exaggerated, perhaps partly out of spite as he was annoyed that the meeting had not been personally arranged by him. Within a month, the matter was regarded as closed, although the anger of the Tsarina was slow to cool. She commiserated with Prince Alexander of Battenberg, who, she said, had been 'victimised by the old fool' Queen Victoria, who had now calmed down after being allowed to vent her spleen. The Tsarina's daughter, the Duchess of Edinburgh, had told her 'that you only have to give her a good fright to make her draw in her horns'.[3]

After the Turkish resistance collapsed at the end of the year, the Sultan sued for peace and the Tsar offered an armistice. Peace was signed at the Treaty of San Stefano in March 1878, but after objections to some of the terms, which proved particularly advantageous to Russia, a congress was held at Berlin in June. One of the terms of this was that the new state of Bulgaria, theoretically autonomous, but in practice under Russian control, would be a principality governed by Prince Alexander of Battenberg.

It was fortunate that Crown Prince Rudolf, only son and heir of the Emperor and Empress of Austria, grew up with a greater sense of royal and imperial obligations than his independently minded mother.

Early in 1878, he made his first visit to England, where he was sent to study political and economic conditions in Britain for a couple of months as part of his preparation for assuming the imperial mantle in the fullness of time. Emperor Francis Joseph, who never once set foot in England during his long life, did not look kindly on the institution of parliament, which curtailed his or any other sovereign's autocratic powers, but he appreciated the value of sending his heir to see and hear the mother of parliaments at work. Britain was also the world's foremost economic power, while Austrian industrialisation was still in its infancy. Rudolf and the Empress Elizabeth accordingly set out for England together, shortly after Christmas 1877, her objective being to spend another hunting season in England.

As they were making an unofficial visit to England, he did not stay at the Austro-Hungarian Embassy in London, but instead went to a hotel in Brook Street. Unlike his mother, he did not need to be told twice that he needed to pay a courtesy call on Queen Victoria and he made an excellent impression. The Queen was 'much pleased with him' and found him very easy to get on with.[4] She seemed so impressed that her cousin Mary, Duchess of Teck, jokingly told Count Beust that she believed Her Majesty was quite in love with the dashing young Crown Prince. However, she declined the Prince of Wales's recommendation that she should confer the Order of the Garter on him, on the grounds that at nineteen he was too young for such an honour.

Empress Elizabeth continued to return to the British Isles for hunting. She had been advised that Ireland was 'a huntsman's paradise', and that sport in the English shires was nothing by comparison. Early in 1879, Lord Langford's house Summerhill, County Meath, was rented for a six-week stay. It was a very insensitive time to go to Ireland, as Home Rule for Ireland was becoming an increasingly contentious issue and it did not bode well for the Consort of Europe's major Catholic monarch to make such a well-publicised foray to Ireland for the purpose of pleasure, thus implying solidarity with the cause of Irish independence. Queen Victoria had little love for the Irish, particularly after the mayor and corporation of Dublin had rejected her gift of a statue of the Prince Consort and after an attempt on the life of the Duke of Edinburgh by a Fenian sympathiser while he was visiting Australia in 1868. Emperor Francis Joseph might normally have been expected to forbid her to put in an appearance in Ireland at such an inopportune time, but he had been advised that news of political discontent in the country was greatly exaggerated by the British press, and moreover he was too chivalrous to refuse his wife anything without good reason.

Perhaps fortunately for Queen Victoria, this time the matter of whether to accord this tactless personality any welcome on to English soil did not arise for Queen Victoria. At Windsor, the court was in mourning for her second daughter Alice, Grand Duchess of Hesse and the Rhine, who had succumbed to diphtheria in December 1878, and was also busy with preparations for the wedding of Arthur, Duke of Connaught, in March. It suited the Empress, and the Austrian Ambassador in London, Count Pista Károlyi, had been instructed that she did not wish to break her journey in London. She arrived in Dover and the imperial train reached Holyhead with her privacy jealously guarded and strictly observed.

All was very different when she sailed into Dublin on the steamer *Shamrock*, where the mayor and corporation were on the platform awaiting her arrival. As she boarded a special train for Summerhill, a large enthusiastic crowd was waving and cheering. As it approached Kilcock Station, a red carpet was laid down from the platform to lead her to her carriage, as an Austrian flag fluttered in welcome from the station mast and from the footbridge flew a green one bearing a gold harp and an inscription: 'Erin cordially welcomes the Empress'. It gave the impression of being anything but a private visit.

She made a half-hearted attempt to appease her conscience with a hasty letter to Queen Victoria, informing her of her arrival and her intention to preserve the strictest incognito while hunting in Ireland: 'Out of respect for the great pain that has befallen Your Majesty's loving, maternal, heart, I did not want to inconvenience you with my visit and, pressed for time, I hastened here'.[5]

She returned to Vienna a month later, but the lure of Summerhill proved too strong and she returned to make what would prove her final visit to Ireland in February 1880. In view of the worsening political situation, with agrarian unrest in the country threatening to curtail hunting activities and the Nationalist leader Charles Stewart Parnell going to the United States of America to raise funds for the independence movement, it was an even more unfortunate time to be going. Queen Victoria was astonished that the Emperor should apparently allow her to make yet another visit, which could only jeopardise Anglo-Austrian relations. That the Empress should be free to go to a country where the British royal family was barely tolerated, and be positively welcomed there, was humiliating. It was inevitable that Parnell would make capital out of Elizabeth's presence, thus inferring to the Americans that Irish nationalism had Habsburg support. Yet it would hardly have done for British ambassadors in courts abroad to acknowledge their problems with Ireland too openly, and the Court of St James had to swallow its pride.

For a while, the Empress was free to do as she wished, commenting with pleasure that the great advantage of Ireland was that it had no Royal Highnesses. However, these carefree days were coming to an end for her. She could not afford to keep up the lease at Summerhill indefinitely, and she asked her secretary to find a suitable residence in Ireland. Fortunately, the Irish special branch of the British intelligence service heard of her intentions almost at once. It was reported to London that such a situation would be intolerable and Emperor Francis Joseph was accordingly notified. He realised that his wife's regular riding expeditions in Ireland had caused quite enough embarrassment to the British and Austrian governments, and the idea that she should have her own residence there was taking matters too far. As he was anxious to establish good relations with Russia, and knew that Britain was perpetually suspicious of Russia's intentions towards India, he did not wish to make an enemy of her. Elizabeth's presence in Ireland had previously been no more than an irritation, but it was now about to assume proportions that could threaten the security of his empire. He ordered her to leave Ireland forthwith and that she must pay a courtesy call on Queen Victoria before returning to Vienna. She obeyed at once, well aware that if he was prepared to go to the lengths of issuing her such orders, then he meant them in earnest.

The subsequent meeting between Queen and Empress at Buckingham Palace was inevitably somewhat strained, for the host evidently understood that her guest was only there under duress. Afterwards, the Queen wrote a little acidly to Crown Princess Frederick William that she had found her most amiable, a little aged, but still very graceful and distinguished-looking, 'only her dress was so tight she could hardly move or sit down'.[6]

Louis, Prince Imperial and, in the eyes of the Bonapartists, his father's successor as Emperor of the French, had been accepted into the Royal Military Academy, Woolwich, in 1872, and passed out two years later. He spoke good English, soon gained a reputation for hard work, and was renowned among his contemporaries as a good sport. While he never lost sight of the possibility that the Third Republic in France might fail, with the approval of Queen, he set his sights on joining the British Army. As the self-proclaimed 'doyenne of sovereigns', the Queen was naturally sympathetic to the idea of another restoration in France. Soon after his father's death, she noted that she thought 'it would be best if the Prince Imperial was ultimately to succeed'.[7]

In her own way, she regarded him as a member of her family. Sir Henry Ponsonby considered that the Prince Imperial and Highland Servant John Brown were the only two people who were quite unafraid of her. After sitting next to the Queen at a luncheon at Osbourne one day, a courtier asked the Prince Imperial whether she terrified him, to which he nonchalantly replied, 'Why should she? We like each other.'[8]

It was also thought that he might have his eyes on a member of the

British royal family, and a hand in marriage—that of the Queen's youngest daughter, Princess Beatrice. How she might have reconciled herself to her shy youngest daughter marrying a devout Catholic and becoming an Empress is a matter for conjecture. Nevertheless, the Queen shared in some measure his view that the Bonapartist cause might be victorious if the Third Republic did not succeed. She also probably thought that if he failed to restore his father's empire, a life as her son-in-law and brother-in-law of the next king would be a very agreeable alternative. As the Queen's constant companion, Beatrice was always by her side on her visits to Camden Place, or when the Empress and her son were together at Osborne or Windsor. The Prince Imperial paid much attention to the Princess on these occasions, while she, who was never completely at ease in the company of young men who were not her brothers, was sometimes seen to blush and stammer and generally show signs of confusion when he engaged her in polite conversation.

There is no evidence as to whether the two mothers hoped, let alone planned, a marriage between them. It was said that, after Empress Eugénie died in 1920, Beatrice wrote to her lady-in-waiting to request the immediate destruction of some of her letters to the Empress, and that a photograph of the Prince Imperial stood on her desk until her death twenty-four years after that.[9] However, many years afterwards, Beatrice's eldest son Alexander, Marquess of Carisbrooke, poured cold water on speculation when he told biographer Harold Kurtz that an oft-quoted story of his mother having hinted to him that she had been in love with the Prince Imperial before she met and married her husband, Prince Henry of Battenberg, was not true.[10]

In February 1879, war broke out in South Africa. Major-General Lord Chelmsford, Commander of British Forces in South Africa, had led a punitive expedition into Zululand and, while going out on reconnaissance, had left much of his army behind undefended. While he was away, the Zulus attacked his camp and almost annihilated his force. At a cabinet meeting, the decision was made to send out reinforcements to avenge British military honour.

The Prince Imperial, now promoted to the rank of lieutenant, had been longing to see active service. Going to war on behalf of Britain against one of the European nations would have caused problems, as one might never know when that nation's friendship would be needed in the future. A war that did not involve rival European interests, but one in which only England was concerned, would be far more suitable, especially as there was every prospect of returning home covered in glory. In addition, his army contemporaries from Woolwich were going out to Africa and he believed that his place was with them.

Without consulting his mother, he wrote to the Duke of Cambridge, asking permission to let him take part in the conflict. When the Empress heard she was appalled, and gave him a warning: '[If anything happened to you] your adherents will not weep for you, they will bear a grudge against you'.[11] She could not dissuade him; his mind was made up. He told her that he was finding his present way of life futile, said that he was not 'a man of pleasure', and cared nothing for going out into society, refusing endless invitations. There was nothing that he could for his own country, he declared with sadness. He was always being reminded that the Orléans princes had seen plenty of fighting while he had seen none.[12]

Having failed to talk him out of it, she could only hope that his request would be refused. Two days later, the Empress met him in the corridor at Camden, looking desperate as he told her that he had been refused and tears came to his eyes—'he, who never cried'. In replying to the Duke, he said that he had looked upon serving in the war as an opportunity for showing his gratitude towards the Queen and the nation: 'In a way that would have been after my own heart. I hoped that it would be in the ranks of our allies that I should first take up arms. Losing this hope, I lose one of the consolations of my exile'.[13]

The Empress Eugénie now gave him her utmost support. Knowing that the Queen was in full agreement with her, she went to see the Duke at the War Office in order to plead his case. The refusal had been a cabinet office decision, but the Duke proposed that he could go as an observer, not as a combatant, attached to the staff of Lord Chelmsford, Commander in South Africa, who was requested to take special care of him. Faced with this decision, the cabinet reluctantly withdrew their opposition to his going to Africa. As Disraeli remarked sardonically, 'what can you do when you have two obstinate women to deal with?'[14]

Mindful of the instructions of the Queen, who insisted that he must not expose himself to any danger, Louis went out to South Africa at the end of February 1879. The Queen was deeply touched that he should wish to repay her kindness in this way. She admitted though that she was glad she was not his mother, and she understood 'how easily in his position he sought suitable employment.'

On 19 June, Queen Victoria and Princess Beatrice were staying at Balmoral when a telegram arrived to inform them of the sudden death of the Prince Imperial. Eighteen days earlier, he had been with a scouting party, attacked by Zulus, and killed. The group had been under the command of Captain Jahleel Carey, who had apparently been among the first to mount his horse and ride off to safety when they were in danger. The others had followed suit, leaving the Prince Imperial to face at least thirty of his foes alone. He tried to vault into the saddle of his already

"NEW CROWNS FOR OLD ONES!"

'New Crowns for Old Ones!' *Punch*'s comment on Queen Victoria's exchanging her British crown for an imperial diadem from Disraeli after the Royal Titles Bill had made her Empress of India in 1876. The cartoon is by Sir John Tenniel.

Queen Victoria and Prince Albert, 1854.

Above left: Leopold I, King of the Belgians.

Above right: Nicholas I, Tsar of Russia.

Sir Robert Peel.

Lord John Russell.

Francis Joseph, Emperor
of Austria.

Queen Victoria investing Napoleon III, Emperor of the French, with the Order of the Garter, April 1855.

Queen Victoria, Prince Albert, Emperor Napoleon III, and Empress Eugénie at the Crystal Palace, April 1855.

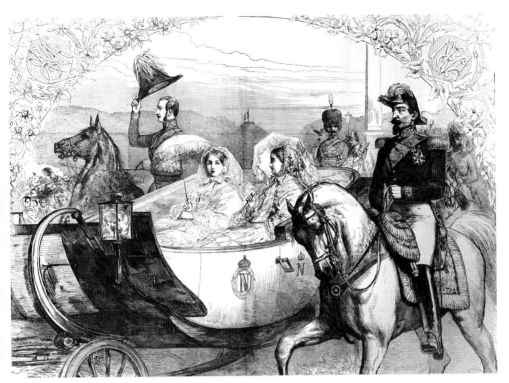

Queen Victoria, Prince Albert, Emperor Napoleon III, and Empress Eugénie during the state visit to Paris, August 1855.

Queen Victoria and Prince Albert with their family at Osborne House, 1857. *Children, left to right*: Prince Alfred; Princesses Louise and Alice; Prince Arthur (front); Princess Beatrice (on the Queen's lap); Victoria, Princess Royal; Prince Leopold; Albert Edward, Prince of Wales.

Queen Victoria and Albert, Prince Consort, 1860.

Prince and Princess Frederick William of Prussia, 1860.

Maximilian, Archduke of Austria and later Emperor of Mexico.

Empress Eugénie of France, shortly after the death of her husband.

Louis, Prince Imperial, Napoleon's and Eugénie's only child.

William I, King of Prussia
and German Emperor.

Augusta, Queen of Prussia
and German Empress.

Francis Joseph, Emperor of Austria.

Alexander II, Tsar of Russia.

Alexander II and his daughter
Grand Duchess Marie, Duchess
of Edinburgh.

THE NEW (NORTH) "STAR."

EEDOM AND LOVE, GO FORTH TO MEET
HE CZAR ON WELCOME'S WINGS;
URS ARE THE SMILES THE GUEST TO GREET
VHO SUCH CREDENTIALS BRINGS.

IN THIS HAND, HIS AND OUR LOVED CHILD,
WHOM TO OUR PRINCE HE GAVE;
IN THAT, THE COLLAR THAT HE FILED
FROM THE NECK OF THE SLAVE.

'The New (North) Star', Alexander II as seen by Sir John Tenniel in *Punch* on his visit to England, May 1874.

Albert Edward, Prince of Wales, in middle age.

Sir Henry Ponsonby, the Queen's private secretary.

Benjamin Disraeli, Earl of
Beaconsfield.

William Ewart Gladstone.

Queen Victoria and Princess Beatrice.

Benjamin Disraeli and Queen Victoria.

The assassination of Tsar Alexander II at St Petersburg, March 1881.

The four sons of Queen Victoria in Highland dress, 1881. *Left to right*: Albert Edward, Prince of Wales; Alfred, Duke of Edinburgh; Arthur, Duke of Connaught; Leopold, Duke of Albany.

Crown Prince Frederick William, later German Emperor Frederick III.

Rudolf and Stephanie,
Crown Prince and Princess of
Austria-Hungary.

Robert Gascoyne-Cecil,
Marquess of Salisbury.

William II, German Emperor.

The Prince and Princess of Wales with their family outside Marlborough House, their London residence, 1889. *Children, left to right*: Prince Albert Victor (later Duke of Clarence); Princess Maud; Louise, Duchess of Fife; Prince George (later King George V); and Princess Victoria.

Prince Otto von Bismarck,
German Imperial Chancellor.

The Empress Frederick
in widowhood.

Queen Victoria and Queen Augusta of Prussia, 1867.

Alexander III and Marie, Tsar and Tsarina of Russia, with their family in 1893.
Children, left to right: Grand Duke Nicholas, the Tsarevich; Grand Duke George; Grand Duchesses Olga and Xenia; and Grand Duke Michael (seated at front).

The Duke and Duchess of York on their wedding day, July 1893.

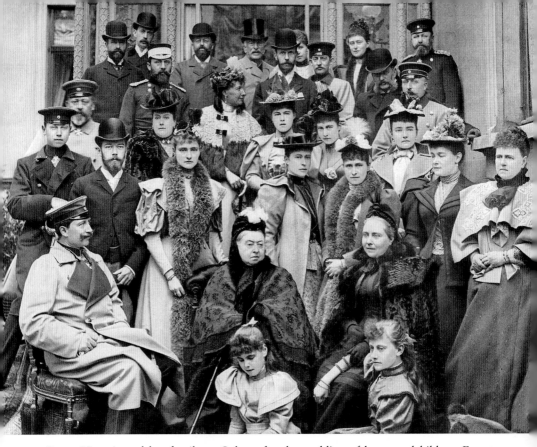

Queen Victoria and her family at Coburg for the wedding of her grandchildren, Ernest, Grand Duke of Hesse, and Princess Victoria Melita of Saxe-Coburg Gotha (neither pictured), April 1894.

Seated, left to right: Emperor William II; Queen Victoria; and Empress Frederick, with Princess Beatrice of Saxe-Coburg Gotha and Princess Feodora of Saxe-Meiningen in front.

First standing row, left to right: Prince Alfred of Saxe-Coburg Gotha; Nicholas, Tsarevich of Russia; Princess Alix of Hesse and the Rhine; Princess Louis of Battenberg; Princess Henry of Prussia; Grand Duchess Vladimir of Russia; Marie, Duchess of Saxe-Coburg Gotha.

Second standing row, left to right: the Prince of Wales; Princess Henry of Battenberg; Princess Philip of Saxe-Coburg Kohary (facing to her left); Charlotte, Duchess of Saxe-Meiningen; Princess Aribert of Anhalt; the Duchess of Connaught.

Two standing rows at back, left to right: Prince Louis of Battenberg; Grand Duke Paul of Russia; Prince Henry of Battenberg; Prince Philip of Saxe-Coburg Kohary; Count Mensdorff; Grand Duke Serge of Russia; Crown Princess Ferdinand of Roumania, formerly Princess Marie of Edinburgh; Crown Prince Ferdinand of Roumania; Grand Duchess Serge of Russia; Grand Duke Vladimir of Russia; the Duke of Saxe-Coburg Gotha.

Grand Duke and Duchess Ernest of Hesse and the Rhine on their wedding day, April 1894.

Lord Rosebery, *c*. 1894.

Queen Victoria with Nicholas II and Alexandra, Tsar and Tsarina of Russia, with their eldest child, Grand Duchess Olga, and the Prince of Wales, 1896.

Prince Alfred of Saxe-Coburg Gotha,
Tsar Nicholas II, Ernest (Grand
Duke of Hesse), and Alfred (Duke of
Saxe-Coburg Gotha), 1896.

Elizabeth, Empress of
Austria-Hungary, 1898.

Queen Victoria and her great-grandchildren, 'the Yorks', 1900. *Left to right*: Princess Mary; Princes Albert (later King George VI); Edward (later King Edward VIII); and Prince Henry (later Duke of Gloucester).

moving horse, something he had been able to do with ease so often before. This time, the strap broke and his arm was struck by a hoof as he fell. He rose to his feet with difficulty as he faced the enemy, a revolver in his left hand, and fired three times, but the shots all went far wide of their target. As he ran at them, he tripped and fell defenceless to the ground. When his body was recovered afterwards, it showed he had seventeen wounds.

'To die in such an awful way is too shocking!' the Queen wrote in her journal. 'Poor dear Empress! her only child, her all, gone! I am really in despair. He was such an amiable, good young man, who would have made such a good Emperor for France one day.'[15] The Empress was stunned: 'I am left alone, the sole remnant of a shipwreck; which proves how vain are the grandeurs of this world'.[16] Carey was court-martialled on 12 June 1879, being accused of 'misbehaviour before the Enemy'. He strenuously defended himself and was found not guilty. However, he never managed to live down the taint of being associated with the death of the prince or having deserted him and, after drifting from one regiment to another, he died in India four years later.

Once the Prince's body had been brought back to England, Queen Victoria was determined that he would be given the most magnificent funeral possible in order to make amends. Benjamin Disraeli had never shared her enthusiasm for the Prince Imperial and feared that such a gesture would be taken as an insult to Republican France. When it appeared that no members of the government would attend the ceremony, she was so angry that they were forced to change their minds and agreed that the Colonial Secretary and the Minister for War would represent the cabinet at what, on her instructions, would be the next best thing to a state funeral. It took place on 12 July at St Mary's Church, Chislehurst. The Queen and Princess Beatrice went to Camden Place, where they knelt before the coffin in the Chapelle Ardente and placed their wreaths upon it, then comforted the Empress as they watched the heartrending procession. Plon-Plon was present as the chief mourner, while the Prince of Wales, the Dukes of Edinburgh, Cambridge, and Connaught were among the pall bearers.

Afterwards, the Prince of Wales noted that he had always favoured a restoration of the French Empire as a guarantee of peace. He had always looked forward to the day 'when [the Prince Imperial] might be called upon to rule the destinies of that great friendly power France', and if he had been called upon to succeed, he believed 'he would have proved an admirable sovereign and that he, like his father, would have been a true and great ally of this country'.[17] It was therefore particularly galling when rumours began to circulate in Paris that the prince had not just been deserted by his cowardly British comrades in arms, but that his senior commanding officers had all had a hand in his assassination, and that even the Prince of Wales was not totally blameless either. Why the British should have had any motive in eliminating the Prince was never made clear. The Empress was infuriated by such whispering and when her mother, the Countess de Montijo, wrote to her daughter to ask her for her views on such a possibility, the Empress replied indignantly. She said that her son died like a hero and that it was extremely hurtful for anybody to insinuate that he had been murdered.[18]

To the end of her life, more than forty years later, the Empress wore black, saying, 'I died in 1879'. Queen Victoria feared that she might suffer a mental or physical collapse under the strain. When she returned to Balmoral in the autumn, she invited her to come and stay at Abergeldie. Both women walked together on the banks of the River Dee and the holiday seemed to do her good. Yet there was to be no respite in her bereavement, for at around the same time she learnt that her mother, aged eighty-five, almost blind, and also heartbroken at the tragic loss of the grandchild of whom she had expected such great things, was dying. Eugénie set out for Madrid at once, having been given permission to travel through France. She reached the Spanish capital the day after her mother had passed away.

In March 1880, she took herself to South Africa on what she described as a pilgrimage, in order to retrace the steps taken by her son during the last few weeks that he had spent out there. Accompanied by General Sir Evelyn Wood, one of the few officers who had taken part in the Zulu War and emerged with his reputation intact, his wife, and two of the Prince Imperial's closest Royal Artillery colleagues (as officers the previous year, who had also been with him at Aldershot), Lieutenants Bigge and Slade, she stayed at Cape Town as guest of the governor, Sir Bartle Frere. They sailed from England on 29 March and were away for about four months. She travelled 800 miles in a horse-drawn carriage and slept for fifty nights under canvas. While they were there, at the Empress's request, Wood spoke to some of the Zulus who had been involved in the fighting. They told him that the Prince had 'fought like a lion' and that they left the medals on his body afterwards, as it was their custom not to take ornaments from the necks of brave men who had died while fighting.[19]

On the night of the first anniversary of her son's death, she knelt in prayer next to a stone cross that had been placed, by order of Queen Victoria, where he fell. Towards the morning, although there was no hint of a breeze in the air, the candles that she had lit suddenly flickered. She believed that his spirit was there with her and she asked if he wanted her to go away. Then she rose and returned to her tent, and a few days later they began to prepare for her journey home.

Wood and Bigge remained her friends for life. She thought the latter was a particularly diligent young man, and it was largely on her recommendation that Queen Victoria appointed him her assistant private secretary shortly afterwards. It proved to be a career for life, as, in 1895, he succeeded Sir Henry Ponsonby as her private secretary, served the next two monarchs in a similar capacity, and was later created Lord Stamfordham by King George V, who once said that 'he taught me how to be King'.

The following year there was some controversy, when Algernon Borthwick, editor of *The Morning Post*, suggested that a fund should be opened to erect a monument to the memory of the Prince Imperial. A memorial being created by the sculptor Edgar Boehm was to be placed in Westminster Abbey. Once the news became known, there were protests that the British public felt it was an inappropriate place. The Zulu War had not been a popular conflict in Britain, and some believed that the Prince Imperial was not a British hero so much as a foreign prince who had gone out to Africa to fight in order to cover himself with glory. Moreover, to honour him in this way would risk causing grave offence to the French. The matter was debated in parliament and a motion against an erection of the statue in the Abbey was carried by a majority of fifteen.

Queen Victoria was furious 'at the language used to England's most faithful ally, as well as the want of feeling and chivalry' shown to the memory of a Prince who had been killed 'because of the cowardly desertion of a British officer'. Empress Eugénie, who had recently returned from a visit to Africa, was very upset when she heard about the debate, her faith in the generosity of the British public was shaken badly and for a while she briefly thought of leaving Britain altogether. Between them, the Queen and Borthwick talked her round. It was the Queen's idea to say that everything had turned out for the best. Tactfully, she said that in her view there had never been a shadow of a doubt that the monument should be situated anywhere other than Windsor, as the chapel was the resting place of so many of her nearest and dearest relations and there it was placed instead.

For the next twenty-eight years, the friendship between Queen and Empress never wavered. Augustin Filon, who had been tutor to the Prince Imperial, thought that no two women could have been more different and that, as time went by, the contrast between them became ever more striking. The Queen, he considered, was 'hard-working and methodical, keen to store facts in her brain and arrange them neatly', while the Empress was impulsive, 'incapable of keeping to a regular routine, quick at seeing truths that might escape more experienced eyes, yet then losing sight of them after much reflection and discussion'. The former was very reserved, the latter highly indiscreet, 'but both were incapable of deceit; they had reached an age when one values sincerity more than anything else'.[20]

The Queen encouraged the Empress not to address her as 'Madam' and 'Your Majesty', but *Ma Soeur*, and to family and close friends they sometimes seemed indeed almost like sisters. The Queen's granddaughter, Princess Marie Louise, was greatly amused one day when she was invited for luncheon. Shortly after she arrived, the Empress and her lady-in-waiting came as well. After the Queen had joined her, they all proceeded to the dining room. As they approached, the Queen asked the Empress to go first: '*Après vous, ma chère soeur.*'

'*Mais non, ma chère soeur, après vous,*' was the gracious answer. So they bowed and curtsied to each other, and then went in to lunch together hand in hand.[21]

Both women being widows who were very lonely at times, the Empress fully understood and respected the Queen's need for the friendship of John Brown, whose rough manners and downright rudeness on several occasions amazed so many of her family and others around her. A week after Brown's death, in March 1883, the Empress was talking to Lady Lintorn Simmons, wife of the Governor of Woolwich. According to the latter's diary, she was both compassionate about the Queen's loss and 'very entertaining' about his position in her Household. 'The fact that he was a servant, and not a gentleman, ought to have prevented any slander,' Lady Simmons noted. 'She added more I was not to repeat.'[22]

The first of several unsuccessful attempts on the life of Tsar Alexander II had been made in April 1866. A little less than fifteen years later, his good fortune finally deserted him. On 13 March 1881, he had been to a military inspection and was returning to the Winer Palace in a closed bulletproof carriage, accompanied by several Cossacks. A member of the 'People's Will', a revolutionary movement whose members had resolved to eliminate him, hurled a bomb in his direction. It killed one of the Cossacks as well as wounding the driver and several nearby spectators, but only causing damage to the carriage. The would-be assassin was captured immediately, but not before he had shouted to somebody else in the crowd who had been there to complete the job if necessary. Meanwhile the Tsar had stepped out, shaken but unhurt, to enquire after the wounded. The guards urged him to return to his carriage and leave the area as soon as possible, but before he had a chance to do so, another person standing nearby threw a second bomb at his feet. He collapsed, bleeding heavily, both legs shattered below the knee, and was carried back to the vehicle, murmuring, 'Home to the palace to die.' Barely conscious and horribly mutilated, he was given the last rites and expired of his wounds later that afternoon.

Although such a tragedy was hardly unexpected, Queen Victoria was 'quite shaken and stunned' when she was brought the news at Windsor: 'Poor, poor Emperor, in spite of his failings, he was a kind and amiable man, and had been a good ruler, wishing to do the best for his country'.[23]

In a letter to the German Crown Princess three days later, she was even more forthright:

A sense of horror thrills me through and through! Where such a criminal succeeds the effect is dreadful. The details are too terrible. No punishment is bad enough for the murderers who planned it; hanging is too good. That he, the mildest and best sovereign Russia had, should be the victim of such fiends is too grievous.[24]

When Tsar Nicholas I had fallen ill and died during the early months of the Crimean War, *The Times* could find nothing complimentary to write on his passing, but it proved more charitable when it came to passing judgment on his son. Though it would be impossible to foresee how posterity would judge the character and activity of Alexander II, its tribute ran:

There is no doubt that his reign will always be regarded as one of the most memorable epochs of Russian history.... He might not have had the genius or energy of Peter the Great or the intelligence and far-sighted political wisdom of Catherine II, but he perhaps did as much as either of those sovereigns towards raising his country to the level of west-European civilisation.[25]

His son, heir, and now successor as Tsar, Alexander III, had forged an indirect link with the British royal family in 1866 when he married Princess Dagmar of Denmark, now Empress Marie Feodorovna. Nevertheless, he had none of his father's respect for Queen Victoria, and doubtless took the side of his sister Marie, Duchess of Edinburgh. She had disliked being at the court of her mother-in-law so much that she now spent as much time as she possibly could either in her husband's country house at Eastwell, Kent, which she did not enjoy much more, or abroad, which was preferable in every way. The widow of Windsor, he told his family, was 'a pampered, sentimental, selfish old woman'.[26] During the first few weeks of his reign, she had some sympathy for 'poor Sasha', who was kept almost a complete prisoner in his palace by stringent security measures protecting him from the terrorists. Nevertheless, as time passed, it became apparent that she had none of the affection and little of the respect for the son that she had afforded to his father. To her, Tsar Alexander III was 'a sovereign whom she does not look upon as a gentleman'.[27]

The Queen's relations with Russia, and in particular with her ruler, would soon sour particularly over the issue of Bulgaria. Prince Alexander of Battenberg, a particular favourite of his uncle, Tsar Alexander II, had been chosen as the Sovereign Prince of Bulgaria after the Congress of Berlin.

With the Tsar's murder, Prince Alexander lost his most powerful protector. He was never on good terms with Alexander III, who had always disliked him and resented his determination to govern without Russian interference.

The situation became complicated when he went travelling throughout the courts of Europe, partly in search of a suitable consort who would strengthen his position by providing him with an heir to the principality. While he was visiting Berlin, he became attached to Princess Victoria of Prussia, the second and eldest unmarried daughter of the German Crown Prince and Princess, and plans were accordingly made for them to become betrothed. Two factors, however, made him *persona non grata* as far as the German Emperor, Empress, and Bismarck were concerned. Firstly, he and his siblings were the children of a morganatic marriage between Prince Alexander of Hesse and Countess Julie von Hauke, a former lady-in-waiting at the Russian court. For the Hohenzollerns to allow one of their princesses to marry a prince who was not of the right lineage—even though he was a sovereign prince of a European state—was out of the question. Secondly, for the Hohenzollerns to identify themselves with a man who seemed to be setting himself up as an independently minded opponent of Russia would conflict sharply with the general direction of German foreign policy.

Crown Prince Frederick William liked the young man, but he felt that allowing his daughter to marry a prince who was not sufficiently royal was not the right thing to do, especially as the idea was opposed so vehemently by his parents and his admittedly semi-estranged eldest son. However, the Crown Princess supported the idea with all her might and championed Prince Alexander so passionately as a son-in-law that gossips at court even started to insinuate that she was perhaps a little in love with 'Sandro' herself. She was supported wholeheartedly by Queen Victoria, who not only admired the prince, but also saw the benefits to England of Bulgaria becoming part of an anti-Russian faction in the Balkans. Time would shortly strengthen her family links with the Battenberg family, for in April 1884 one of Alexander's brothers, Louis, married the Queen's eldest Hessian granddaughter, Princess Victoria, and another, Henry, married her youngest daughter, Princess Beatrice, fifteen months later.

Although he was very popular in Bulgaria, Prince Alexander's rule incurred the wrath of St Petersburg and, on 21 August 1886, he was taken prisoner and forced by a Russian coup by gunpoint to abdicate. Queen Victoria was shocked and incensed by the behaviour of 'these Russian fiends', and 'at the terrible treatment to which a reigning Prince and respected by all but Russians (by a good many of them too) the Paul-like Tsar's first cousin [has been subjected], and are furious with the language of the so-called official organs of the German Government'.[28, 29] Her rage against the Tsar, whose sanity she brought into question, knew no bounds.

The Queen often had very firm views about who her granddaughters should marry and was sometimes equally vehement about the unsuitability of certain potential husbands. Her profound distrust of the Romanov family was not easily appeased. Any favourable, if temporary impression resulting from the visit of Tsar Alexander II to England in 1874 had not survived the ensuing Russo-Turkish War, or the persecution of Jews in Russia during the first years of his reign, which had bitterly inflamed British feeling. To add to this was an incident in which British India had been threatened by the sudden arrival of a Russian diplomatic mission in Afghanistan, when a new Amir, exiled in Russia for several years, had entered the country just after an unsuccessful British invasion and seized power.

Memories of the tragic fate of another Hessian princess who had married into the family and been profoundly unhappy, Tsar Alexander II's ill-fated consort Marie, came back to haunt her. The delicate health of the consumptive Marie had proved unequal to the fierce Russian climate, but she had lived long enough to experience the humiliation of seeing her husband flaunt his mistress, Katherine Dolgorouky, and flaunt their illegitimate children at court. Since the death of her daughter Alice at Darmstadt, the Queen had done her best to take Alice's place as a mother to the four surviving daughters and one son. When it seemed likely that the second daughter Elizabeth ('Ella') was likely to marry Tsar Alexander III's brother Grand Duke Serge, she was very concerned. Russia, she was convinced, was no place for one of her favourite granddaughters, and she warned Ella's elder sister Princess Victoria strongly about what she called 'the very bad state of Society & its total want of principle, from the Grand Dukes downwards'. She thought that Serge and his youngest brother Paul were exceptions to this rule, while adding that she had heard 'the former [has] not improved of late'. Above all, she feared that her 'sweet but undecided & inexperienced Ella, with her lovely face, may be misled & get into difficulties & troubles—wh[ich] might have painful consequences'.[30]

It was, however, to no avail. The more Ella saw of Serge, the more she liked him and felt they had much in common as personalities—religious, serious-minded, and cultural. She was determined not to be pressured into marrying any other equally eligible prince that her grandmother had in mind for her. By October 1883, she had made up her mind. Crown Princess Frederick William, who was always more readily able to see the good in others and was never afraid of putting a different view to her mother, assured her that she could quite well understand her reservations about the marriage, stating:

Serge will captivate you when you know him I am sure. There is something quiet and gentle, in fact rather melancholy about him, and his appearance and manners have something high bred and *distingué* which one misses in some of his brothers.[31]

In February 1884, Ella and Serge were formally betrothed and the wedding took place four months later.

After the Prince Imperial was buried at Chislehurst, the Empress decided she wanted to build a mausoleum in which her husband and son could find a permanent resting place. Initially she hoped she might be able to acquire a site near St Mary's Church, where they had briefly been laid to rest. When that proved impracticable, she moved from Camden Place to a mansion at Farnborough in Hampshire. St Michael's Abbey was built nearby, and, in 1888, both bodies were interred there. Queen Victoria took a keen interest in the progress of the building and presented two enormous sarcophagi, hewn from red Aberdeen granite, to be installed in the transepts to the left and right of the altar in the crypt. A third would be placed on an archway above the altar, where the body of the Empress joined the others some three decades later.

Although she never ceased to mourn the deaths of her husband and their only child, and always dressed in black, the irrepressible Empress, who celebrated her sixtieth birthday in May 1886, seemed quite rejuvenated at times. Farnborough Hill always remained her home for the rest of her ninety-four years, but she also built herself a villa at Cap Martin, near Monaco, where she would spend every winter. After buying a yacht, she sailed round the coasts of Britain and Scandinavia, then cruised the Mediterranean. She visited several European countries and Egypt, where in her eightieth year she went sightseeing on a donkey under the blazing sun.

As ever, she remained a very self-effacing woman, completely withdrawn from public life, declining all invitations to lay foundation stones, open exhibitions, or become patron of any charities. It was as if she was determined not to try and become a rival to the Queen, whom she always respected and admired. She made a brief return to Paris in 1883 to perform what she said would be her 'last political act'. Plon-Plon had demanded a plebiscite in France, which he fondly hoped would lead to the overthrow of the existing government and presumably a restoration of the empire, with him as emperor. Instead, he was arrested and imprisoned for a few days. The Bonapartist Party intended to disassociate themselves from him and his actions in future, especially as the imperial succession, such as it was, had passed from the Prince Imperial to Plon-Plon's son Victor. She begged with members of the party not to exclude him, but to forgive him. Though she was unsuccessful, she did at least manage to bring about a temporary reconciliation between him and his sons.

'It Does Seem Like an Impossible Dream'

For several years, Queen Victoria and her family had eagerly awaited the day when her eldest son-in-law would succeed his father as German Emperor. With the passing years, it was increasingly evident that Bismarck was firmly entrenched as Chancellor. There were many differences between him and the imperial heir, but, despite the conservatism of one and the liberal sympathies of the other, there was an ingrained mutual respect. Crown Prince and Princess Frederick William could not but acknowledge that he had helped to bring about the unity of the German Empire, even though they might have deplored his methods and his policy of 'blood and iron'. Yet the Crown Prince's health was not as robust as that of his father. He suffered from severe colds and coughs each winter, as well as an increasing tendency to depression, telling friends and family that he would never rule and that the succession would skip a generation. On his fiftieth birthday, he noted despondently in his diary that he felt acutely how he was ageing and that if he did not have his wife and children as his all, he 'would long since have wished to be out of this world'.[1] He was dismayed by years of being treated as a virtual political pariah by the official world in Germany, by the differences between his eldest son Prince William who had become increasingly estranged from his parents, and also by his own father's ostracism. The elderly Emperor was increasingly dismissive of the son and heir, whom he regarded as dangerous and accused of being a supporter of parties who were hostile to the state, telling Empress Augusta that if he was not the Crown Prince, 'he would be worth getting rid of'. He appeared to be treating his grandson William as heir instead, giving him preferential treatment when it came to sending a representative of the Hohenzollerns on important visits abroad, such as meetings with the Tsar of Russia. The Crown Princess shared her husband's irritation that 'such things [were] always arranged between the Emperor and William without consulting or informing [them]', which in their view was a source of 'endless mischief and endless harm'.[2] In March 1887, the Crown Prince told the governor of Alsace-Lorraine that although he was an Emperor-in-waiting he was bitterly frustrated at hearing nothing about home or foreign policy from official sources and learnt everything through the newspapers, 'and that with the Emperor being ninety years old'.[3]

Throughout Germany, Britain, and Europe, during his long apprenticeship as heir-in-waiting, Crown Prince Frederick William had acquired a reputation as a forward-thinking personality at odds with the ingrained conservatism of his father and uncles as well as most of the German military elite. His views on contemporary issues such as anti-Semitism, socialism, and religious toleration, and interest in the fine arts, all marked him out as a liberal. Nonetheless, doubts were entertained as to whether he would remain thus once he ascended the throne. In London, *The Economist* suggested that during his reign he would exercise immense authority, but he had been kept almost entirely out of public life; while most Germans believed him to be a liberal, some suspected that, when he succeeded his father, 'he will show himself a true Hohenzollern'.[4] Much as he loathed the butchery of war and the waste of life that he had witnessed on the battlefield, he was still a product of the dynasty of 'soldier kings', which personified a love of all things military. To the end of his days, he retained a particular interest in the passage of any bills through the Reichstag dealing with the army and with the minutiae of detail such as soldiers' and officers' uniforms and procedures for drill on the parade ground. It was a fascination that even the Crown Princess sometimes felt bordered on the obsessive.

A heavy smoker throughout his adult life, the Crown Prince had been prone to sore throats and losing his voice for short periods during the winter. When the same thing happened yet again during the winter of 1886, nobody attached any significance to it for several weeks. It was not until those weeks turned into months and he was still cancelling appointments well into the new year that his physician, Dr Wegner, suspected it might be something more serious this time. On 6 March, at his request, Professor Karl Gerhardt, a throat specialist, examined the Crown Prince's throat and discovered a small growth on the left vocal cord that he tried to remove surgically. At first he met with little success. This came at an inconvenient time for, two weeks later, various European royalties, including the Prince of Wales and Crown Prince Rudolf of Austria, were gathering at Berlin for the celebrations of Emperor William's ninetieth birthday. It was alleged that, during the festivities, the elderly and now possibly senile Emperor quipped that he would not die, since the Crown Prince was still alive.[5] Notwithstanding his own personal feelings about the parent who seemed well-nigh immortal, it was an occasion for family and national solidarity and, as befitted his position as heir, the Crown Prince delivered a generous speech of congratulation to the assembled company. As he did so, it was noticed that his normally resonant voice sounded unusually hoarse.

After a month, which involved several sessions of painful treatment, the lesion was removed and the Crown Prince was given permission to recuperate at the spa resort of Bad Ems. No one could be certain that the growth would not return after a few weeks. At first the Crown Prince made a good recovery and his voice returned to normal, but by the beginning of May the old symptoms had returned. When he returned to Berlin in May for examination, Gerhardt discovered that the growth on his vocal cord was there once again—and larger than before. Consultation with further specialists accordingly took place, and they decided it would be necessary to seek the advice of a renowned British laryngologist, Dr Morell Mackenzie. At the request of the German doctors and of Bismarck himself, he was summoned from London in May and arrived in Berlin to take charge of the case.

Within a few days of his beginning his treatment of the Crown Prince, arguments began between him and the German doctors, all of whom insisted that an immediate operation on the throat was vital. Mackenzie insisted that if they did operate, the Crown Prince would almost certainly die. For once, the Crown Princess had an unexpected ally in her old adversary Bismarck, who for years had disparaged the Crown Prince, but was now appalled by the possibility that the immature and headstrong Prince William, whose head had been turned by a clique of flatterers among the military staff, might succeed his grandfather and ascend the throne long before he was ready to do so. The Chancellor agreed with her wholeheartedly that the risk of death after an immediate operation was too terrible to contemplate. They would rather take a chance on the possibility that the natural order of things would follow and that the elderly Emperor would predecease his son, even if it meant that the latter was dying when he succeeded.

In Britain, plans were being made for the celebration of Queen Victoria's jubilee to mark her fifty years on the throne the following month. The Crown Prince and Princess had been invited and were determined to go. Once his illness became common knowledge throughout Berlin, his eldest son, Prince William, took it for granted that he and his wife would be officially representing Prussia at the festivities instead as his father would probably not be well enough to attend. He therefore asked his grandfather Emperor William to appoint him as the Hohenzollerns' official representative in London that summer, a request that the Emperor granted without bothering to consult his son. Deeply upset at being passed over in this unthinking manner, the Crown Prince wrote to Queen Victoria, confirming his intention to be there and requesting that she consider him as the official representative of the family. The Queen was more than happy to oblige and to reprimand her grandson for his presumption—a scolding that he took with very bad grace. Such plans fitted in perfectly with the planned medical treatment, for Mackenzie had recommended that, if the Crown Prince came to England, he could be treated as a private patient in his surgery. Several warning voices were raised against this plan, particularly from those who feared that the Emperor did not have long to live, and there would be grave difficulties if he died while his son was abroad, was to have a relapse, and was too ill to return to Berlin. Although the Crown Princess was increasingly worried by her husband's condition, and 'struggling between hopes and fears', she maintained that 'one cannot be kept a prisoner here, or be prevented from following a useful course by the fear of what might happen'.[6]

As the Crown Prince was heir to the throne, the Emperor's permission for such questions as to whether any operations could take place, or whether his son could go abroad in order to receive medical treatment, was always required. Whenever he was consulted, he always responded in a curiously detached manner, as if to emphasise the fact that he did not really care for his son any more. On being urged by Bismarck to receive the doctors before deciding whether to permit a life-threatening operation on the heir to go ahead, he complained that this would be inconvenient as the Crown Prince was meant to be going to inspect troops in Potsdam. Even Bismarck was astonished by such a heartless response and insisted that His Majesty had to become involved. The Emperor reluctantly conceded, but only as long as the doctors arrived early so that it would not interfere with or delay the inspection. Later, when asked to grant permission for the Crown Prince to travel to London, the Emperor assented, remarking casually that this would perhaps be his son's final wish.

Of all those taking part in the procession for the jubilee service of thanksgiving at Westminster Abbey on 21 June, no one looked more magnificent than Crown Prince Frederick William in his gleaming white Cuirassier uniform, towering above those riding next to him. It still known to very few that he could barely speak above a whisper, and that the doctors suspected his throat trouble to be cancer of the larynx. At the end of the service, all the princes and princesses present moved forward to pay the Queen homage. When she stepped down from the coronation chair, Crown Prince Frederick William happened to be standing near her. Impulsively she embraced him, lingering on his arm in a moment of deep emotion.

The other imperial heir from Europe at the jubilee, Crown Prince Rudolf, had met the Crown Prince and the Prince of Wales at Emperor William's birthday celebrations three months earlier. At the time, European affairs were overshadowed by a quarrel between Austria and Russia in the Balkans, complicated by Tsar Alexander III's conviction that England had completely withdrawn from European affairs and was too ill-equipped to dare or even consider going to war. Crown Prince Rudolf was keen for a closer understanding between England and Austria, and told the Crown Prince and Princess that the Austrian government dreaded not being able to secure any such agreement. He believed that 'if Germany helps Austria against Russia, the French will instantly attack Germany and that the coming war will be extremely serious!'[7] Fortunately, the threat of war had receded by the time they met in London.

As the official representative at the celebrations of the Austro-Hungarian Empire, the thoroughly Anglophile Crown Prince Rudolf was thrilled at his meeting with Queen Victoria, whom he had long since greatly admired at a distance. He reported to his wife, Crown Princess Stephanie, who had been unable to come with him, that she 'was most friendly, and bestowed on me the Order of the Garter, pinning it on herself, and fondling me as she did so, so that I could hardly refrain from laughing'.[8] For the Order of the Garter to be conferred on a prince who was not a reigning sovereign, or not related to the Queen, was an exceptional honour. He made an excellent impression on the Queen, as well as on everyone else. It was noticed that when they went into dinner at Buckingham Palace she walked in on his arm, in front of several crowned heads.

Although very much a man of the world, Crown Prince Rudolf showed a little more decorum than his host one evening while they were in London that week. The Prince of Wales took him and several other friends to supper in a public restaurant, where an orchestra was providing the entertainment. At about 2 a.m., with the party in full swing, the heir to the throne asked the leader if they would play the 'Can-Can', Offenbach's high-kicking dance from *Orpheus in the Underworld*. Although it had been popular for some years, it was still not considered right by some sections of respectable society, but the Prince of Wales entered fully into the spirit of the occasion with the Duchess of Manchester as his partner. Crown Prince Rudolf whispered discreetly to one of the party to order the waiters to leave, as they should not 'see their future King making such a clown of himself'.[9]

Crown Prince and Princess Frederick William stayed in Britain for the rest of the summer, spending part of their time at Osborne and the rest at Braemar, near Balmoral, the Queen's Highland residence. The newly knighted Sir Morell Mackenzie advised them that they ought to avoid the bitter weather of Berlin over the winter, so, on leaving Britain in September, they went first to Toblach in the Austrian Tyrol, then to Venice and Baveno. At the time, the patient and his family were still hoping that the trouble was not cancer and by the end of the month the Crown Prince was writing from Venice to his old tutor Professor Karl Schellbach that his convalescence was 'in full swing', but it was still necessary for him to spend his time in a milder autumn than that of Germany. Mackenzie, he said, was convinced that the real trouble had been overcome and that it was only necessary for him to strengthen his health by avoiding speaking and catching cold, 'so that [he] may be able to return to [his] duties at home by the beginning of the winter'.[10] Meanwhile, in Berlin, the Emperor received the Crown Prince's chamberlain, who had just returned from Britain, but he showed no interest in the medical reports and instead grumbled about how much his son's protracted stay abroad was costing the exchequer.

At the beginning of November, the Crown Prince and Princess moved further south to San Remo, on the Italian coast and close to the French border. To their dismay, once they had arrived, the Crown Prince did not improve, but instead he lost colour and appetite and found the heat irritating. For some weeks, the rumours that he was suffering from cancer of the larynx had been growing and after a further examination, Mackenzie, who had for several months been in denial, had to admit that this was almost certainly the case.

Moreover, the Crown Prince and Princess had the additional cross to bear in the increasing estrangement from their eldest son and heir. Prince William not only showed contempt for his parents' liberal leanings in favour of the ultra-conservative politics of his grandfather and Prince Bismarck, but also began to behave unpleasantly as if he was the Emperor-in-waiting. Endlessly fawned upon and flattered by the reactionary elements at court and the military establishment, he became more arrogant and dismissive of his parents' ways than ever. Such sympathy as he felt for his seriously ill father and desperately worried mother was concealed too well. He seemed to regard his father as a noble, but helpless victim, totally at the mercy of a steely wife who according to her detractors gave every appearance of looking after her own interests as well as those of her British homeland. After he had an angry conversation with the chamberlain Count von Radolinski in July 1887, a few weeks after the jubilee celebrations, the latter was convinced that the young prince hated his mother. Shortly after his parents arrived at San Remo, he took it upon himself to warn the German Foreign Office not to send any confidential information to the Crown Prince, because the Crown Princess was opening and screening his correspondence and would certainly pass on any information of interest to their counterparts in London.

Over Christmas and the new year, the Crown Prince rallied a little and, in spite of the German doctors' comments, Mackenzie appeared unconvinced that his patient was suffering from cancer after all. In an article in the *British Medical Journal* for the first week of January, he noted that in his view the symptoms were more compatible with 'the more severe form of chronic laryngitis', and a few days later he told Queen Victoria that he believed there was nothing malignant about the disease.[11] A few days later, his condition worsened again and, after one particularly bad night when he was in danger of suffocation and speedy death, an immediate tracheotomy was decided upon and performed by Dr Bramann. By this stage, it was clear that his life could only be prolonged by a matter of weeks. Since late the previous year, he had been in constant pain, unable to speak at all except in a hoarse whisper, and reduced to writing everything he wanted to say on a pad of paper that he always kept within reach.

The ninety-year-old Emperor had been ailing ever since he caught a severe cold during a naval inspection the previous summer. Some wondered whether the son would predecease the father. Nevertheless, it was intended that the Crown Prince should stay at San Remo and not return to Berlin until the spring, by which time the weather would have improved, but it was not to be. On 9 March, while taking his regular morning walk in the garden at San Remo, he was handed a telegram that brought him the news that Emperor William had just passed away, within two weeks of what would have been his ninety-first birthday.

'My OWN dear Empress Victoria it does seem an impossible dream, may God bless her!' the Queen wrote to her daughter as soon as she was brought the news of her son-in-law's accession, 'You know how little I care for rank or Titles—but I cannot deny that after all that has been done & said, I am thankful & proud that dear Fritz & you sh[oul]d have come to the throne'.[12] Like so many others, she had feared that he would not survive his father. Now that he had come into his inheritance and would not enjoy it for long, she begged her daughter to be firm. She should not accept any interference or impudence from her elder children—particularly William, now Crown Prince—and remind them that in the previous reign they had always spoken of the Emperor and Empress with great respect and needed 'to remember who they are now'.

The new sovereign announced that he intended to reign as Emperor Frederick III. He, the Empress, and their entourage returned to Berlin that same week, but it was evident to all that the disease was too far advanced for there to be any hope of recovery. Their existence was made worse by the tactless behaviour of Crown Prince William, surrounded by toadies who already had an eye on their own advancement during the forthcoming reign. Despite his political differences with the new Emperor, Bismarck still believed that it was in nobody's interests for Prince—now Crown Prince—William to ascend the throne while he was still so immature and headstrong. Aware that he had to prepare himself for the normal course of events, he asked the German doctors how much longer he had to put up with such uncertainty. They assured him that the Emperor would not last the summer out.

Since his departure from Balmoral the previous year, Queen Victoria had been determined to visit her stricken son-in-law again, for what she knew would be the last time. If Emperor William had survived a few weeks longer, they might have met at San Remo, for she had arrived at Florence within a fortnight of Emperor Frederick's accession. When she publicly announced her intention of coming to Berlin with Prince and Princess Henry of Battenberg, Bismarck and his son Herbert, who was his father's Minister for Foreign Affairs, were convinced that she was coming to insist on the betrothal of her granddaughter Princess Victoria of Prussia to the former Prince of Bulgaria. Nothing was further from the Queen's mind, for she was aware that, although her daughter and granddaughter were still hoping that it would be possible, she had warned them not to pursue the idea in defiance of Crown Prince William's opposition. From the beginning, he had made his opposition to any thoughts of the marriage perfectly clear, even to the extent of threatening to put a bullet through the head of 'the Battenberger' if he as much as set foot inside German territory again. Moreover, the Queen had found out that Prince Alexander was weary of the official German opposition to his plans with Princess Victoria and he had not only given up the idea, but also fallen in love with an opera singer, Joanna Loisinger, whom he would marry early the following year. Sir Edward Malet, the British Ambassador in Berlin, was anxious to preserve good Anglo-German relations, even at the expense of appeasing the Bismarcks and the Crown Prince. He wrote to Lord Salisbury, British Prime Minister, to persuade the Queen to postpone her visit. With some indignation, she pointed out that her journey was to have no political significance and it was merely a family visit so she could see her daughter and son-in-law.

As they travelled across Europe, the train halted at Innsbruck so the Queen could pay a brief visit at his request to Emperor Francis Joseph of Austria, who had travelled seventeen hours in full uniform in order to come and see her. His desire to meet her was partly inspired by courtesy towards a fellow-sovereign passing through his territory, and partly by a desire to further Anglo-Austrian harmony, following the excellent impression Rudolf had made at the jubilee. The Queen was not altogether pleased, for the last thing she intended to do was to give Bismarck the impression that her journey was being undertaken for anything other than private reasons.

However, to decline Emperor Francis Joseph's invitation would be to commit the same breach of royal etiquette that Empress Elizabeth had done so habitually in England. On the afternoon of 23 April, a boiling hot day, the royal train pulled into Innsbruck and, although the four of them sat down to lunch in a room at the station, she 'unfortunately had a very bad sick headache and could eat next to nothing'. However, the Emperor, she noted, 'was most kind' and told her how happy he was at the good state of Anglo-Austrian relations, which he hoped would continue, so that in the event of war they would be able to act together. Russia, he said, was 'incomprehensible' and he thought Bismarck 'much too weak and yielding to Russia, which was a great mistake'.[13]

On her arrival at Berlin, the Queen went straight to the Emperor's sickbed. The Empress noted sadly that it was the first time she had ever had her mother to stay under her roof—and now it was for the most poignant of reasons. Though he was rather the worse for sleepless nights, the sight of his mother-in-law cheered him up as he sat up in bed, propped up on his pillows. She sat beside the bed, holding his hand as she talked about the family and he wrote at intervals on his pad, passing it to her.

Despite Lord Salisbury's fears that Her Majesty would surely be exposed to fierce anti-German demonstrations in the street, the Queen was received enthusiastically every time she appeared in public. When the Empress took her seat beside her mother, shouts of 'long live the Empress!' were evident as well. At her request, the Queen had an audience with Bismarck on the day after her arrival. The thought of coming face to face with her—which he had done once before, very briefly, at Versailles in 1855—made him quite ill at ease. He need not have worried, for the meeting went very smoothly. The sole record of their conversation, which lasted a little more than an hour, was that made by the Queen in her journal afterwards. They discussed international affairs and the possibility of war with a Franco-Russian alliance if Austria should be attacked with Germany being bound by her treaty obligations to defend her. Otherwise they kept to uncontroversial matters, such as her anxiety about the inexperience of her grandson William, who would surely be Emperor within a few weeks. Bismarck assured her that, although the young prince knew nothing about civil affairs, 'should he be thrown into the water, he would be able to swim'. She asked him to stand by her daughter and he promised faithfully he would, as 'hers was a hard fate'. Above all, he assured her that he was not contemplating any form of regency, as he knew it would upset the Emperor.[14]

The Queen's published journal made no reference of any possible marriage between Princess Victoria of Prussia and the former Prince of Bulgaria, which she knew it was no longer worth pursuing and about which she had made her views clear to the Empress. However, as the Queen's journals were transcribed after her death by Princess Beatrice and the originals destroyed, it was possible that the subject was mentioned, if only briefly. After they had finished, Bismarck walked out of the room, smiling with admiration and mopping his brow, as he exclaimed, 'What a woman! One could do business with her!'[15]

On the last day of her visit, the Queen saw the Emperor again as she told him with a heavy heart that he would have to do what she knew would never come to pass—that he must repay the visit and come to see her in England once he was better.

For the next six weeks, his decline was evident to all around him. By a supreme effort of will, he was able to attend the wedding of his second son, Prince Henry, to his cousin Princess Irene, the third daughter of Louis, Grand Duke of Hesse and the Rhine, on 24 May. However, he leaned on a stick for support the whole time he was present and every step he took caused him great agony. On the morning of 15 June, members of the family were warned that the end was near and they gathered in the sickroom as he breathed his last.

At the time, Queen Victoria was at Balmoral. Early in the morning, she had received a telegram to say that he could only last another few hours and soon afterwards Princess Beatrice brought her another from her eldest grandson, now Emperor William II, telling her it was all over. Although she had been preparing herself for the news for several weeks, she was grieved at the realisation that the curtain had fallen on thirty years of hope. 'Feel very miserable and upset', she wrote in her journal. 'None of my own sons could be a greater loss.... My poor child's whole future gone, ruined, which they had prepared themselves for nearly thirty years!'[16]

While she had often been dismayed at the unfilial conduct of her eldest grandson over the last few years, she was ready to make allowances for him. At once she telegraphed him: 'Do all you can for your poor dear mother and try to follow in your best noblest and kindest of father's footsteps'.[17] It was an optimistic appeal to his better nature, for the young sovereign had no intention of doing any such thing. During the previous twenty-four hours, as Emperor Frederick lay dying, the then Crown Prince William had filled the grounds and corridors of Friedrichskron—the former Neue Palais, which Frederick had recently renamed after himself, where he had been born and where he had returned to end his days—with troops in readiness for a virtual state of siege. The building was effectively sealed off from the outside world by armed guards and orders were issued that neither doctors nor members of the imperial family could leave without a signed permit, while all outgoing letters, telegrams, and parcels were to be checked and censored. The Emperor had to be dissuaded from issuing an order for the immediate arrest of Dr Mackenzie. He had been prepared for the secret removal of some if not all of his parents' private correspondence, knowing that it would not show him in a very favourable light, but though his soldiers ransacked every desk they could lay their hands on, they could find nothing. Knowing better than to trust their son, during the previous year, the then Crown Prince and Princess had ensured that everything was or would soon be in safe storage at Windsor.

In defiance of his father's express instructions and his grief-stricken mother's pleas, Emperor William permitted a post-mortem to be held. He was determined to uphold the name of German medicine by proving that the German doctors' diagnosis had been right and that Mackenzie was at fault. According to the hurried examination, conducted with a verdict pronounced on the evidence of the naked eye, the whole of the larynx apart from the epiglottis had been destroyed and it consisted of one large, flat, gangrenous ulcer, with patches of septic broncho-pneumonia present in the lungs.[18]

The funeral of Emperor William I in March had been held a week after his death in order to give everyone who wanted to attend adequate time for preparation. In contrast, the obsequies for his son were rushed through and he was buried three days later, on 18 June, at the Friedenskirche, Potsdam. No invitations were sent out to other European sovereigns or princes, though, as the sad event had been anticipated for several weeks, some representatives had been chosen by their heads of state to attend and were ready to travel to Berlin with as little notice as possible. Among them were the Prince and Princess of Wales and their elder son, Albert Victor; the Empress's brother-in-law, the Marquis of Lorne; her uncle, Ernest, Duke of Saxe-Coburg Gotha; and from Russia, Tsar Alexander III's brother, Grand Duke Vladimir. While waiting for the coffin to arrive at the start of the ceremony, the clergymen and military officers stood around laughing and chattering with each other. Chancellor Bismarck was not among them and had sent his son Herbert to represent him. To discourage members of the public who wanted to pay their last respects to 'our Fritz', whose reign they hoped would have been the start of a new era in German history, the Emperor had the route of the procession cordoned off by soldiers. The Empress could not face attending her husband's official funeral, and she and her three younger daughters held a small private service of their own instead the same day.

Just as hard to bear as the loss of her beloved husband was the realisation that all their political efforts had failed. 'We had a mission, we felt it and we knew it, we were Papa's and your children!' she wrote that same day to her mother. 'We were faithful to what we believed and we knew to be right. We loved Germany—we wished to see her strong and great, not only with the sword, but in all that was righteous, in culture, in progress and in liberty'.[19]

Princess Louis of Battenberg was prepared to make allowances for her cousin's behaviour. She pitied him sincerely. 'He is so young for his position, & greatly needs a wise & honest friend to help him,' she wrote to her grandmother the day after Emperor Frederick's death:

> I greatly fear, that for want of such a one, his faults rather than his good qualities will develop. When I think how warm hearted & nice he was as a boy, how greatly he changed during the last years, I cannot but think it is a great measure the fault of his surroundings.[20]

Queen Victoria was appalled by Emperor William's behaviour towards his mother and the memory of his father, and by the supine behaviour of Empress Augusta Victoria ('Dona'), who showed no sympathy to the bereaved mother-in-law who had always treated her with such kindness, but went along unthinkingly with everything her husband said and did.

Unlike her granddaughter, the Queen was for the moment less inclined to be charitable towards him. 'It is too dreadful for us all to think of Willy & Bismarck & Dona—being the supreme head of all now!' she wrote to the princess the following month. 'Two so unfit & one so wicked'.[21] She and Lord Salisbury had both been astonished by the lack of any mention of Britain in his first speech from the throne and felt uneasy by the indications of a new understanding with Russia, at a point when Anglo-Russian relations were at a low ebb. When she heard of the young Emperor's travelling plans, she wrote to him with some annoyance, saying that she trusted he would not pay any official visits to other countries for several months as it was still less than a month since his father had died and they should still be in mourning. He replied high-handedly that his meeting with the Tsar of Russia would 'be of good effect for the peace of Europe & for the rest & quiet' of his allies. If it had been possible, he would have waited longer, 'but state interest goes before personal feelings, & the fate which sometimes hangs over nations does not wait until the etiquette of court mournings has been fulfilled'.[22]

While he was in Russia, the Emperor and his entourage did not hold back from criticising the Queen to Tsar Alexander III, who had never been an admirer of her in the first place. Herbert Bismarck told him that in the English royal family 'and its closest offshoots' there was 'a kind of cult of the family principle', with Queen Victoria being looked upon 'as a kind of absolute head of all members of the Coburg tribe and all its offshoots'. Moreover, it was Britain's intention to 'create discord and conflict on the continent and to goad the other great powers for England's benefit'. The

Prince of Wales, he asserted, had already attempted to 'blacken' the name of Emperor William to the Tsar in order to create mutual distrust and the Queen had written to the Emperor three days before their departure for Russia to advise him strongly against his journey. As he had had enough of 'this uninvited tutelage', he sent the Queen such a plain answer that such a situation was unlikely to recur. It said much about the character of Herbert Bismarck that he was prepared to speak with such lack of restraint about personal relationships within the royal family to another sovereign. Notwithstanding the antipathy between Tsar Alexander and Queen Victoria, it may be wondered what the Tsarina—who was presumably told of these exchanges by her husband—thought of this, in view of the fact that she had always been close to her sister the Princess of Wales and, no matter what her opinion of Queen Victoria might have been, liked and respected the brother-in-law who had always been prepared to defend Danish interests to the best of his ability.[23]

Without her husband, the Empress Frederick was denied the chance to be more than an unofficial ambassador for the country or empire over which he had reigned so briefly. She had to accept that she was no longer of any significance in diplomatic relations between Britain and Germany. Neither Queen Victoria nor the Prince of Wales, the two closest members of her family, were officially obliged to treat her as of political importance, although in private they insisted on showing her every possible courtesy. The Queen showed a full understanding of her predicament: 'You are far more sorely tried than me. I had not the agony of seeing another fill the place of my angel husband which I always felt I never could have borne'. To her it was 'a misfortune untold and to the world at large', and 'far more dreadful to [her] than the loss of [her] own children'.[24]

The Empress was convinced that the Emperor Frederick was missed less in Germany than in Britain. 'My beloved husband was cheered and gratified beyond measure by the affectionate sympathy shown him from England during his illness', she wrote to Lord Napier two months after his death, 'Now he is taken from us, and my life is left a blank, but I feel gratefully that he is mourned and appreciated in my own dear home he loved so well'.[25]

That autumn, Emperor William paid a visit to Emperor Francis Joseph in Vienna. Having heard that the Prince of Wales was also due to visit the city at the same time, he refused to meet his uncle there and the Prince was obliged to postpone his visit. What became known as 'the Vienna incident' provoked deep hostility. At first, the Prince of Wales was extremely disappointed. He had genuinely looked forward to meeting his nephew and Colonel Leopold Swaine, an attaché at the British Embassy in Berlin, said he had never seen the Prince so upset about anything.[26] A few days later, his sadness had turned to fury. 'William the Great', he commented angrily, needed to learn that he was 'living in the nineteenth century and not in the Middle Ages'.[27] The episode resulted in a stout defence of her son from an infuriated Queen Victoria, whose patience with the grandson for whom she was generally ready to make allowances had now almost reached breaking point.

Speaking on behalf of her son and herself, she wrote to Lord Salisbury:

> [I have always] been very intimate with our grandson and nephew and to pretend that he is to be treated in private as well as in public as 'his Imperial Majesty' is perfect madness! He has been treated just as we should have treated his beloved father and even grandfather, and as the Queen herself was always treated by her dear uncle King Leopold. If he has such notions, he better never come here. The Queen will not swallow this affront...

She was anxious that what should have remained a private family issue should have as little impact as possible on matters of state, but feared that such an escalation would be unavoidable if matters continued on their present course. With regard to the political relations of the British and German governments, she continued:

> [I fully agree] that this should not be affected (if possible) by these miserable personal quarrels; but the Queen much fears that, with such a hot-headed, conceited, and wrongheaded young man, devoid of all feeling, this may at ANY moment become impossible.[28]

Shortly after the Emperor's death, the Queen had urged her daughter to return to England for a visit. The latter did not want to make it appear as if she was running away, but, after having endured endless humiliations in Germany for the last few months, she was almost at the end of her tether. The constant barrage of attacks on her husband's memory and on her personally, and the callous behaviour of her eldest son and Bismarck, had come close to unnerving her completely. On 29 September, the anniversary of her betrothal at Balmoral, she admitted in a letter to her mother that the previous day she 'felt very near putting an end to [herself]'.[29]

The latest cross she had to bear was Sir Morell Mackenzie's vindication of his handling of the case. The German doctors had defended themselves in a pamphlet attacking Mackenzie, but instead of responding with a dignified silence he felt obliged to try and clear his name with a book, *The Fatal Illness of Frederick the Noble*. Published on 15 October in English and German, it was not confined to a discussion of the medical issues, but, in an attempt to exonerate himself, he sharply criticised the German doctors' incompetence and mistreatment of their patient. The British medical establishment censured him for airing his views so publicly and, while the Empress remained supportive of him, it was one more controversy that made her life in Berlin very uncomfortable.

Lord Salisbury told the Queen that it was too soon to think of letting the Empress return to England, no matter how briefly, and that to receive Her Imperial Majesty at such a point in time would risk undermining Anglo-German relations. She retorted that it would be 'impossible, heartless and cruel' to put any obstacles in her daughter's way as it would be purely a family visit and that to postpone it would be a cowardly action that would only encourage the Bismarcks and the Emperor in their disgraceful behaviour towards her.[30] Her grandson had angered her with his 'passion for travel', and his 'unfeeling & indecent conduct in rushing ab[ou]t so early uninvited to other Courts, his marked slights & rudeness to England & his relatives'.[31] Altogether, in his first few months as Emperor he had made a bad impression in Britain and throughout Europe, in not observing a decent interval of mourning for his father. Such a reputation, so thoughtlessly acquired, would take him time to live down.

On 19 November, the Empress and her three younger daughters, Victoria, Sophie, and Margaret, arrived in England for three months. Though as a matter of course she never went further than her front door when welcoming even her most exalted guests to England, this time she made the journey to Gravesend to meet her daughter and granddaughters as they landed from the yacht *Victoria and Albert*. Nothing was too much trouble for the widowed Empress, whose brightest hopes had been dashed so tragically, and she hoped that when he heard of this reception the Emperor would be shamed into treating her with more respect when she went home.

Meanwhile, another imperial tragedy was about to unfold with a devastating effect on all those who were closely involved. When the Prince of Wales was informed in September 1888 that his presence was not required in Vienna while Emperor William was there, an alternative programme had to be drawn up for his entertainment prior to the arrival of the new Emperor. Arrangements were made for him to go to Bucharest at the beginning of October and stay with King Carol and Queen Elizabeth of Roumania. However, he could hardly leave Vienna at a moment's notice and while he was there the host country had to accommodate him the best she could without offending her illustrious Hohenzollern ally. Royalties throughout Europe were well aware of the British heir's boundless energy, his abhorrence of going to bed before the small hours, and his ill-concealed boredom if not kept active. The problem was particularly acute in Vienna, where dinners at the Hofburg were over by what he considered the unbelievably early time of 10 p.m. Francis Joseph was always at his desk by 5 a.m. the next day, and late nights were not part of his routine. The task of acting as host fell to Crown Prince Rudolf, who was only thirty years old, but astonished by his friend's stamina. 'Wales', he wrote to his wife, Crown Princess Stephanie, was 'in great fettle, wants to see everything and will not allow himself to be left out in the cold. Nothing seems to tire the old boy. I long for a rest.'[32]

Crown Prince Rudolf and the Prince of Wales had long been friends, and the Habsburg heir had also been a friend and admirer of the late Emperor Frederick. He was one of several European royalties who had regarded Frederick's premature death and the accession of William II to the imperial throne as a tragedy for Europe. To his wife, he said he wanted to invite 'Wales' to a bear shoot in October after his return from Roumania. Sardonically, he added that he had no intention of inviting Emperor William II, unless it was 'in order to arrange a neat hunting accident which would remove him from the world'.[33] Perhaps he recalled the demise of another William II, who had met a sudden death in England while out hunting several centuries earlier. Rudolf had never liked William. In 1883, he had called the Prussian heir 'a dyed-in-the-wool Junker and reactionary', who never spoke of parliament except as 'that pig-sty', or the opposition deputies except as 'dogs who must be handled with a whip'.[34]

Shortly before he left Vienna later that week, in order to accommodate his nephew's wishes, the Prince of Wales attended military manoeuvres with Emperor Francis Joseph at Belovar. The occasion demanded several hours in the saddle and, with his portly figure and chronic breathlessness (to say nothing of a tight-fitting Hungarian uniform that was evidently not up to the task required), it was not an ideal situation for him and the Emperor appreciated the effort the British heir was making. To his mistress, Katherine Schratt, the Emperor wrote with admiration that 'the plump fellow kept up the whole time and lasted out incredibly. But he did get pretty stiff, and as he had split his red Hussar trousers and had nothing on underneath, it was all rather unpleasant for him'.[35]

Before he returned from Central Europe to England, the Prince of Wales was in good spirits as he waved farewell to Crown Prince Rudolf. He could not have imagined that they had just seen each other for the last time. The Austrian heir had been deeply upset not only by the death of Emperor Frederick III, but also by the state of affairs within the Habsburg Empire and within Europe in general. He was suffering from gonorrhoea, heavily dependent on morphine, and his marriage to Crown Princess Stephanie had virtually collapsed in all but name. His entourage were increasingly worried by his absent-minded attitude at military parades and other public ceremonies, as well as a sudden complete lack of interest in serious books and thirst for scholarship.

Another blow fell when Emperor William sent Emperor Francis Joseph a letter, drafted by Bismarck, demanding for the sake of Austro-German relations that the Crown Prince of Austria-Hungary should be dismissed from the post of Inspector of Infantry, to which he had recently been appointed. It was unwarranted interference, but the Habsburg Emperor, mindful of maintaining good relations with Germany, did not destroy the letter on reading, as he might well have done. Instead, he invited his son to an official interview, told him about the German Emperor's complaints, and asked if he would be willing to resign of his own accord in the interests of good relations. A bitterly angry and demoralised Crown Prince Rudolf insisted that he was carrying out his duties conscientiously and refused to consider resignation. At around the same time, although not necessarily on this particular occasion, he asked his father for permission to divorce his wife, but the Emperor would not hear of it. The Prince of Wales later reported to Queen Victoria that it was as a result of one of these scenes, or possibly a combination of both, which led directly to 'the catastrophe'.

On 31 January 1889, people throughout Europe were shocked by the news that the thirty-year-old Crown Prince of Austria-Hungary had been found dead at his hunting lodge at Mayerling. As the news was broken to his deeply distressed parents, wife, and sister, initial reports suggested that he had probably been poisoned. The public were informed first that he had died of apoplexy and then that he had been suffering from some form of mental disturbance during the last few weeks of his life and had killed himself in a moment of mental derangement. Only later did it gradually emerge that he did not die alone, and that the body of his mistress, Marie Vetsera, had been found next to his. It was apparent that they had made a suicide pact and that he shot her, then himself.

As she could never forget how Rudolf had charmed her when he attended the jubilee celebrations in June 1887, Queen Victoria was particularly shocked and 'terribly upset', and she telegraphed Sir Augustus Paget, the British Ambassador at Vienna, for any details he could gather, no matter how distressing. To Lord Salisbury, she wrote that the Prince had seen a friend from Vienna, a great personal friend of the Emperor, and he knew all the details, which he said were too shocking to write: 'But there is no doubt that the poor Crown Prince was quite off his head'.[36] Lord Salisbury was apparently one of those who did not believe the suicide theory, and believed or had been led to suppose that Rudolf's death was a carefully contrived assassination, staged to look as if he had pulled the trigger himself. Rumour had it that he had been killed either by agents of Count Taaffe, the Austrian Minister-President, or an execution squad acting under instructions from the Emperor's cousin Archduke Albrecht, Inspector General of the Austrian army, because he was deeply involved in treason against the state and that nobody would think he had been eliminated thus as he was a potential suicide. It was also whispered that French or Hungarian patriots had put him to death because they had exacted from him a promise to help their countries on which he had reneged; or that he was the victim of a forester who had been cuckolded. To some, the suicide theory concealed an even more scandalous reason, which the Austrian government and court were desperate to conceal.

At Buckingham Palace, the blinds were drawn as a mark of respect, while full mourning was ordered for a fortnight. Special masses were said for the repose of the soul of the prince in the Austrian Chapel at Berkeley Square. However, owing to the scandalous circumstances of his private life and death, the Queen felt unable to grant the Prince of Wales or any other member of the royal family her permission to attend the funeral in Vienna. She was represented by Paget, and the Prince of Wales by Major-General Keith Fraser, a military attaché at the British Embassy. The Prince was at least able to send a wreath in memory of the friend whom he greatly mourned. Just as the Emperor Frederick's death had put an end to any prospect of a liberal German empire, seven months later Rudolf's shocking demise had dealt a similar blow to such chance as there might have been of a liberal Austria.[37]

'I Really Cannot Go about Keeping Everyone in Order'

For several months, the behaviour of Emperor William II seemed calculated to give offence to his relations in England. He continued to make personal attacks on the English in general and his mother in particular. To King Humbert of Italy, he ridiculed the Empress Frederick mercilessly as 'that fat, dumpy little person who seeks influence'.[1] Almost a year after his father's death, he was still telling his associates in Germany that an English doctor killed his father, and an English doctor had been responsible for his deformed arm and hand: 'This we owe to my mother who would not have Germans about her!'[2]

As the new year dawned, Queen Victoria remained firm in defence of the Prince of Wales and resolute that she could not allow the Emperor to be received in England. 'William must not come this year,' she wrote to him, 'you could not meet him, and I could not after all he has said and done. He would not meet with a very cordial reception by anyone, I am sure.'[3] Yet William was desperate to be invited. He still gave his relations in England the impression that he felt he had done nothing wrong, and therefore had nothing to apologise for. Colonel Swaine at the embassy in Berlin advised Sir Henry Ponsonby that it was imperative for Queen Victoria to treat His Imperial Highness as Emperor, and he would remain her grandson: 'Treat the Emperor as grandson and he is lost as such for ever'.[4] Moreover, the British government was obliged to put state expediency before the personal feelings of the royal family by building bridges between Britain and the country that had long been her traditional ally. The Prince of Wales admitted that there were political advantages in such a visit, but he resolutely refused to receive his nephew until the latter had expressed at least a word of regret for the Vienna incident. With regard to the Emperor coming during the summer, he conceded: 'Of course it would be the proper & right thing that he should having visited the chief countries of Europe excepting England'. He wanted complete harmony to exist between England and Germany, and if they remained friends and allies they could do more to keep the world at peace than any other two nations:

> But if one's nearest Relations abuse one—& are rude to one—it is impossible to 'pocket it' without a murmur. The result is coldness & later enmity, & all this is so unnecessary & deplorable.[5]

At the end of February, the Queen was still insisting to the Prime Minister that she hoped the Emperor would postpone his visit for another year, 'as it is still too soon after all that has passed and will be very disagreeable to The Queen'. If he really intended to come this year, he would have to apologise to the Prince of Wales first.[6] Lord Salisbury, who had little admiration or respect for the Prince, stressed that, for reasons of international politics, an unqualified reconciliation between the two royal families and a warmer relationship between Britain and Germany was highly desirable if not essential. From a telegram that he had received from the Emperor, it was clear, he told the Queen, that he earnestly desired to be received back into Her Majesty's favour once more. It may have been connected with the fact that his relations with Russia were now less satisfactory than they had been, 'but it is also probable that he has now thoroughly awakened from the temporary intoxication of last summer. It is [Her] Majesty's interest to make his penitential return as easy to him as possible'. There could be disastrous consequences for the standing of the British monarchy, which would rise from a British refusal, including the withdrawal of the German Ambassador to London, Paul von Hatzfeldt, if no visit was to take place.[7]

With some misgivings, and despite her feeling that the Prince of Wales was clearly owed an apology after the humiliating way he had been treated during the Vienna incident the previous autumn, the Queen was persuaded to draw a line under the matter. She reluctantly conceded that the 'rude boy' should visit her at Osborne in his yacht, but not in London, so that it would be more of a family than an official occasion, and that it should take place at the end of July. Even so, she felt obliged to warn her grandson that the Prince of Wales would not be present at their conversations unless he had reached some understanding with his uncle first, otherwise his place would have to be taken by the Duke of Edinburgh as the second of her sons. The Empress Frederick was extremely hurt when she learned of this, especially as she only heard from her son Prince Henry that the Emperor had told him 'that he was going to have a glorious reception, great preparations would be made for him', that he would be accorded a naval review and would be bringing his fleet. She realised that it was the wish of Lord Salisbury:

> It is also, I suppose & believe, very right & proper & necessary. But you can imagine what a stab it gives me! The thought that W. who has so trampled upon me, & on his beloved father's memory, should now be received … in my own dear home![8]

The matter of mediation between uncle and nephew had still not been settled, but the Prince of Wales was still furious and would not be easily appeased. He declined the proposal brought to him by Swaine that he should first write to William, to which the latter would send a conciliatory reply. The Prince also refused to accept Hatzfeldt's suggestion that he should simply let the unpleasant business rest until both men had had the opportunity to express their mutual regret over the misunderstanding once they met. The Prince of Wales then asked his brother-in-law, Prince Christian of Schleswig-Holstein, who had always got on well with the Emperor, to mediate for him during his forthcoming visit to Berlin. However, the Prince of Wales's private secretary, Sir Francis Knollys, expressed the view that nobody would be in a better position to settle the family quarrel than the Queen herself.

At the end of March, with the full agreement of Bismarck and the Emperor and much to the surprise of the British government and the German Ambassador, Herbert Bismarck came to London on a mission to try and restore Anglo-German relations and to prepare the ground for the visit that his master particularly wanted to pay at around the end of July. This was all the more pressing in view of the danger of a military confrontation on the continent, and of the fear of a French invasion of Italy. According to Alfred von Waldersee, recently appointed Chief of the German Imperial General Staff and one of the Emperor's inner circle, it was the German Minister for Foreign Affairs' aim to try and bring about a lasting Anglo-German union against Russia. Herbert Bismarck had explicit instructions from Emperor William to make clear his pleasure at the kind invitation he had received. In conversations with Lord Salisbury, he stressed that in his view it was important that England and Germany should appear united before the world and pointed to the significance of the Emperor's forthcoming visit in this regard. He then drew Salisbury's attention to the danger of the British monarchy being seen in open opposition to public opinion as embodied in parliament. It was the Emperor's wish, he reiterated, to spend a quiet few days on a family visit at Osborne, as well as two or three further days after that in visiting ports, arsenals, and other matters of military interest. He then spoke in a conciliatory manner of the Emperor's great veneration and affection for the Queen, and tactfully described the death of Emperor Frederick III as 'an appalling calamity'. With regard to the Prince of Wales, 'he betrayed some soreness, and was evidently disappointed that his visit to England had not produced some sign of favour or relenting on the part of his Royal Highness'.[9]

The Prince of Wales was prepared to use the negotiating skills of Prince Christian, who had already planned to go to Berlin in a few days' time, in order to achieve a mutually satisfactory outcome with the Emperor. In discussions with Prince Christian and Herbert Bismarck, the Emperor claimed repeatedly that he had never expressed a wish not to see the Prince of Wales in Vienna the previous year, but Christian still thought he detected 'a certain indisposition' towards the Prince of Wales. Above all, the Emperor remained inflexible on the matter of offering a written explanation. He said he could not write to the Prince of Wales as it was not a simple matter between uncle and nephew, but between Emperor and Prince of Wales. The next day, a weary Prince Christian asked Malet to telegraph the Prince of Wales to say that the Emperor was keen to settle the quarrel, but was not prepared to take the first step by writing. He suggested that they should involve the Austrian Foreign Secretary, Count Gustav Kálnoky, and ask him how he had gained the apparently false impression that the Emperor had not wanted to see the Prince. Malet thought that this would only cause more trouble and asked the Prince of Wales to send a cipher telegram expressing his satisfaction with the Emperor's explanation that Kálnoky must have been given the wrong impression. With this, he hoped that the whole tedious matter could finally be laid to rest.

The Prince of Wales was not satisfied. If the whole affair had been based on a misunderstanding from the start, he said, then the Emperor could perfectly well 'write a few lines saying he regretted that [the Prince] was under the impression that he was averse to seeing [the Prince] in Vienna'.[10]. The Emperor refused, on the grounds that he did not know whether Bismarck would permit it. The Prince of Wales was adamant that, in asking for a few lines instead of a vague verbal message, he was not making an excessive demand. If the Emperor would not comply, he would regard it as proof that he Emperor did not wish to make it up with him and he would ask the Queen's permission to absent himself when His Majesty came to England that summer.[11] To Prince Christian, he reiterated that he had a duty to protect his own dignity; if William would not write a letter, and if he should therefore stay away during the visit of the Emperor and his Fleet, he would take care 'that everyone knows the reason'.[12]

Queen Victoria fully shared her son's view that it was only right that he should receive a few words in writing from his nephew. The Empress Frederick also agreed. She thought her son's behaviour was a result not of

malevolence, but of embarrassment, and considered it incomprehensible
that he had not long since managed to settle the matter with a few simple
lines to his uncle. Salisbury, his senior ministers, and advisers of the crown
had further reasons for settling the dispute as speedily as possible. They
wanted to avoid any rupture with Germany arising out of non-political
difference, and Ponsonby warned the Queen that it could pose a danger to
the standing of the monarchy at home if republican agitators seized upon
the royal family quarrel to further their case among the lower classes.[13]

By this time the Prince of Wales had had more than enough of the
wretched affair. Sir Francis Knollys and Sir Henry Ponsonby reverted
between them to the suggestion that the only person who could bring
about a reconciliation was Queen Victoria herself, a suggestion with
which the Prince readily agreed, writing to the Empress Frederick that he
intended to 'leave the matter entirely in dear Mama's hands'.[14] Ponsonby
therefore drafted a letter for her to send to the Emperor, drawn up by
Lord Salisbury. She made several corrections to it in her own hand, on
the grounds that the wording to it proposed by the Prime Minister simply
accepted the Emperor's denial and in effect forced them to accept the lies.
She crossed out a passage that would have given the impression that the
Emperor's visit was awaited with pleasure in Britain, and to the dismay of
her Prime Minister she added one expressing the hope that the Emperor
would order an official investigation into the Vienna incident.

Although he was still deeply hurt, the Prince of Wales agreed at length
to the draft as altered by the Queen, accepting that she had stood solidly
by him. He also let it be known that, if Lord Salisbury raised any objection
to the Queen's amendments, he would refuse to dine with him on the
Queen's seventieth birthday dinner. The family had come to the end of their
willingness to compromise any further. Advisers at court were convinced
that her letter would have the desired effect. Ponsonby conceded that
nobody could force the Germans to launch an enquiry, but believed that
otherwise 'all will come right'.

Unfortunately, Emperor William was in no mood to compromise
either. In his reply, he declared that the whole affair had been 'absolutely
invented' and was 'a fixed idea which originated either in uncle Bertie's
own imagination or in somebody else's, who put it into his head'. He was
glad that at last the affair was over, evidently unaware that the Queen, the
Prince of Wales, and Knollys were all still extremely annoyed with him.[15]

There was a theory that the Emperor had not been responsible for and
therefore nothing to do with the Vienna incident. It was possible that the
Bismarcks, father and son, and possibly the late Crown Prince Rudolf,
with his contempt for the Emperor, had been behind it all the time. At
the same time, it was insulting to suggest that the Prince of Wales had

imagined it all. As the Prince had decided not to forgo his visit to the Isle of Wight that summer after all, it would be impossible for him to avoid meeting the Emperor, but it was agreed that any contact between them would have to be restricted to the minimum possible. If the Prince was to receive the Emperor, it would look as though he was welcoming him and that was out of the question. The general sense of anger at Windsor was exacerbated when the Empress Frederick reported that the Emperor was boasting that he could do 'what he liked with his Grandmama'.[16]

The Queen intended to send the Emperor another letter trying to persuade him to offer some explanation for his insulting behaviour in a manner that would prove acceptable to the Prince of Wales. Lord Salisbury proposed that she should declare herself 'very satisfied' with his letter, with the exception of the sentence pertaining to the Vienna incident having been his uncle's imagination. The Queen and the Prince of Wales both redrafted the letter in rather more blunt terms, but by now Salisbury had had more than enough. He now strongly advised against replying to the Emperor's letter at all, saying that if an answer must be sent, it would have to be his original draft. What the Queen wanted to say privately to her grandson was her own personal affair.

The Prime Minister's attitude was deeply resented in the royal family and generally at court. The Prince was furious, writing to the Empress Frederick that Salisbury had given their mother 'the worst possible advice, making [them] virtually to "eat humble pie!" What a triumph for the Bismarcks, as well as for Willy!'[17] Others, particularly Prince Christian and Knollys, felt that the Prime Minister had sacrificed the heir on the altar of political expediency. Yet it was the culmination of several months of refusal by either side to give way, and there was no way out but compromise of one kind or another. A constitutional government had to prevail over personal wishes in matters of politics. The Queen and her heir might be offended, but Britain as a nation had at least earned the gratitude of a notoriously hard-to-please European sovereign.

Shortly before the Emperor's accession, Salisbury—and, one assumes, the Queen and other members of the family as well—had, however, been warned by one of her surgeons that Prince William, as he was then, 'was not, and never would be, a normal man'. He would always be subject to 'sudden accesses of anger,' incapable of forming reasonable or temperate judgments, and 'some of his actions would probably be those of a man not wholly sane'.[18] This was probably a coded reference to the possibility of porphyria, and the Prime Minister was more prepared than his sovereign and her heir to make allowances for his mental instability.

As a constitutional sovereign first and foremost, the Queen had no choice but to accept her Prime Minister's judgement as binding. In June, she made Emperor William a British admiral, for which he was effusively grateful. For him, wearing the same uniform as St Vincent and Nelson was enough to make him feel quite giddy. He assured Sir Edward Malet that he would immediately set to work in order to select a regiment fit for the great honour of having Her Majesty as honorary colonel: 'I feel something like Macbeth must have felt when he was suddenly received by the witches with the cry of "All hail, who art Thane of Glamis and of Cawdor too"'.[19]

Despite everything that had happened, grandmother and grandson had a deep bond of mutual respect that would never be erased, come what may. As the Duchess of Edinburgh had commented to the Emperor's sister Charlotte, Hereditary Princess of Saxe-Meiningen, it made no difference how much Queen Victoria might denounce 'that dreadful tyrant', as soon as he arrived in England again it would 'all disappear'.[20] The Emperor might express his occasional impatience with her, but she always remained his 'unparalleled grandmama'. 'How I love my Grandmother, I cannot describe for you', he wrote to his friend Philipp zu Eulenburg, 'she is the sum total of all that is noble, good and intelligent. With her and my feelings for her, England is inextricably connected'.[21]

In August, the Emperor came to spend a few days in England, accompanied by his brother Prince Henry among others. As was so often the case, as soon as he set foot in England, he fell under the spell of his grandmother's charm and was on his best behaviour throughout. The Queen reviewed the German Fleet, he presented to her a deputation of four officers of her regiment, she bestowed on Prince Henry the Order of the Garter, and the Emperor conferred on his cousin Prince George of Wales the Order of the Black Eagle. Matters went better than anyone involved had dared to expect, and after his departure the Prince of Wales's private secretary Sir Francis Knollys told Lord Salisbury that relations between the Emperor and Prince were excellent. It was almost as if the unpleasant events of the previous two years or so had never happened.

If he could, as his mother put it, do 'what he liked with his Grandmama', he did not refrain from taking liberties with other members of the family as well. In June 1891, the Prince of Wales was called as a witness in a legal action brought by Sir William Gordon-Cumming, who had been accused of cheating at the illegal game of baccarat at a house party at Tranby Croft, Yorkshire, the previous year, at which both men had been among the guests. Gordon-Cumming was determined to clear his name and the Prince was implicated as he had been among the players and signatories to a pledge signed by Gordon-Cumming, in which he promised never to play cards for money again. He had moreover gone against military regulations, which stipulated that all serving officers, including Field-Marshal HRH The Prince of Wales, had to order any fellow-officers accused of dishonourable conduct to refer his case directly to his commanding officer. To a casual observer, it was almost as if the heir to the throne was on trial. Although she felt angry and humiliated by the affair, the Queen stood solidly by him, but the German Emperor was among those who joined in with those taking the moral high ground. He sent a letter to Queen Victoria—which has not been preserved—protesting against the impropriety of anyone holding the honorary rank of a Colonel of Prussian Hussars becoming embroiled with men young enough to be his children in a gambling squabble.[22] To the Prince of Wales, this lofty missive from his nephew was probably even more infuriating than a leader in *The Times* expressing a wish that he too would also sign a pledge that he would never again play cards for money.

Throughout the next few years, the German Emperor would outstay his welcome in England more than once. Few, if any, servants at court in England really looked forward to his next appearance. One of Queen Victoria's more sharp-tongued ladies-in-waiting, Marie Mallet, noted in her diary that they were all dreading what he would say and do the next time:

> The more I hear of him the more I dislike him, he must be such a despot and so terribly vain. However, poor man, he has a most insipid and boring wife who he does not care for and from whom he escapes by prancing to the four corners of the world.[23]

Having thoroughly relished his first visit as Emperor to the Isle of Wight, and fancying his prowess as a yachtsman, he suddenly showed an interest in the sport that rapidly became something of an obsession. He purchased an English America's Cup contender, the *Thistle*, rechristened her the *Meteor*, and with an English captain and all-English crew began to race. It was with his success with this first *Meteor*—he later commissioned a second with the same name—which prompted the Prince of Wales, a yachting enthusiast of some years' standing and Commodore of the Royal Yacht Squadron, to order his yacht the *Britannia* in an effort to keep up with his nephew's insatiable thirst for competition.

For four consecutive summers, from 1892 to 1895, the Emperor could be relied on to put in an appearance at the Regatta, combining his racing activities with a visit to the Queen at Osborne House. In the spring of 1892, Lord Salisbury was complaining about his unpredictability, telling Sir Henry Ponsonby that 'if he is in this excitable mood he may be dangerous and that a few hours' conversation with the Queen can appease him'. He hoped the Queen would make an effort to go and visit him while she was on the European mainland, visiting the family of Ernest, Grand Duke of Hesse—who had succeeded his father Louis, who had died about a month earlier—at Darmstadt, and then going to stay at Hyères on the French Mediterranean coast. Much as she loved her often infuriating imperial grandson, she baulked at the prospect, protesting that she 'really cannot go about keeping everyone in order'.[24] As the court was still mourning the deaths of the Grand Duke and also the Prince and Princess of Wales's eldest son 'Eddy', Prince Albert Victor, Duke of Clarence, the Queen did not particularly want another visit from the Emperor that summer. She never invited him, she insisted to Ponsonby in June, and 'she w[ou]ld be very thankful if he did not come'.[25] Nevertheless, come he did, although mindful of the bereavements that had cast such a gloom over the family earlier that year, he was on his best behaviour at Cowes. Even the Prince of Wales conceded that for once he was 'not in the least grand, and very quiet, and most amiable in every respect'.[26]

All the same, it was not forgotten that he had failed to attend a memorial service for the Duke of Clarence in Berlin, and had refused to let his brother Prince Henry come and attend the funeral in England. Four years earlier, about three weeks before their father's death, Prince Henry, who had married his cousin Princess Irene of Hesse about three weeks before his father's death, had formerly been inclined to side, less than wholeheartedly, with his brother during most family arguments and issues against their mother. Now, under the influence of his more conciliatory and pro-English wife, he was becoming more amenable. Having become a regular visitor to England, he was particularly liked and respected by Queen Victoria, the Prince of Wales, and his other cousins. The Emperor was jealous of his more easy-going brother's popularity at Windsor and Sandringham, and also tried to forbid him from attending the Duke of York's wedding in England in June 1893 until pressure persuaded him to think again and give in.

From 1893 onwards, when he came to Cowes, the job of acting as host to the Emperor every time fell on the Prince of Wales. It was not a duty he relished, for his nephew became increasingly obsessed with the sport, making endless trouble about handicaps and rulings, implying that the committee was unduly favouring the Prince of Wales and other yachtsmen. Whenever he was engaged in a race, he could also be tiresomely single-minded.

That same summer, as the *Meteor* and the *Britannia* were racing each other around the Isle of Wight, the wind suddenly dropped and both yachts were becalmed. On board the *Britannia*, the Prince became anxious about a full-dress dinner that the Queen was hosting that evening in honour of the Emperor, knowing that if they arrived late his mother would take it as gross discourtesy. From his yacht he signalled the *Meteor*, proposing that they abandon the race and return by train at once so that they would both be back at Osborne in time for dinner. The Emperor nonchalantly replied that the race had to be fought out, as it did not matter what time they reached Cowes. Although the breeze revived a little later, the yachts did not reach their moorings for several hours, and uncle and nephew did not reach Osborne House until about 10 p.m., one in a considerably more relaxed state of mind than the other. The Queen had finished dinner by the time the Emperor hurried up, kissed hands, and apologised profusely. She greeted him with 'a thin smile'. His uncle came a few minutes later, taking cover momentarily behind a pillar to wipe the perspiration from his bow, then came forward and bowed to his mother. She gave him a stiff nod.[27]

In spite of this, or perhaps because of it, as the Emperor returned home in August 1893, Francis Knollys told Gladstone's secretary, Algernon West, that His Imperial Majesty's visit had been a great success: '[He had enjoyed everything] immensely; so much so indeed, that I am afraid it will tempt him to repeat his visit very frequently'.[28]

In August 1895, the Emperor excelled himself with what was an astonishing display of tactlessness, even by his standards. At the start of the month, he arrived at Cowes escorted by his two latest and fastest warships, the *Wörth* and the *Weissenburg*, both named after German victories in the Franco-Prussian War. Two days later, he celebrated the twenty-fifth anniversary of the Battle of Wörth by delivering on board a sabre-rattling speech that infuriated those who were there. It also caused adverse comment in the British and French press, the more so as it had been made in British waters on what should have been a purely social occasion free from politics. While the Emperor was dining with the Prince of Wales, the discussion centred partly on negotiations then in progress for a more clearly defined frontier between British India and French Indochina. The Emperor jokingly suggested that a breakdown in talks might lead to war. Either forgetting or disregarding the fact that the Prince of Wales had never seen active service in his life, despite having in vain asked Queen Victoria on at least one occasion to be allowed to do so, he thumped his uncle on the back, saying, 'So you'll soon be off to India again, and we'll see at last what you're really good for as a soldier!'[29]

During the previous two seasons, the *Britannia* again triumphed over the *Meteor*, but not without the Emperor complaining—he was tired of losing. During this year, just before the start of the race for the Queen's Cup, he announced that he was dissatisfied with the handicapping and was accordingly withdrawing the *Meteor*. It was the last time he ever raced at the Isle of Wight. The Prince of Wales was heartily relieved to see the last of his nephew's obsession with yachting, but he too had had enough. In 1897, he sold the *Britannia* as his experience of 'the Boss of Cowes' had completely taken the fun out of his sporting activities. It had once been a pleasant holiday for him, he admitted, but 'now that the Kaiser has taken command there, it is nothing but a nuisance'.[30]

The Emperor rarely let slip by a chance to humiliate or irritate his uncle, 'the old peacock', in some way. Such petty exchanges might be commonplace among families, but when they involved two of the most important European royal personalities, the consequences could be incalculable. One theory that has been suggested is that William may have been trying to discredit him in order to position himself to wear the English crown. As Queen Victoria's grandson, the Emperor was in the order of succession line to the British throne, albeit a long way down. Somehow he had managed to convince himself that, if her eldest son was judged to be unsuitable to succeed his mother, then he (William) would be invited to take his place.[31] Although the idea sounds almost implausibly far-fetched by twentieth-century standards, there had been a precedent, most notably the deposition of King James II in 1688 and his displacement by his daughter Princess Mary and her husband William, Prince of Orange. Nonetheless, such a situation belonged to a very different age, as well as ignoring the simple fact that, when King Edward VII ascended the throne in January 1901, his son and heir, Prince George, Duke of York, already had three sons who were next in the order of succession after him. For William Hohenzollern to contemplate being offered the British crown in all seriousness suggests a disturbing sense of exaggerated ambition.

Even the ever-patient Lord Salisbury, who had been so anxious to help build bridges between His Imperial Majesty and his warring relations in England at first, had evidently had enough. Having long since counselled treating the Emperor with the greatest consideration, he evidently disregarded this advice shortly after forming a new government in August 1895. A meeting had been arranged between both men to discuss the Eastern question, and the consequences that the possible collapse of the Ottoman Empire might have throughout Western Europe. Salisbury was willing to talk about ways of partitioning the affected territories, but arrived two hours late at a meeting they had scheduled, and when he did arrive proved thoroughly non-committal, not to say uncommunicative. The Emperor proposed that they should convene again the next day, and Salisbury agreed but failed to turn up. Later, he sent his apologies, explaining that he had had a meeting with the Queen at the same time, had not received the Emperor's message, and—not very convincingly— that he had been caught up in the rain. The Emperor therefore made plans for a third meeting, yet once again the Prime Minister did not arrive, on the grounds that he had to be in London early. One member of the imperial entourage suggested to Baron von Holstein (the German Minister for Foreign Affairs) that the real reason was because Salisbury could not bear the thought of seeing him again.[32]

In stark contrast to the brash, exhibitionistic behaviour of the mercurial Emperor William was the quiet demeanour of his near-contemporary and the Prince of Wales's other imperial nephew, Grand Duke Nicholas, Tsarevich of Russia. He had already been to England once, when he was just five years old, accompanying his parents on their visit in the summer of 1873. On the summer reunions between the British and Russian royal families at Denmark, he had formed a close friendship with the sons and daughters of the Prince and Princess of Wales and, when Prince George of Wales was preparing for his marriage to Princess Victoria Mary of Teck in July 1893, he particularly asked whether 'Nicky' could be included among the guests coming to England for the occasion.

Queen Victoria gave her consent and the Tsarevich was invited, not only to the ceremony, but also to stay at the Wales' London residence, Marlborough House. Always ready to play the part of a conscientious host, the Prince of Wales had ensured that there would never be a dull moment for the Russian heir. The Tsarevich wrote regularly to his mother, Empress Marie Feodorovna, telling her that he was delighted with London, which he had never thought he would like so much, and with a faint note of weariness that 'Uncle Bertie is in very good spirits and very friendly, almost too much so'.[33] 'Uncle Bertie' was indeed a little overwhelming at times. The constant round of garden parties, dinners, luncheons, visits to tailors, bootmakers, and hatters became exhausting after a while, especially in the heat of what was proving to be an unusually hot summer. Nicholas's spirits were not improved when it was noticed that he bore a remarkable resemblance to his cousin George. Only three years apart, both were of similar height, had similar beards, and also dressed alike. 'Everyone finds a great resemblance between George and me, I am tired of hearing this again and again', he complained.[34] At one garden party, George was asked for his opinion of London, while Nicholas was congratulated on his forthcoming wedding.

He also succeeded in softening Queen Victoria's views towards the Romanovs and Russia a little. The visits to England of the previous Tsars had done nothing to alter her lifelong antipathy to the country, except possibly on a very short-term basis, and although it had been some years since they were both at war—or in the case of the Russo-Turkish dispute, very close to fighting— political differences still remained. At the time, both nations were locked in a dispute over Russia's claim to the Pamir mountains in Central Asia, and the British Foreign Secretary, Lord Rosebery, was threatening to send forces out there in order to defend British interests. The Queen received the Tsarevich at Windsor, and invested him with the Order of the Garter, an honour that completely took him by surprise.

In turn, she was surprised to find him totally unlike his father—polite, unassertive, even shy. She noted that he was 'charming and wonderfully like Georgie. He always speaks English, and almost without a fault, having had an English tutor, a Mr Heath, who is still with him. He is very simple and unaffected'.[35] In turn, he described her affectionately, if perhaps not too flatteringly as 'a big round ball on wobbly legs', who was 'remarkably kind' to him.[36]

In April 1894, Queen Victoria paid what would be the last of her seven visits to the ancestral home of Coburg, in what would be a prelude to a second marriage alliance between her family and the Russian Empire. The occasion was the wedding of two of her grandchildren, a match that she had helped to bring about and which would, much to the consternation of many of the family, end in divorce within less than a year of her death. The Queen had long regarded herself as another mother to the five surviving children of her second daughter, Alice, Grand Duchess of Hesse and the Rhine. Soon after Ernest, the only son among them, succeeded his father as Grand Duke in March 1892, he fell in love with his cousin, Princess Victoria Melita, second daughter of the Duke and Duchess of Edinburgh. The marriage just over two years later proved to be one of the last great gatherings of European royalty on the mainland in the nineteenth century. It was, however, slightly overshadowed by speculation as to whether the groom's youngest sister, Alix, who was known to take her religion very seriously, was prepared to change her faith in order to marry the Tsarevich, for whom she was considered to be the ideal wife. It had been over three years since rumours had first reached her that 'Nicky' was falling in love with her and that her elder sister, Ella—married to Tsar Alexander III's younger brother, Grand Duke Serge—was doing her best to encourage the match. At first, the Queen was not at all pleased, as she wrote very firmly to Princess Louis of Battenberg:

I had your assurance that nothing was to be feared in that quarter, but I know it for certain, that in spite of all your (Papa's Ernie's & your) objections & still more contrary to the positive wish of his Parents who do not wish him to marry A. as they feel, as everyone must do, for the youngest Sister to marry the son of the Er. [Emperor]—would never answer, & lead to no happiness,—well in spite of all this behind all your backs, Ella & S. [Serge] do all they can to bring it about, encouraging & even urging the Boy to do it!

Adding to her convictions was her belief that the state of Russia was 'so rotten that at any moment something dreadful might happen' and that the wife of the heir to the throne would find herself in a particularly difficult position.[37] The omens for an Anglo-Russian marriage were certainly not promising, for the union between the Duke of Edinburgh and the Tsar's sister had been the least happy match among all her children. Moreover, she had never forgiven the Tsar for the way he behaved towards the former Prince of Bulgaria, who had married and retired into private life in Austria, broken in health and destined to die at an early age. She had heard all about it from the Princess of Wales, who had been told by her sister the Tsarina. Shortly afterwards, there were rumours that the Tsarevich might instead marry Princess Margaret of Prussia, the German Emperor's youngest sister, and Alix would marry the Duke of Clarence, but neither of these came to anything. Nicholas was unimpressed by Margaret, a level-headed if rather plain young woman, while Alix failed to warm to 'Eddy', and, in Queen Victoria's words, in turning him down she refused 'the g[rea]test position there is!'[38]

On the morning after the wedding of Ernest and Victoria Melita, Ella came to see the Queen, 'much agitated', to tell her that they were indeed engaged and wished to come in and see her. She admitted to being 'thunderstruck', as though she knew Nicholas had particularly wished for it, she thought Alix 'was not sure of her mind'. People were pleased at the betrothal, she noted, 'which has the drawback that Russia is so far away, the position a difficult one, as well as the question of religion'.[39] It seemed remarkable that 'gentle simple Alicky' would be 'the great Empress of Russia'. For the next few days, until they returned to their respective countries, she invited the two young people for morning coffee in her rooms each day. She also made them pose regularly for photographs, all notable for showing a resolutely unsmiling Alix.

Having regarded herself as a second mother to her motherless Hessian grandchildren ever since the death of Alice in December 1878, the Queen worried constantly about Alix and the future that lay ahead of her as Empress of Russia. She wrote regularly to Nicholas, impressing on him her concerns for his future wife's health and her nerves. While she had no doubt that they were genuinely devoted to each other, it was as if she genuinely feared the desperately shy, independently minded young woman was ill-equipped for such a role in life. That summer, she invited both of them to England for a few weeks. While staying with her at Windsor, they accompanied her to White Lodge for the christening of the Duke and Duchess of York's eldest son Edward. Alix also met the Bishop of Ripon Dr Boyd Carpenter, who could instruct her in points in common between the Orthodox Church and the Church of England, and the Tsar's new confessor, Father Yanishev, who could coach her in her new faith.

The diffident youth of twenty-five, quite unprepared for his inheritance, had met with the Queen's unqualified approval. After they had gone, she wrote to Empress Frederick that she had 'never met a more amiable, simple young man, affectionate, sensible and liberal-minded'. Alicky, she added, was 'very fortunate, only the position is an anxiety'.[40]

They were to be married in November and everyone assumed that they would have the benefit of a period of grace before succeeding to the imperial throne of Russia. It therefore came as a tremendous shock to everyone when the health of the Tsarevich's great bear-like father suddenly began to fail. Only those closest to him had been aware that he was never really the same again after the family had narrowly escaped death during an accident in 1888, when their train had been derailed, due not to sabotage by terrorists (as had at first been suspected), but by the carriages travelling too fast. Over twenty people were killed and many more seriously injured. In order to allow the family and other survivors to crawl out of the wreckage, it was alleged, the Tsar held the roof up— although this version of events has sometimes been disputed. Nevertheless, the trauma of the accident, if not the physical strain he suffered while the family were being rescued, severely affected him for the rest of his days.

Early in 1894, he celebrated his forty-ninth birthday, but he had aged beyond his years, and that autumn he fell ill with nephritis. Despite careful attention from his physicians, it was soon apparent that he was dying. He and the family moved to Livadia in the Crimea, the palace where he could benefit from milder weather, but the doctors could do little if anything else to make his last few weeks more comfortable. By the time Alix arrived to meet her betrothed's father so he could give her his blessing, he was almost blind and so weak that he struggled to get into his uniform, but he considered that to receive her in anything less would show a lack of respect.

On 30 October, in response to a personal appeal from the Tsarina, the Prince and Princess of Wales left London for Livadia. As they stopped at the British Embassy in Vienna two days later, they learnt that the Tsar had just passed away. Before proceeding to Russia, they sent a telegram to the Duke of York asking him to come and join them as well 'out of respect for poor dear Uncle Sasha's memory'.[41]

Although there was little love lost between the two sovereigns, who had not met since the younger was still only heir to the throne, Queen Victoria was deeply concerned. She was at Balmoral when Princess Beatrice brought her a telegram informing them. Although it had been expected, 'the news seemed almost incredible and very sad'. Her immediate thoughts were with her granddaughter Alix and Nicholas:

> What a terrible load of responsibility and anxiety has been laid upon the poor children! I had hoped and trusted they would have many years of comparative quiet and happiness before ascending to this thorny throne.[42]

Nicholas was appalled at the responsibility that had been thrust on him with so little warning. His father had always regarded him as a mere boy and had done nothing to prepare him for the business or experience of being a sovereign. As Princess Louis of Battenberg observed, the dominating personality of Tsar Alexander III 'had stunted any gifts for initiative' in his son.[43] He admitted in desperation to his cousin Alexander that he knew nothing of the business of ruling. His sister Olga recalled that he said he did not know what would become of them all, and admitted to her that he was wholly unfit to reign. It was to be a chilling foretaste of his reign as a whole.

On 8 November, the Russian imperial family, accompanied by the Prince and Princess of Wales, left Livadia on their three-day journey to Moscow in the imperial train. It was a harsh journey, which took them from the spring-like Crimea to the snow-covered ground on the streets of the capital.

For the time being, the Prince of Wales would prove the temporary salvation of the shell-shocked, temporarily rudderless family. While the Princess took care of her sister, the distraught widow Empress Marie Feodorovna, her husband took charge of befriending and encouraging the new Tsar, as well as taking responsibility for the funeral arrangements and everything else that needed to be done. 'I cannot tell you what awful and trying times we are living through now!' the Tsar wrote to Queen Victoria. 'Your dear kind telegrams touched us all, more than words can say!'[44] He readily acknowledged how much the presence of Alexandra of Denmark (his aunt Alix) and his uncle Bertie had helped them all, not least in assisting his mother in her grief. It was left to his sister Olga, who probably shared in some measure their late father's antipathy to Queen Victoria, to wonder 'what his tiresome old mother would have said had she seen everybody accept uncle Bertie's authority in Russia of all places'.[45] While the Queen could not be there, she took a keen interest, demanding regular reports and wanting to know every detail possible. Some of them found her persistent curiosity rather wearing, none more than the Prince of Wales's equerry, Sir Arthur Ellis, who grumbled about 'the old, tiresome woman at Windsor Castle' in persistently telegraphing them for yet more letters.[46]

The Prince was one of sixty-one European royalties present at the funeral at Kazan Cathedral that November. Throughout the ceremonies, at which there were no pews so everybody had to stand throughout, the Prince stood next to the Tsar. Like the rest of the Romanovs, he kissed the lips of the dead Tsar, though the corpse was already decomposing despite having been embalmed, admittedly not until three days after death. His friend Lord Carrington, Lord Chamberlain of the Household, admitted that the dead man's face 'looked a dreadful colour and the smell was awful'.[47]

The Prince of Wales could not help but compare the new sovereign with another European ruler of the same generation, and favourably so. Tsar Nicholas II, he observed, was 'quite touching' in his deference to his mother the Dowager Tsarina, who was still first lady of the Russian empire, 'and hardly likes to assume his new position! It is such a contrast to another Emperor and his conduct to his mother!'[48] Ironically, though not surprisingly, Tsar Nicholas and Emperor William were distantly related. As great-great-grandsons of Tsar Paul, they were third cousins, and through William's great-aunt Charlotte, sister of Emperor William I and consort of Tsar Nicholas I, great-grandfather of Nicholas II, they were also second cousins once removed.

Alix had been received into the Orthodox Church on the day after Tsar Alexander III's death, and it was decided that their wedding would need to be held as soon as reasonably possible after the funeral. Many a superstitious Russian feared that it would be a bad omen for their ruler's bride to follow a coffin. The ceremony took place at the Chapel of the Winter Palace on 26 November, one week after the funeral. The day before, Queen Victoria wrote ominously to the Empress Frederick that 'poor dear Alicky's fate' would be sealed: 'No two people were ever more devoted as she and he are and this is one consolation I have, for otherwise the dangers and responsibilities fill me with anxiety'.[49]

The Duke of York wrote to his grandmother afterwards, telling her that the bride 'went through it all with so much modesty but was so graceful and dignified at the same time, she certainly made a most excellent impression'. He never saw two people, he went on, more in love with each other or happier than they were, and when they drove from the Winter Palace to the cathedral 'they got a tremendous reception and ovation from the large crowds in the streets, the cheering was most hearty and reminded me of England'.[50]

There was certainly no lack of goodwill towards the married couple, but the Duke's words were possibly somewhat gilded. Others thought that the Tsar looked very pale and worn throughout the solemn, even gloomy ceremony, while Alix, struggling with the weight of the traditional silver brocade and cloth of her ermine-lined, diamond-encrusted wedding dress (which required eight pages to lift it) came across as looking uncomfortable and as unsmiling as ever. Her cousin Marie, Crown Princess of Roumania, who never really liked her, observed with more than a grain of truth that 'no joy seemed to uplift her, not even pride', and that 'she was all dignity but she had about her no warmth'.[51] Everything about the wedding, said Sir Arthur Ellis, 'had the appearance of a forced air of mock festivity', with all mourning put aside 'and an effort to appear cheerful—which was manifestly put on'.[52]

It was an ominous beginning to the next chapter of the Romanov dynasty, and some of those present at the chapel may have been struck by a presentiment that the Russian Empire was or would soon be doomed.

'So Important that We should Understand Each Other'

With the accession of Tsar Nicholas II to the Russian throne, Queen Victoria and Lord Rosebery, who had become Prime Minister on the resignation and retirement of Gladstone in March 1894, both saw a golden opportunity for closer Anglo-Russian relations at the start of what could be the beginning of a new era. With this in mind, Rosebery had asked the Prince of Wales to do what he could in furthering a close relationship with the young Tsar.

Prince Albert Edward had never shared his mother's distaste for Russia. Ever since he was a young man, he had always made it clear that he would be only to happy to do whatever he could in promoting good relations with the Romanov empire, especially after the ill-feeling caused by the Crimean War and the conflict with Turkey two decades later had subsided, and above all as the Princess of Wales's favourite sister had been married to Tsar Alexander III. The latter's funeral had resulted in his fourth visit to Russia, and while he was there he had several long conversations with Minister for Foreign Affairs Nikolai Giers. When he told Lord Carrington that he had reservations about his nephew's autocratic outlook and lack of worldly sense, the latter said he feared a revolution in Russia was inevitable. The Prince refrained from agreeing with this gloomy prognostication, though he added that it was always necessary to move with the times and he hoped the new sovereign would have the wisdom to realise as much.[1]

After the repressive thirteen years of the reign and rule of Tsar Alexander III, following on a period twice that length of his more enlightened, but sadly doomed father and predecessor, all heads in Europe looked towards Russia to see what direction the young new ruler would follow. Queen Victoria and Emperor William II both hoped that, with his close family relations, he would lean towards them. After what had been a very successful visit by the Prince of Wales, almost a triumph if such a term could be used to describe a sojourn that included the death and funeral of a ruler, the British entourage thought and hoped they could detect signs of a new liberal dawn in the Romanov dominions. In particular, the Tsar had received a deputation from Poland, a much-persecuted land, and told its representatives that in his own eyes all subjects were equal and alike. It was a promising start, but also a false harbinger of the state of things to come. Disillusion set in soon afterwards, when he made a speech attacking 'senseless dreams' of democracy and declaring that he would maintain the principle of autocracy just as firmly as it had been preserved by his father. Like his father before him, Nicholas accepted as law the ultra-reactionary views of Konstantin Pobedonostsev, Chief Procurator of the Holy Synod of the Russian Orthodox Church.

Nevertheless, he told the British ambassador in St Petersburg, Sir Frank Lascelles, how fond he was of his English relations and how he accepted the necessity of enjoying cordial relations with the country. Family ties were cemented through regular correspondence between Queen Victoria and the Tsar and Tsarina, which was, however, destroyed by the latter after her grandmother's death. When their first daughter, Grand Duchess Olga, was born in November 1895, they asked the Queen if she would consent to becoming her godmother, a request to which she was glad to agree.

As there was no longer any difference of opinion between either nation, the Tsar said they should be able to act in perfect harmony towards solving issues and problems throughout the world. One particular outstanding bone of contention was a territorial dispute over the Pamir boundaries in the Himalayas, which after festering for some time was settled by a Pamir boundary commission, which paved the way for formal acknowledgement of Russian and British colonial possessions in Central Eurasia, ratified by a convention a few years later. Less success crowned British attempts to resolve tension in the Ottoman empire and later in the Far East. When the British government invited Russia to bring pressure to bear on the Ottoman government after its partial responsibility for several massacres of the Armenians, a Christian minority ethnic group within the Turkish empire pressing for self-government, the Russians declined to cooperate, despite claiming to be staunch defenders of Christians within the empire. Not long afterwards, the British cabinet sought help in backing a call for an armistice in the Far East, where the Chinese had been soundly defeated in a war with Japan and were asking the great powers to intervene. Russia declared it was not in her interest to let Japan establish a foothold in China, a neighbour of Russia. A further bone of contention arose when the Russians, realising that the Japanese had plans to annex the Northern Chinese province of

Manchuria (on which they had their own designs), demanded that the British back their plan to evict them. As British interests were not directly involved, their ministers refused to become involved.

Queen Victoria diplomatically wrote to Tsar Nicholas, saying that she and her government regretted they could not side with Russia, 'but the feeling was so strong in this Country that it was impossible'. She did, however, take the opportunity of complaining about 'violent and offensive articles against England in the Russian press' by a journalist whom she understood to be known personally to the Tsar.[2] In mitigation, he answered that he could not prevent people from putting their opinions openly in the newspapers, a less than convincing excuse as the Russian press was notoriously the most rigidly censored in the world at that time. He pointed out with some justification that the British press was openly critical of his country's regime, although he was incorrect in believing that the British government controlled the papers in quite the same way. He probably had in mind instances such as an article by Leo Tolstoy about the persecution of a pacifist sect, whose members were beaten and starved for refusing to do military service, published by *The Times* in October 1895.[3]

The hostility of the Russian press continued unabated and, in his final audience with the Tsar as British ambassador at St Petersburg before leaving to take up a similar post at Berlin, Lascelles told him how much the British deprecated this, adding that such articles would surely not be written if the views they expressed did not find favour with the majority of the people, in other words the Russian ministers who controlled the media. To this, the Tsar could only give a rather non-committal reply that the press had 'very little importance' in Russia.

In the autumn of 1896, shortly after England and Russia had signed an agreement on the disputed Pamir territory, reports that Russian troops had been sight on the borders of Tibet were received by the foreign office in London. These were followed by rumours that the Russians had made a secret loan worth about £8,000,000 to China, which was facing a large war indemnity after being defeated in a war with Japan. Russia had in turn demanded trading concessions and approval for extending the trans-Siberian railway though Manchuria, a Northern Chinese province extending into the Russian territory of Siberia. The British government was suspicious of any such Russo-Chinese arrangements, especially as it had done quite handsomely from helping the Chinese imperial government with loans and other financial trading arrangement and suspected the Russian Foreign Minister Prince Lobanov-Rostovsky of intriguing with other foreign powers and trying to unite them against England. All this seemed to be confirmed in April 1896, when Queen Victoria learned from Lord Salisbury that Russia was 'urging and encouraging France against us with regard to Egypt'. While the Prime Minister was adamant that 'there was no sensible statesman in England who was not anxious for a good understanding with Russia', the general anti-Russian feeling in Britain was very strong, and any signs of hostility or unfriendliness from Russia would make it very difficult for the British government.[4] Thoroughly prejudiced against the British, Lobanov-Rostovsky refused to cooperate with Lord Salisbury's administration as he was convinced that his ministry's objective was to create tension in Eastern Europe, with the added aim of taking part of Turkish territory should the Ottoman Empire crumble completely. At the same time, Russia was keen to pursue an expansionist policy in Asia and the Far East, where Britain was her only significant rival.

From Berlin, Emperor William saw Germany's chance to create a formidable friendship and alliance with Russia that would detach her from her allegiance to the French and the British. Although no friend of Britain, Tsar Alexander III had also long had an antipathy to William, dismissing him as *'un garcon mal élevé et de mauvaise foi'* ('an ill-bred youngster of bad faith'), but William sensed that the more new malleable, eager-to-please-everyone Tsar would be easier to persuade.[5] His ambassador and several of his ministers shared his view that what had been a traditional shared amity between Germany and Russia could easily be rekindled as long as the comparatively fresh Franco-Russian alliance could be weakened and then left to wither on the vine. The 'unnatural love affair' between the French Republic and autocratic Russia, they believed, simply defied logic.

One problem that Queen Victoria and her government always faced was that it was always impossible to find out exactly what was happening with regard to Russian government policy. No one was responsible for coordinating action, as individual ministers reported to the Tsar and acted unilaterally, quite often in contravention of each other. As an autocracy, Russia felt no obligation to explain or justify its policies, either to its subjects or to foreign governments, while the Russian press was an unreliable source of information and existed largely if not wholly to disseminate ministerial propaganda. Tsar Nicholas II was inscrutable and inaccessible, and no one ever knew whether he was really the autocrat following in the footsteps of his father that he always claimed to be or whether he was merely leaving government up to his ministers as they saw fit. Moreover, he soon acquired a reputation for avoiding confrontation and contradiction, and almost always agreed with the last person to whom he had spoken.

Unfailingly charming to everyone he met, in stark contrast to his late father, Tsar Nicholas II was the epitome of good-natured politeness to the Germans just as much as he always was to Queen Victoria. To every German representative who visited St Petersburg, and in his correspondence with Emperor William, he complained about English perfidy, giving the impression that he could be easily detached from the likelihood of Anglo-Russian friendship, if not Anglo-French bonds as well. The second factor was likely to prove more problematic, especially in view of the generous French loans being advanced to Russia. Had he realised it, Emperor William would have done well to hold back a little and appreciate that his excessive attempts at manipulating the Tsar, to say nothing of his bright and breezy behaviour, his slapping him on the back and playfully poking him in the ribs whenever they met for conversation, were proving counter-productive. Tsar Nicholas resented his pushy attitude just as much as his parents had been revolted by his personification of all they loathed about Bismarck's *nouveau riche* imperial Germany.

In September 1896, a few months after their coronation at Moscow that had been thoroughly tainted by the disaster of Khodynka Field, at which over a thousand spectators died in the stampede to obtain free gifts at the customary distribution, the young Tsar and Tsarina came to stay with Queen Victoria on her Scottish holiday. This was one of a series of courtesy visits they were making on fellow sovereigns in Austria, Germany, and Denmark.

Like most of the Queen's family, the Tsar would find her Highland paradise a joyless and tedious place at the best of times. In driving rain, the Russian imperial yacht *Standart* anchored at Leith and the Prince of Wales came aboard to escort his mother's guests to Balmoral. Drenched after a ride in the open carriages, they reached their destination after dark where the Queen was waiting for them on the castle steps, surrounded by Highlanders with flaming torches. She had noted that the day on which they arrived coincided with the anniversary of the fall of Sebastopol, and had arranged for an exhibition of trophies won from the Imperial Russian army during the campaign. It was not the most tactful of gestures.

All the same, as a family reunion it was a modest success, although during his talks with the Queen the Tsar remained non-committal when it came to any discussion of political issues. For part of the time, he was under the wing of the Prince of Wales for sporting activities. This had evidently not been the Tsar's choice, as he told his mother: 'They seem to consider it necessary to take me out shooting all day long with the gentlemen. The weather is awful, rain and wind every day and on top of it no luck at all'.[6] He was thoroughly relieved when the Prince grew tired of his enforced time at Balmoral, where the Queen was careful to exclude him from the more serious conversations on political and foreign affairs that she held with the Tsar, her Prime Minister, and other ministers of the crown. With some relief, the Tsar assured his mother that he had an easier time after 'uncle Bertie' had left, as he was no longer obliged to go out shooting in all weathers. 'Granny' was kinder and more amiable, and sent Lord Salisbury to discuss European matters with him in depth. The Prime Minister may have found him a pleasant contrast to the ever thin-skinned and excitable German emperor, although he had his doubts as to whether Nicholas was the right man to wield such power. To his friend Canon Gordon, he wrote:

> [How remarkable it is] that in spite of the progress of democratic ideas, the weight of individual personalities, for good or evil, is greater than ever. Now every turn in the humours of the Emperor Nicholas or the Emperor William, or the Sultan of Turkey is watched and interpreted— the fate of many thousands of lives depends on them.[7]

Although the Queen might have considered it 'quite like a dream having dear Alicky & Nicky here', after their departure, she can hardly have seen anything to alter her initial conviction that their reign in Russia would not be a guaranteed success. For much of her reign, she had regarded the Romanovs with caution at best and an antipathy at worst. As her great-grandson Louis of Battenberg, later Earl Mountbatten of Burma, would say many years later, the 'liberal-minded constitutional monarch' in her was convinced 'that absolute autocracy was wrong and was bound to end in tears, which it did'.[8]

While she had her doubts as to whether he was resolute enough to be a successful autocrat, she did not live long enough to form any definitive impressions of the character of Tsar Nicholas II. She was aware that he was not the strongest of characters and, being ever-anxious to please, was liable to be influenced unduly by the more dominant forces around him. In March 1899, she felt impelled to warn him that Emperor William was taking 'every opportunity' of impressing on Lascelles, former British Ambassador to Russia and now filling the same post in Berlin, that Russia was 'doing all in her power' to work against England, to the extent of offering alliances with Germany against England. She did not believe a word of it, any more than Lascelles or Lord Salisbury did. Nevertheless, she was afraid:

> William may go and tell you things against us to you, just as he does about you to us. If so, pray do tell me openly and confidentially. It is so important that we should understand each other, and that such mischievous and unstraightforward proceedings should be put a stop to.[9]

She knew that her grandson in Berlin could not always be relied on to mean just what he said, and that his utterances were capable of causing no end of trouble.

Her eldest son, who survived her by nine years, was an excellent judge of character and had formed an accurate impression of the Tsar. While he had been in Russia for the funeral of Tsar Alexander III, the Prince of Wales had liked what he saw. He thought that the young new sovereign's liking for the English royal family, and the close kinship of his wife-to-be, seemed 'a promising foundation on which to rear a political union' between both nations. To a friend, he wrote that his character and personality 'give assurance of the benefits which would come of an alliance'.[10] Within a few years, he had seen enough to revise his opinions and was rather less charitable, thinking his Russian nephew 'weak as water and unable to make up his mind to do anything'.[11] The last thing he wanted was for him to be at the mercy of the German Emperor. Perhaps the most perceptive verdict on the Tsar came from his sister-in-law, Princess Louis of Battenberg. Under other circumstances, she wrote, he 'would have made a remarkably good constitutional Sovereign, for he was in no way narrow minded, nor obsessed by his high position. If one could have boiled down Nicky and William [the German Emperor] in one pot you would have produced an ideal Emperor for Russia'.[12]

Emperor William II had particularly wanted and expected to be a guest at Queen Victoria's diamond jubilee celebrations in London in June 1897, not in his capacity as a reigning sovereign, but as her eldest grandchild. He was advised gently, but firmly that an invitation would not be forthcoming.

His standing in England, which had never been very high, had plummeted during the last year or so. In January 1896, he had sent a telegram to Paul Kruger, President of the Transvaal Republic in South Africa, congratulating him on repulsing the Jameson Raid—a sortie by 600 British irregulars from Cape Colony into the Transvaal meant to trigger an anti-government uprising by the mainly British expatriate miners, which turned into a disaster with over sixty raiders and only one Boer killed. It had caused much British indignation and led to severe tension with Germany. More recently, he had sided with Turkey in her differences with Greece over the possession of Crete. The prospect or possibility of war—initially a local one, but which could also embroil other nations and spread—had arisen over a dispute between Greece and Crete, which was part of the Turkish Empire, but boasted a predominantly Greek population. After riots and a state approaching civil war on the island, the Greek government sent troops to help protect their indigenous inhabitants, who were seeking union with their mother country. This led to Greece and Turkey making preparations for war, until Lord Salisbury proposed a compromise on behalf of the powers that, while Crete could not be annexed to Greece, self-government free of the Turkish yoke should be established, and meanwhile Greek troops were to leave the island forthwith. Turkey accepted this solution, but Greece refused to remove her army of occupation until the following month, when she was compelled to accept Cretan autonomy, remove her forces, and pay the Turks a heavy indemnity.

While this was going on, the Emperor went against family loyalties by snubbing King George of Greece (the Princess of Wales's brother) and the King's daughter-in-law, Crown Princess Sophie (his own sister), thus outraging British feeling that was overwhelmingly pro-Greek. The Empress Frederick was frantic with worry over Germany's encouragement of the Turks. She believed that 'the three Emperors are all agreed and on the WRONG tack, and it grieves me bitterly to think that dear England is so bound and so died down that she cannot act as she would wish'. Emperor William's 'personal hatred to Greece and enmity to the King and whole Royal family is well known everywhere.... Oh, if Fritz had been spared, all this would never have happened! Germany would have mediated and appeased, and England could have gone hand in hand with her!!'[13] Queen Victoria could do no more than send messages of support to her daughter and her granddaughter. To the Empress Frederick, she stated: 'How my heart bleeds for our darling Sophie and you as well. And to think of William's shameful behaviour, for he it is who has urged this on!'[14]

As early as January 1897, she was assuring her private secretary, Sir Arthur Bigge, that 'there is not the slightest fear of the Queen's giving way about the Emperor William's coming here, in June'.[15] She could not but help compare his behaviour with that of the more gentle-natured Tsar Nicholas II, the 'dear young Emperor' in St Petersburg, whom she found so much more sensible and amenable, as well as far more eager to promote good relations with Britain.

Emperor William resented his exclusion from the occasion bitterly. Even at the beginning of June, he was still expressing his disappointment as if hoping for a change of heart on her part and a last-minute invitation after all, as he told her that he felt 'like a charger chained in the stables who hears the bugle sounding, stomps and chomps his bit, because he cannot follow his regiment'.[16] It was to no avail. Instead, his mother, brother, and three of his sisters took part in the jubilee festivities without him.

In retrospect, it was probably fortunate for William that he did not go after all as he would not have received a particularly warm welcome. As it was, the crowds groaned audibly when a German general rode by in the procession through London to St Paul's Cathedral for the service of thanksgiving. When Prince Henry passed, a cockney voice informed him loudly that, if he wanted to send a telegram to Kruger, he would find a post office round the corner. Less restraint would doubtless have been shown if it had been his elder brother instead.

By the 1890s, the meetings between Queen and Empress Eugénie had fallen into a regular pattern. Each summer, the Empress spent a few weeks at Osborne and a short time at Balmoral in the autumn. In the spring, they would meet in the south of France. The Queen went regularly to Cimiez, near Nice, close to Cyrnos, the Empress's villa at Cap Martin, and would sometimes drive over to see her. Accompanied by the widowed Princess Beatrice and a couple of ladies, she would drive from Cimiez to arrive at Cyrnos shortly before luncheon, where the Empress was waiting to welcome them. After lunch, they would go strolling through the garden. These walks were evidently enjoyed more by the Empress, who was still very sprightly for her seventy years, than by the Queen, who had always been impervious to cold, but disliked heat—even more so with age. Increasingly lame in her last years, she now rarely walked, but was generally wheeled in her chair. At length, they reached a narrow terrace overlooking the sea, in the shelter of a clump of flowering shrubs where they would settle down in a semi-circle of armchairs. It was the Empress's favourite part of the garden, she would say, as she so loved the view of the coastline from this location.[17]

At other times, they would exchange visits at Windsor and at Farnborough Hill. Much as the deterioration in Anglo-French relations before the outbreak of the Boer War in October 1899 saddened them both, it did nothing to disturb their bonds of friendship. Neither, fortunately, did a difference of opinions involving the Empress's native country, Spain, the previous year. War between Spain and the United States of America broke out in April 1898 after American intervention in the Cuban War of Independence. Revolts had been occurring in Cuba, a Spanish colony, for several years and war was declared after Spain refused to surrender control of the island. The Empress had fervently hoped that Spain and the Cuban rebels would reach an understanding without armed conflict, but this was not to be realised. Shortly after the declaration of war, Lord Salisbury made a speech in which he asserted that England would remain neutral in the dispute, but her sympathies could hardly be on the side of moribund nations that were 'drawing nearer and nearer to their fate'. When pressed as to which nations he was referring to, he insisted that he did not imply Spain, but instead the republics in South and Central America.

The Empress was shocked by his words. She thought that the Prime Minister's attitude to other countries was one of 'if you are weak we admire you and if you are strong we help you', and that if Spain was defeated the Spanish monarchy would not survive for long. Events would prove her wrong, for after a ten-week conflict the victorious Americans negotiated and made peace at the Treaty of Paris, which brought the curtain down on the Spanish Empire not only in Cuba, but also in Puerto Rico and the Philippines.

Even so, she was moved for once to make a direct appeal to Queen Victoria. She hoped that a gesture of monarchical and European solidarity led by Europe's longest-reigning sovereign would strengthen and give invaluable moral support to the Spanish government and throne. Writing angrily to her niece Maria, Duchess of Alba, she said that she had spoken to the Queen of the plight of King Alfonso XIII, at that time a boy of twelve, and his mother Maria Christina, Queen-Regent: 'She listened to me, her eyes were full of sympathy, but she did not utter one word. She had become the constitutional sovereign once more, with her Ministers being the sole organ of policy: it is infuriating!'[18] The Empress fully understood her friend's limitations and her anger soon cooled, but it was one of the few occasions when the woman who had once acted as Regent of France while her husband was at the head of his army during war bitterly lamented how the Queen had to bow to the judgment of her ministers.

To the Queen's eldest children, the Prince of Wales and the Empress Frederick, the Empress remained a staunch friend. For the first few years of her widowhood, the Empress Frederick was a regular visitor to Farnborough. After she was diagnosed with what would prove to be incurable cancer of the spine, Empress Eugénie offered her villa at Cap Martin for the winter. By that time, she was unable to travel far, although she was very grateful for the offer. Empress Eugénie had little contact with Emperor William II, although he had paid her a visit at Farnborough in 1894, escorted there by Arthur, Duke of Connaught. The occasion was a success, for, although his tactless and overbearing behaviour frequently infuriated members of his family, the Emperor could always be charming when necessary.

The opportunities for a royal rendezvous on the Riviera—ironically, in Republican France—had also made possible two more meetings of Anglo-Austrian crowned heads. During the first fifty-eight years of her reign, Queen Victoria and Emperor Francis Joseph had met only twice, with almost a quarter of a century separating both occasions. As the Queen approached her diamond jubilee in June 1897, they were to meet twice within the space of a year.

For three successive winters, Empress Elizabeth had stayed at Cap Martin in the south of France. Over the years, she had become more obsessed than ever about her figure and punished herself with endless new 'cures' so immoderately that she suffered from digestive disorders. She was regularly trying them with so little moderation that they did her more harm than good. During the last few years of her life, she was taking little nourishment apart from milk and, as it had to be as pure as possible, a special herd of cows was bought and maintained at Vienna for the purpose. When he felt able to leave Austria for a few days at a time, the Emperor would come south to keep her company and try to persuade her to follow a more normal diet, as he was often in despair about her dietary fads, remarking that the incessant cures were 'really terrible'. For him to take a holiday himself was out of the question; even when he stayed at Cap Martin, the Emperor, renowned for his early rising, had drafted about fifty telegrams and read a pile of despatches by 6 a.m. each day when his adjutant came on duty.

In March 1896, it was rumoured that Queen Victoria was also about to take a winter holiday on the Riviera, and would stay at the Grand Hotel de Cimiez. To her youngest daughter, Archduchess Valerie, the Empress wrote that the Queen had taken the whole hotel and two villas as she was bringing a suite of about seventy people, including her Indian servants. 'It must be a great pleasure to travel like a circus', was her comment.[19] There was more unconscious envy than mere cynicism in her words, for Elizabeth was fascinated by these oriental servants in their exotic costumes. Even now, as in her younger days, the colourful and unconventional still held an allure for her.

Queen, Emperor, and Empress met on 13 March. The Queen noted in her journal that the Empress was much altered and had lost all her former beauty, apart from her figure that still remained the same as when they had last met seventeen years earlier. As ever, she found the Emperor 'very kind', and she asked him if he would accept the Colonelcy in Chief of the King's 1st Dragoon Guards, with which he was most pleased. Sensing that both would like to have a little time for conversation on their own, the Empress left them alone after a brief greeting. As ever, the rest of their conversation turned to political matters. He told her that he hoped their countries would remain on the best of terms, while they could not bind themselves to any particular action beforehand. In view of the troubled state of affairs in the Balkans and the ever-unpredictable speeches of Emperor William II, 'he regretted the state of Turkey, William's imprudence, but trusted England and Germany would always keep well together'.[20]

It had been a sad meeting. Queen Victoria noticed what the Archduchess Valerie had seen for herself in the miserable weeks following their son's suicide, that the Emperor and Empress had drifted so far apart in personality and temperament that by now they had hardly anything in common except for their shared grief. She could, however, take some consolation in the fact that the Emperor might act as a counter-balance to the German Emperor by providing a stabilising influence in the Austro-German alliance as a friend of Britain, as long as he had the determination and the energy to keep the younger men and advisers around him under control.

A year later, Queen and Emperor met at Cimiez for what would be the final time. On her spring holiday in March 1897, he called on her after luncheon. Their conversation centred chiefly on the issue of Crete, which they feared could provide the spark for another conflict if mishandled. 'He is distressed at the Cretan troubles', she wrote, 'but rejoices greatly at the union of the Great Powers, and thinks there can be no general war'.[21]

Aside from these largely social meetings, Queen Victoria had as little contact with the Habsburgs in Austria-Hungary at this stage in her reign as she had had in her early years. However, she looked with sadness on the various tragedies that had darkened the family and had nothing but sympathy for the lonely Emperor. Of his three brothers, he had lost one to a firing squad in Mexico, another to typhoid after drinking from contaminated water in the River Jordan on a visit to Palestine, and had to banish the youngest from Vienna after his open homosexuality and propensity for cross-dressing had threatened to embroil the throne in major scandal. His only son had killed his mistress and then himself in an apparent suicide pact, while his wife had long spent much of her life travelling around Europe, anxious to put as much distance between herself and her husband's empire as she could. She suffered a further tragedy in May 1897, when her favourite sister, Sophie, Duchess of Alençon, was working at a stall in a charity bazaar in Paris and fire suddenly broke out in the building; after bravely insisting that the girls who were working for her should be saved first, Sophie paid the ultimate price herself and was burned to death.

On 10 September 1898, Empress Elizabeth and her lady-in-waiting, Countess Sztáray, were in Geneva walking along the quay to catch a ferry to Montreux. Suddenly, a young man appeared to bump into her and stumble as he attacked her, knocking her over. Only after he had run away and she was helped to her feet was it realised that he had stabbed her in the chest with a steel file. She collapsed, lost consciousness, and was dead within the hour.

Crowned heads and royalties throughout Europe were shocked by the assassination. Queen Victoria sent a telegram to Emperor Francis Joseph expressing her sympathy and horror. After her body was brought back to Vienna and the funeral took place, he wrote what was to be his last letter to Queen Victoria, stating: 'The only thing that can give me comfort is so affectionate a remembrance as I have just received from you'.[22]

The last two years of Queen Victoria's life were in various ways difficult and sad ones for the family. In January 1899, Emperor William informed Sir Frank Lascelles that France and Russia had invited Germany to join them in a coalition against Britain, but he had no intention of doing so. Anglo-French tensions had made such a possibility more than likely.

The same month was marked by a small if significant personal milestone. On 27 January, the Emperor completed his fourth decade. 'William's fortieth birthday', the Queen noted in her journal, 'I wish he were more prudent and less impulsive at such an age!'[23]

As she penned these words, another family tragedy was beginning. While the Duke and Duchess of Saxe-Coburg Gotha (the Duke of Edinburgh having somewhat reluctantly succeeded his childless uncle Ernest to the ducal title in 1893) were celebrating their silver wedding—a somewhat joyless occasion it might be assumed as their marriage had long since ceased to be a happy one—their son and heir, another Prince Alfred, wasting away from what were probably the effects of venereal disease, was barred from meeting friends and family as he was in the throes of mortal agony—self-inflicted shotgun wounds, from which he died a few days later at the age of twenty-four. The Prince of Wales had long since renounced the Coburg succession for himself and his issue, and, as the third brother, Arthur, Duke of Connaught, was therefore now heir. The reigning Duke had been in poor health for several years and seemed unlikely to survive his son for long. Without consulting the Emperor, Queen Victoria gave her full approval to Arthur taking up his position as heir presumptive. The Emperor was angry at not being asked his permission and he insisted that the Duke and his eldest son would have to go and live in Germany and enter the German army, or else the Reichstag might pass a law that declared foreign princes ineligible to succeed to German thrones. Now in his late forties, the Duke made no secret of his reluctance at having to uproot himself and his family from England.

At a meeting with the Dukes of Connaught and Saxe-Coburg in April, the Emperor denied threatening to introduce any bill preventing the succession of foreign princes, but insisted that national sentiment required the heir to the duchy to serve in the German army and have his principal residence in the empire. Queen Victoria was annoyed with the Emperor, who had been 'tiresome and has interfered', and deprecated his 'threats' to Lord Salisbury. The issue was settled some weeks later when the Duke of Connaught renounced the succession for himself and his son in favour of his fifteen-year-old nephew Prince Charles of Albany, only son of Queen Victoria's youngest son Prince Leopold, who had died fifteen years earlier. Charles would succeed sooner than anticipated, for Duke Alfred succumbed to throat cancer in July 1900.

No sooner was one bone of contention decided than another one arose. Britain, the United States of America, and Germany were involved in a dispute over control over the Samoa Islands in the Pacific. Following civil war, a tripartite convention had resolved the issue with the islands being ultimately divided between Germany and America, and Britain giving up her claims in exchange for concessions on colonial territories in Africa. The matter had not been concluded without stalemate for some weeks, during which the Emperor declared that Germany was being snubbed. In May, he wrote Queen Victoria a long anguished tirade, accusing Lord Salisbury and his government of 'high-handed treatment' and giving the impression that the Prime Minister despised Germany. For years he had been the one true friend of Britain throughout Europe, and now public feeling in Germany against Britain had been inflamed, merely 'on account of a stupid island which is a hairpin to England compared to the thousands of square miles she is annexing right and left unopposed every year'.[24]

The Queen immediately put him in his place, replying that she sincerely doubted 'if any Sovereign ever wrote in such terms to another Sovereign, and that Sovereign his own Grandmother, about their Prime Minister'.[25] She had never personally attacked or complained of Prince Bismarck, who had died the previous year, although she regarded him as a bitter enemy of England whose attitude caused great harm to the relations between both countries.

The dispute continued throughout the summer and was settled by autumn. By mid-September, Count Paul von Hatzfeldt at the German Embassy feared that Anglo-German relations might reach the point of no return unless there was some demonstration of friendship. At length, after persuasion from cabinet colleagues, Lord Salisbury conceded and Germany was permitted to acquire the Samoan Island of Upolu. Delighted with this latest acquisition, another 'success for world policy' as he saw it, the Emperor agreed to visit Windsor later in the year.

Accompanied by the Empress, two of his sons, and a large suite, including Count Bernhard von Bülow (his Minister for Foreign Affairs and future Chancellor), the Emperor arrived on 20 November. It was not a propitious time, for five weeks earlier war had broken out in South Africa between the British and the Boers. Public opinion throughout Europe, especially in Germany as well as in France, was overwhelmingly on the side of the Boers. Emperor Francis Joseph had been almost alone in Austria and in fact in Europe, by his expression of sympathy and support for the English, during the conflict, and making no secret of his opinion in the presence of foreign diplomats.

While he was in Berlin, Emperor William had recently taken advantage of the patriotic mood in his empire to announce a second navy law in order to build up the German fleet. However, after a few days at Windsor, he was suddenly transformed into the respectful grandson of Queen Victoria, even more English than the English. Each morning he pointed to the tower, telling his somewhat resentful military entourage that 'from this tower the world is ruled'.[26] They were so used to seeing him in military uniform every day that to them it seemed oddly out of character that he should for once be dressed all the time like the English country gentleman, which he sometimes said he had always aspired to be or, as one less charitable observer would have it, 'like a Bank Holiday tripper to Margate'.

Lord Salisbury was in mourning for his wife, who had died at Hatfield on the day the Emperor arrived, so perhaps it was fortuitous that this time he did not have a chance to see the man about whose government he had been so critical. He did, however, have meetings and talks with two of the senior ministers, Arthur Balfour and Joseph Chamberlain. Queen Victoria was relieved to find that, when she complained to her grandson, he and Bülow strongly deprecated 'shameful attacks' on England in the German press, blaming it on the '"poison" which Bismarck poured into the ears of the people'; that Bismarck had hated England, 'and wished for an alliance with Russia'. If he had not dismissed Bismarck, the Emperor went on, 'he does not know what would have happened' and he personally wished 'for a better understanding with [the British]'.[27]

Four days later, when the Emperor and Empress left Windsor to pay the Prince and Princess of Wales a brief visit at Sandringham, Queen Victoria's verdict was overwhelmingly positive as she later reported to the Empress Frederick:

[Both of them had been] extremely amiable & kind & I had a good deal of talk with William on all subjects & found him very sensible & most anxious that all should go well between the 2 countries & that they should be on the best of terms.[28]

When talking to his grandmother's senior ministers, the Emperor was more guarded. Joseph Chamberlain, the Colonial Secretary, suggested to him the idea of an Anglo-German-American alliance. He was reluctant to commit himself, on the grounds that it would be contrary to the traditions of all three nations and also that it might threaten conflict with Russia. When it came to the matter of limited Anglo-German cooperation in areas such as Morocco and Asia Minor, where there was a personal conflict of interests, he was ready to be more accommodating. If there could be no alliance, he suggested, they could at least come to 'an understanding'.

One year later, it seemed as if such an understanding was well within reach. After Salisbury's government won an election in October 1900, he retained the premiership, but resigned as Foreign Secretary on health grounds, appointing Lord Lansdowne to the post instead. Chamberlain was particularly sympathetic to the idea of an alliance between both countries and, in the first few days of January 1901, he discussed the subject with the Duke of Devonshire. To government ministers, Britain's 'splendid isolation' was no longer sustainable in the modern age and it was imperative that England had to look for allies elsewhere, either Russia or France, or the Triple Alliance. Chamberlain preferred the latter, news that Berlin received with guarded welcome.

There were, however, signs that the Victorian era was in its last days. The royal family had been increasingly concerned by the state of Queen Victoria's health, which appeared to have been declining over the last few weeks. The deaths of her son Alfred, Duke of Saxe-Coburg Gotha, in July, and of her grandson Prince Christian Victor of Schleswig-Holstein to enteric fever while he was serving with the army on the campaign in South Africa in October, and constant worry over the progress of the war, had taken their toll. She became increasingly listless, her once remarkable memory was failing as was her eyesight and she gradually lost her once tremendous appetite. Shortly before Christmas 1900, she and the court left the mainland as usual to spend the festive season at Osborne House. For the last few years she had always written a special letter to Empress Eugénie, but this time she was too ill and weary to wield the pen herself and instead she dictated it to Princess Beatrice. On New Year's Day 1901, she sent her old friend a card, inscribed with 'one almost illegible word'.

A fortnight later, Arthur, Duke of Connaught, was in Berlin with the Emperor, attending bicentenary celebrations for the Kingdom of Prussia, when he was summoned home by telegram, warning him that she was not expected to last for more than a few days. The Emperor had always retained close personal contact with her personal physician, Sir James Reid, on the subject of her personal health and he also received a wire, informing him that 'disquieting symptoms have developed which cause considerable anxiety'.[29] He cancelled all his engagements at once, and on 19 January telegraphed to the Prince of Wales, confirming that he would reach London the following evening. The Duke was on better terms with his nephew than the rest of his family and, while it 'might be an expression of his kindness of heart', he was aware that his presence there would be viewed with mixed feelings at best. He therefore tactfully suggested to Bülow that the Emperor ought to consider carefully whether it would be in his interests to leave Germany. Nevertheless, William, for once assuming the role of grandson in preference to that of Emperor, insisted that his proper place at such a time was by her side. Throughout the journey he masked his feelings beneath a display of high spirits and banter, explaining to his suite that 'Uncle Arthur is so downhearted we must cheer him up'.[30]

He was clearly motivated by a love and admiration for his grandmother that years of disagreements and occasional irritation had never been able to efface, though a sense of ambition lay at the heart of it. In a sense, he saw himself as the Queen's successor as a natural leader of the family, of a dynasty that extended to almost every monarchy throughout Europe. Any natural leadership in the family, he probably believed, would fall to him rather than his uncle, the Prince of Wales, for whom he had all too little respect.[31]

The Emperor and the Duke took their place together at the hushed vigil at Osborne with the Queen's children and many of the grandchildren. The most obvious absentee was the Empress Frederick, who was now seriously unwell and for whom there was no question of travelling overseas (shortly afterwards she wrote to her eldest brother, saying that it was her 'ardent wish' to come to England shortly and rent a house at Bournemouth for a few months, the inference being that she wanted to die in her homeland, but the doctors forbade her to do so because she was so ill).[32] By the time the Emperor arrived, his grandmother's mind was wandering and she mistook him for 'Fritz', his father, who had been dead for twelve years.

As news spread throughout Europe of the Queen's condition, all attention was being focussed on the family drama at Osborne. Newspapers carried regular bulletins on the latest news of the Queen's condition. Public functions and private gatherings were cancelled, while court balls planned in Vienna and St Petersburg were called off as their Emperors asked anxiously as to her state of health. By the morning of 22 January, it was evident that she had only a few hours left. Her remaining strength ebbed away as Emperor William helped to support her with his right arm. She passed away early in the evening.

At the age of fifty-nine, the man who had been Prince of Wales since birth finally came into his inheritance. Despite his mother's hopes that he would reign as King Albert or Albert Edward, at the meeting of the Privy Council at St James's Palace to hear the Archbishop of Canterbury read out the oath of accession, he told them that he had resolved to be known by the name of Edward, as borne by six previous Kings of England. Meanwhile, Emperor William remained behind at Osborne in charge of the arrangements. At his suggestion, a Union Jack was draped on the walls of the room where his grandmother's coffin lay in state. Though he would have celebrated his forty-second birthday on 27 January, he requested that no special notice should be taken of it as mourning for 'his unparalleled grandmama' must come first.

In Berlin, the Empress Augusta Victoria strongly disapproved of her husband's visit to England. Reluctant to acknowledge the deep emotional bond between him and his recently deceased grandmother, she asked Bülow to see if he could dissuade him from staying in England for the funeral, insisting that he could quite easily arrange for the Crown Prince or Prince Henry, or both, to attend instead. Her main reason, she said, was that the Empress Frederick was particularly anxious to see him again, but this was to no avail. In reply, he telegraphed her stating:

> [My aunts are] quite alone and I must help them with many things, I must give them my advice, whenever advice is necessary. They are so kind to me, they treat me like a brother and a friend instead of like a nephew.[33]

Three days later, the Empress heard that her husband had been made an English field-marshal by King Edward VII and she immediately saw it as evidence of 'English scheming'. Her concerns were shared by Holstein and Bülow, who tried to prevail on Baron Hermann von Eckardstein at the German Embassy in London to restrain him from discussing an alliance or any other political matters with British ministers while on what was supposed to be a mere family visit. When approached in this vein, the Emperor promised he would do no more than discuss Anglo-German relations in general terms. This did not stop him from advising Bülow a couple of days later that he intended to propose an alliance all the same. His senior ministers advised him to stay his hand for a while, as with hostile powers on all sides and the possibility of defeat in the South African war, Britain would need all the allies she could find in Europe and the price Germany could ask for an alliance would rise accordingly.

Even so, his motives for staying in England were clearly connected first and foremost with the farewell to his grandmother. He remained for her funeral at Windsor on 2 February and her internment in the mausoleum two days later. King Edward was touched by his nephew's uncharacteristically subdued behaviour and wrote to the Empress Frederick that his 'touching and simple demeanour, up to the last, will never be forgotten by [himself] or anyone'.[34]

Empress Eugénie was likewise grieved at the loss of her friend, 'a support in [her] chequered life'. It was the end of an era for her, as it was for the rest of her family and country. Now, she said, she felt 'even more than ever a foreigner, alone in this land', very saddened and discouraged at the loss of a woman whose friendship had sustained her for almost half a century.[35] As she was suffering from bronchitis at the time, she was not well enough to go to Osborne and see the Queen's remains or attend the funeral service. However, she found reassurance in the continued friendship and solicitude of King Edward VII. In a message to the Empress, he assured her that his 'dear mother was deeply attached to [her]'.[36] It was appropriate, and significant, that three years later the Entente Cordiale would be established between Britain and France and that the King would play a leading role in the new alliance between both countries.

On his last day in England, at Marlborough House, the King proposed the health of Emperor William. The latter answered in ringing terms of 'the two Teutonic nations' that would stand together to help in keeping peace throughout the world. They should form an Anglo-German alliance, he declared, with Britain keeping watch on the seas and Germany on the land: 'With such an alliance, not a mouse would stir in Europe without our permission, and the nations would, in time, come to see the necessity of reducing their armaments'.[37] Although he had sometimes spoken very harshly about her in moments of impatience, the Emperor revered the memory of Queen Victoria for the rest of his days. To his officers, he sometimes opined that she was one of the two wisest and best sovereigns who had ever lived, the other being his grandfather William I. As a sovereign, he took both of them as his exemplars, and, whenever he found himself in a difficult position, he asked himself how they would have acted under similar circumstances.[38]

Britain might have enjoyed 'splendid isolation' during the last years of the nineteenth century and the last two decades of Queen Victoria's reign, but for much of that time she had enjoyed peaceful, if sometimes uneasy relations with the imperial powers on mainland Europe. In August 1914, only one of those empires, Russia, was a British ally. After war broke out with Britain, Russia, and the French Republic in one armed camp and Germany and Austria in the other, Emperor William was filled with bitterness against his fellow crowned heads and cousins, King George V of Britain and Tsar Nicholas II of Russia. 'To think that George and Nicky should have played me false!' he was alleged to have said. 'If my grandmother had been alive, she would never have allowed it'.[39]

Endnotes

Abbreviations

A   Prince Albert, subsequently Prince Consort
E   Prince of Wales, later King Edward VII
F   Emperor Frederick III, as Prince, Crown Prince and Emperor
FJ   Emperor Francis Joseph
HP   Sir Henry Ponsonby
L   King Leopold I
N   Tsar Nicholas II, as Tsarevich and Tsar
OS   Old Style (relating to Russian calendar)
QV   Queen Victoria
QVJ   Queen Victoria's Journal
S   Marquess of Salisbury
V   Victoria, as Princess Royal, Crown Princess, Empress Victoria, and Empress Frederick
VH   Princess Victoria of Hesse, later Princess Louis of Battenberg
W   Emperor William II, as Prince, Crown Prince and Emperor

Prologue

1. Lee, S., *King Edward VII,* Vol. I, 402
2. Longford, E., *Victoria R.I.*, p. 404, QV to HP, 27.1.1873
3. QV, *Letters 1862-85*, ii, 452, QVJ, 25.4.1876
4. QV, *Advice to a Grand-daughter*, 56, QV to VH, 21.9.1883
5. Derby, Earl of, *The Derby Diaries*, p. 269, 16.1.1876
6. Longford, E., p. 404
7. Lee, S., Vol. I, p. 403
8. Duff, D., *Victoria Travels*, p. 12
9. Longford, E., p. 407

Chapter 1

1. Woodham-Smith, C., 176-7; QV, *Girlhood*, Vol. II, pp. 187-191, QVJ 27-29.5.1839
2. Fulford, R., *The Prince Consort*, p. 85
3. Martin, Sir T., *The Life of HRH The Prince Consort*, Vol. I, 215
4. *Ibid.* 216
5. Cecil, A., *Queen Victoria and her Prime Ministers*, p. 165
6. QV, *Letters 1837-61*, Vol. I, pp. 14-5, QV to L, 9.6.1844; Martin, Sir, T., Vol. I, pp. 222-3

7. *Ibid.*
8. *Ibid.* Vol. I, p. 12, QV to L, 4.6.1844; Martin, Sir T., Vol. I., p. 219
9. *Ibid.* Vol. II, p. 106, QV to L, 29.9.1846
10. *Ibid.* Vol. II, pp. 155-6, QV to L, 1.3.1848
11. *Ibid.* Vol. II, p. 206, QV to L, 19.12.1848
12. Van der Kiste, J., *Windsor and Habsburg*, QV to FJ, 5.5.1851
13. QV, *Letters 1837-61*, Vol. II, p. 334, QV to L, 4.12.1851
14. *Ibid.* Vol. II, p. 360, QV to L, 20.1.1852
15. Seward, D., *Eugénie*, p. xii
16. Kurtz, H., *The Empress Eugénie*, p. 45
17. Van der Kiste, J., *Windsor and Habsburg*, p. 24, QVJ, 6.3.1853
18. *Ibid.* p. 24, QVJ, 17.3.1854
19. Van der Kiste, J., *Emperor Francis Joseph*, p. 31, QV to L, 28.8.1853

Chapter 2

1. QV, *Letters 1837-61*, Vol. II, p. 452, QV to Lord Aberdeen, 25.9.1853
2. *Ibid.*, Vol. II, p. 453, Lord Aberdeen to QV, 6.10.1853
3. *The Times*, 20.6.1854
4. QV, *Letters 1837-61*, Vol. III, pp. 34-5, QV to Lord Aberdeen, 26.6.1855
5. Martin, Sir T., *The Life of HRH The Prince Consort*, Vol. II, p. 104, A to QV, 6.9.1854
6. *Ibid.*, Vol. III, p. 107
7. QV, *Leaves from a Journal*, p. 16
8. QV, *Letters 1837-61*, Vol. III, p. 49, QV to Earl of Clarendon, 10.10.1854
9. *Ibid.*, Vol. III, p. 113, QV to A, 4.3.1855
10. *The Times*, 3.3.1855
11. QV, *Leaves from a Journal*, p. 31, 16.4.1855
12. QV, *Letters 1837-61*, Vol. III, p. 117, QV to L, 17.4.1855
13. QV, *Leaves from a Journal*, p. 51, QVJ, 19.4.1855
14. Guest, I., *Napoleon III in England*, p. 116
15. QV, *Leaves from a Journal*, p. 39, QVJ, 17.4.1855
16. Aronson, T., *Queen Victoria and the Bonapartes*, p. 40
17. QV, *Leaves from a Journal*, p. 66, QVJ, 21.4.1855
18. QV, *Letters 1837-61*, Vol. III, pp. 122-3, QV, Memorandum 2.5.1855
19. Connell, B., *Regina v. Palmerston*, p. 175, Lord Palmerston to QV, 26.4.1855
20. Aronson, T., *Queen Victoria and the Bonapartes*, p. 51
21. Villiers, G., *A Vanished Victorian*, p. 259
22. QV, *Leaves from a Journal*, p. 88, QVJ, 20.8.1855
23. *Ibid.* p. 19
24. *Ibid.* p. 116, QVJ, 24.8.1855
25. *Ibid.* p. 128, QVJ, 25.8.1855
26. *Ibid.* p. 143, QVJ, 27.8.1855
27. Barkeley, R., *The Empress Frederick*, p. 30, quoting Helmuth von Moltke, *Briefe an seine Braut und Frau* (1894)
28. QV, *Letters 1837-61*, Vol. III, p. 147, QV to KL, 22.9.1855
29. Corti, E.C.C., *The English Empress*, p. 24, A to F, 15.10.1855
30. *The Times*, 3.10.1855
31. Corti, E. C. C., *The English Empress*, p. 24, A to F, 1.11.1855
32. Van der Kiste, J., *Frederick III*, p. 30; Van der Kiste, J., *Dearest Vicky, Darling Fritz*, p. 27, F to A, 22.10.1855
33. Martin, Sir T., Vol. III, p. 388, A to F, 25.10.1855
34. Connell, B., p. 235, QV to Lord Palmerston, 26.3.1856
35. Anon, *Empress Frederick: A Memoir*, pp. 41-2, Bismarck to Gerlach, 8.4.1856
36. Lowe, C., *A Tale of a 'Times' Correspondent*, p. 83
37. QV, *Letters 1837-61*, Vol. III, pp. 203-4, Earl Granville to QV, 20.8.1856
38. Kurtz, H., *The Empress Eugénie*, p. 103
39. Martin, Sir T., Vol. IV, p. 96, Emperor Napoleon III to QV, 15.8.1857
40. Aronson, T., *Queen Victoria and the Bonapartes*, p. 89

Chapter 3

1. QV, *Letters 1837-61*, Vol. III, p. 253, QV to Earl of Clarendon, 25.10.1857
2. Greville, C. C. F., *The Greville Diary*, II, p. 583, 26.1.1858
3. Martin, Sir T., *The Life of HRH The Prince Consort*, Vol. IV, p. 176, A to V, 17.2.1858
4. QV, *Dearest Child*, p. 110, QV to V, 6.6.1858
5. Martin, Sir T., Vol. IV, p. 271, QVJ, 4.8.1858
6. *Ibid.* p. 272, A's diary
7. *Ibid.* p. 273
8. *Ibid.* p. 278, A to Duchess of Kent, 11.8.1858
9. QV, *Letters 1837-61*, Vol. III, p. 306, QV to L, 17.12.1858
10. *Ibid.* p. 314, QV to L, 2.2.1859
11. QV, *Dearest Child*, p. 201, QV to V, 13.7.1859
12. Albert, *Letters*, p. 338; Albert, *Prince Consort and his Brother*, pp. 196-7, A to Ernest, Duke of Saxe-Coburg Gotha, 18.6.1859
13. QV, *Dearest Child*, p. 285, QV to V, 24.11.1860
14. Corti, E. C. C., *The English Empress*, p. 65, A to Ernest Stockmar, 16.1.1861
15. *Ibid.* p. 66, A to V, 17.1.1861
16. Martin, Sir T., Vol. V, p. 306, King William I to A, 10.3.1861
17. *Ibid.* p. 19, F to A, 27.4.1861
18. Kollander, P. A., *Frederick III*, p. 15, A to F, 1.5.1861
19. Müller, F. L., *Our Fritz.*, p. 67, A to F, 1.5.1861
20. Martin, Sir T., Vol. V, p. 415
21. Weintraub, S., *Albert, Uncrowned King*, p. 430
22. QV, *Letters 1837-61*, Vol. III, pp. 473-4, QV to KL, 20.12.1861
23. Müller, F. L., p. 20, F to V, 17.3.1862
24. QV, *Letters 1862-85*, Vol. I, p. 45, QVJ, 17.9.1862
25. Müller, F. L., p. 85, F to V, 19.9.1862
26. von Poschinger, M., *Life of the Emperor Frederick*, p. 142
27. QV, *Dearest Mama*, p. 25, QV to V, 8.6.1863
28. Victoria, Consort of Frederick III, *Letters of the Empress Frederick*, p. 41; QV, *Letters 1837-61*, Vol. I, p. 87, V to QV, 8.6.1863
29. QV, *Dearest Mama*, pp. 262-3, QV to V, 5.9.1863
30. *Ibid.* p. 264, V to QV, 8.9.1863
31. *Ibid.* p. 319, QV to V, 9.4.1864
32. *Ibid.* p. 249
33. QV, *Letters 1862-85*, Vol. I, p. 356, Duke of Cambridge to QV, 7.7.1866
34. *Ibid.* QV to Duke of Cambridge, 8.7.1866
35. QV, *Your Dear Letter*, p. 98, QV to V, 24.9.1866
36. QV, *Letters 1862-85*, Vol. I, p. 440, QVJ, 4.7.1867
37. *Ibid.* p. 448, QV to Lord Stanley, 18.7.1867
38. Aronson, T., *Queen Victoria and the Bonapartes*, p. 125
39. Arthur, Sir G., *Concerning Queen Victoria and her Son*, p. 144

Chapter 4

1. QV, *Your Dear Letter*, p. 289, QV to V, 1.8.1870
2. Ridley, J., *Bertie*, p. 137, E to QV, 21.7.1870
3. Magnus, P., *King Edward the Seventh*, p. 110, E to QV, 20.7.1870
4. QV, *Letters 1862-85*, Vol. II, p. 89, QVJ, 28.11.1870
5. *Ibid.* p. 93, Vol. I, QVJ, 5.12.1870
6. Müller, F. L., *Our Fritz*, p. 25
7. QV, *Letters 1862-85*, Vol. II, p. 110, King William I to QV, 14.1.1871
8. Seward, D., *Eugénie*, p. 266
9. QV, *Letters 1862-85*, Vol. II, pp. 104-5, V to QV, 4.1.1871
10. *Ibid.* p. 106, Lord Granville to QV, 7.1.1871
11. *Ibid.* p. 106-7, HP to QV, 8.1.1871

12. *Ibid*. p. 124, QVJ, 27.3.1871
13. St Aubyn, G., *Edward VII*, p. 409
14. QV, *Letters 1862-85*, Vol. II, p. 155, QVJ, 31.7.1871
15. Seward, D., p. 268, quoting Paléologue, *Les Entretiens de l'Impératrice Eugénie*, p. 237
16. QV, *Letters 1862-85*, Vol. II, p. 236, QVJ, 9.1.1873
17. Lee, S., *King Edward VII*, Vol. I, p. 340
18. Magnus, P., p. 126, W. E. Gladstone to Lord Granville, 15.1.1873
19. QV, *Dearest Child*, p. 39, QV to V, 10.2.1858
20. Abrash, M., *Slavonic & East European Review*, QV to Tsar Alexander II in August 1871
21. Abrash, M., QV to Lord Granville, 19.7.1872 and 8.8.1872
22. Van der Kiste, J., *Romanovs 1818-1959*, p. 59, QVJ, 21.6.1873
23. Abrash, M., QV to HP, 7.6.1873
24. Buchanan, M., *Queen Victoria's Relations*, p. 115
25. QV, *Dearest Child*, p. 133, QV to V, 27.9.1858
26. *Punch*, 6.5.1874
27. QV, *Letters 1862-85*, Vol. II, p. 337, QVJ 13.5.1874
28. Van der Kiste, J., *Romanovs 1818-1959*, p. 68, QV to Tsar Alexander II, 20.5.1874
29. QV, *Darling Child*, p. 145, QV to V, 2.8.1874
30. Haslip, J., *The Lonely Empress*, p. 269
31. QV, *Darling Child*, p. 145, QV to V, 3.8.1874
32. Corti, E. C. C., *Elizabeth, Empress*, p. 210
33. QV, *Darling Child*, pp. 205-6, QV to V, 1.3.1876, pp. 175-6
34. Corti, E. C. C., *Elizabeth, Empress*, p. 222

Chapter 5

1. QV, *Letters 1862-85*, Vol. II, p. 473, Duke of Edinburgh to QV, 31.7.1876
2. Corti, E. C. C., *Downfall of Three Dynasties*, p. 242, Empress Marie to Prince Alexander of Hesse, 12.4.1878
3. *Ibid*. p. 243, Empress Marie to Prince Alexander of Hesse, 7.5.1878
4. Van der Kiste, J., *Windsor and Habsburg*, pp. 77-8, QV to E, 12.1.1878
5. *Ibid*. pp. 84-5, EE to QV, 22.2.1879
6. QV, *Darling Child*, p. 68, QV to V, 12.3.1880
7. Kurtz, H., *The Empress Eugénie*, p. 289
8. *Ibid*.
9. Dennison, M., *The Last Princess*, pp. 90-1
10. Kurtz, H., p. 289; Dennison, M., p. 91
11. Kurtz, H., p. 296
12. Seward, D., *Eugénie*, p. 280
13. Kurtz, H., p. 296, Prince Imperial to Duke of Cambridge, 21.2.1879
14. Aronson, T., *Queen Victoria and the Bonapartes*, p. 169
15. QV, *Letters 1862-85*, Vol. III, p. 27, QVJ, 19.6.1879
16. Duff, D., *The Shy Princess*, p. 89
17. Lee, S., *King Edward VII*, Vol. I, p. 341
18. Aronson, T., *Queen Victoria and the Bonapartes*, p. 183
19. Kurtz, H., p. 317
20. Seward, D., p. 266, quoting Filon, *Souvenirs sur L'Impératrice*, p. 255
21. Marie Louise, Princess, *My Memories of Six Reigns*, p. 148
22. Longford, E., *Victoria R.I.*, p. 344
23. QV, *Letters 1862-85*, Vol. III, p. 202, QVJ, 13.3.1881
24. QV, *Beloved Mama*, p. 97, QV to V, 16.3.1881
25. *The Times*, 14.3.1881
26. Vorres, I., *The Last Grand-Duchess*, p. 54
27. Massie, R. K., *Nicholas and Alexandra*, p. 25
28. QV, *Letters 1886-1901*, Vol. I, p. 179, QV to MS, 22.8.1886
29. *Ibid*. p. 196, Vol. I, QV to MS, 1.9.1886
30. QV, *Advice to a Grand-daughter*, p. 55, QV to VH, 21.9.1883
31. QV, *Beloved Mama*, p. 153, V to QV, 15.12.1883

Chapter 6

1. Müller, F. L., *Our Fritz*, p. 30
2. Victoria, Consort of Frederick III, *Letters of the Empress Frederick*, p. 207, V to QV, 11.8.1886
3. Müller, F. L., pp. 25-6
4. *Economist*, 23.6.1883; Müller, F. L., p. 82
5. Müller, F. L., p. 29
6. Victoria, Consort of Frederick III, *Letters of the Empress Frederick*, p. 239, V to QV, 3.6.1887
7. *Ibid.* pp. 210-11, V to QV, 17.3.1887
8. Stephanie of Belgium, Princess, *I was to be Empress*, p. 210
9. Aronson, T., *Grandmama of Europe*, p. 28
10. von Poschinger, M., *Life of the Emperor Frederick*, pp. 436-7, F to Professor Schellbach, 28.9.1887
11. Müller, F. L., p. 202
12. QV, *Beloved and Darling Child*, p. 64, QV to V, 10.3.1888
13. QV, *Letters 1886-1901*, Vol. I, p. 400, QVJ, 23.4.1888
14. *Ibid.* Vol. I, pp. 404-5, QVJ, 25.4.1888
15. QV, *Further Letters*, p. 268
16. QV, *Letters 1886-1901*, Vol. I, p. 417, QVJ, 15.6.1888
17. *Ibid.* Vol. I, p. 417, QV to William II, 15.6.1888
18. Reid, M., *Ask Sir James*, p. 101
19. Victoria, Consort of Frederick III, *Letters of the Empress Frederick*, p. 320, V to QV, 18.6.1888
20. Hough, R., *Louis and Victoria*, p. 143, VH to QV, 16.6.1888
21. *Ibid.* p. 144; QV, *Advice to a Grand-daughter*, p. 95, QV to VH, 4.7.1888
22. Röhl, J. C. G., *Wilhelm II: Kaiser's Personal Monarchy*, p. 30, W to QV, 6.7.1888
23. *Ibid.* p. 34, Memorandum by Herbert Bismarck, 26.7.1888
24. QV, *Beloved and Darling Child*, p. 72, QV to V, 15.6.1888; Corti, E. C. C., *English Empress*, p. 281
25. Van der Kiste, J., *Dearest Vicky, Darling Fritz*, p. 235, V to Lord Napier, 11.8.1888
26. Ridley, J., *Bertie*, p. 254, Arthur Ellis to Colonel Swaine, 12.9.1888
27. Magnus, P., *Kinf Edward the Seventh*, p. 209
28. QV, *Letters 1886-1901*, Vol. I, p. 441, QV to S, 15.10.1888
29. Victoria, Consort of Frederick III, *Letters of the Empress Frederick*, p. 346, V to QV, 29.9.1888
30. QV, *Letters 1886-1901*, I, p. 443, QV to S, 24.10.1888
31. Röhl, J. C. G., *Wilhelm II: Kaiser's Personal Monarchy*, p. 48, QV to Sir Theodore Martin, 4.11.1888
32. Listowel, J., *A Habsburg Tragedy*, p. 183, Crown Prince Rudolf to Crown Princess Stephanie, 12.9.1888
33. Cassels, L., *Clash of Generations*, p. 185, Crown Prince Rudolf to Crown Princess Stephanie, 12.9.1888
34. Röhl, J. C. G., & Sombart, N., *Kaiser Wilhelm II*, p. 33
35. Brook-Shepherd, G., *Royal Sunset*, p. 77, FJ to Katherine Schratt, 16.9.1888
36. Haslip, J., *The Lonely Empress*, p. 404
37. Ridley, J., *Bertie*, p. 259

Chapter 7

1. von Holstein, F., *The Holstein Papers*, II, p. 382
2. Pakula, H., *An Uncommon Woman*, p. 510, V to QV, 27.4.1889
3. QV, *Letters 1886-1901*, Vol. I, pp. 467-8, QV to Malet, 7.2.1889
4. Sinclair, A., *The Other Victoria*, p. 231, Leopold Swaine to HP, 8.3.1889
5. Röhl, J. C. G., *Wilhelm II: Kaiser's Personal Monarchy*, p. 90, E to QV, 8.2.1889
6. *Ibid.* p. 90, QV to S, 27.2.1889

7. *Ibid.* p. 91, S to QV, 9.3.1889
8. Pakula, H., p. 517, V to QV, 7.3.1889
9. QV, *Letters 1886-1901*, Vol. I, pp. 484-5, S to QV, 29.3.1889
10. Pakula, H., p. 517, E to Prince Christian, 10.4.1889
11. *Ibid.* p. 95, E to S, 16.4.1889
12. *Ibid.* p. 95, E to Prince Christian, 19.4.1889
13. *Ibid.* p. 97, HP to QV, 13.5.1889
14. Ridley, J., *Bertie*, p. 260, E to V, 15.5.1889
15. Röhl, J. C. G., *Wilhelm II: Kaiser's Personal Monarchy*, p. 98, W to QV, 28.5.1889
16. *Ibid.* p. 99, V to QV, 3.6.1889
17. Magnus, P., *King Edward the Seventh*, p. 213, E to V, 8.6.1889
18. Röhl, J. C. G., *Kaiser and his Court*, p. 21; Röhl, J. C. G., Warren, M., and Hunt, D., *Purple Secret*, p. 223
19. QV, *Letters 1886-1901*, Vol. I, p. 504, W to Sir Edward Malet, 14.6.1889
20. Röhl, J. C. G., *Wilhelm II: Kaiser's Personal Monarchy*, p. 641, Duchess of Edinburgh to Princess Charlotte, probably July 1889
21. Kohut, T. A., *Wilhelm II and the Germans*, p. 202
22. Magnus, P., p. 228
23. Mallet, M., *Life with Queen Victoria*, p. 52, 21.4.1891
24. Ponsonby, A., *Henry Ponsonby, Queen Victoria's Private Secretary*, p. 297, HP to Lady Ponsonby, 17.4.1892
25. Carter, M., *The Three Emperors*, p. 160, QV to HP, 15.6.1892
26. Magnus, P., p. 240, E to W.E. Gladstone, 5.8.1892
27. von Eckardstein, H., *Ten Years at the Court of St James*, p. 45
28. St Aubyn, G., *Edward VII, Prince and King*, p. 284
29. von Eckardstein, H., p. 56
30. *Ibid.* p. 55
31. Bartone, C. M., *Royal Pains*, p. 20
32. Carter, M., pp. 174-5
33. Nicholas II, Tsar, *Secret Letters*, p. 71, N to Empress Marie, 24.6.1893 (OS)
34. Carter. M., p. 132, N's diary, 20.6.1893 (OS)
35. QV, *Letters 1886-1901*, Vol. II, p. 269, QVJ, 1.7.1893
36. Carter, M., p. 133, N's diary, 19.6.1893 (OS)
37. QV, *Advice to a Grand-daughter*, p. 110, QV to VH, 29.12.1890
38. Pope-Hennessy, J., *Queen Mary, 1867-1953*, p. 196, QV to V, 7.5.90
39. QV, *Letters 1886-1901*, Vol. II, p. 395, QVJ, 20.4.1894
40. Corti, E. C. C., *English Empress*, p. 348, QV to V, 22.7.1894
41. Magnus, P., p. 246, E to Duke of York, 1.11.1894
42. QV, *Letters 1886-1901*, Vol. II, p. 438, QVJ, 1.11.1894
43. Duff, D., *Hessian Tapestry*, p. 248
44. Maylunas, A., & Mironenko, S., *A Lifelong Passion*, N to QV, 30.10.1894 (OS)
45. Vorres, I., *The Last Grand-Duchess*, p. 68
46. St Aubyn, G., *Edward VII*, p. 299
47. Magnus, P., p. 248
48. St Aubyn, G., *Edward VII*, p. 297, E to Viscount Knollys, 9.11.1894
49. QV, *Beloved and Darling Child*, p. 173, QV to V, 25.11.1894
50. Carter, M., p. 143, Duke of York to QV, 28.11.1894
51. Marie, Queen of Roumania, *The Story of My Life*, Vol. I, p. 68
52. Carter, M., p. 143, E to QV, 28.11.1894

Chapter 8

1. Magnus, P., *King Edward the Seventh*, p. 247
2. Carter, M., *The Three Emperors*, pp. 178-9, QV to N, 15.5.1895
3. *Ibid.* p. 179
4. QV, *Letters 1886-1901*, Vol. III, p. 39, QVJ, 6.4.1896
5. Bennett, D., *Vicky*, p. 271n
6. Nicholas II, Tsar, *Secret Letters*, pp. 119-20, N to Empress Marie, 14.10.1896

7. Roberts, A., *Salisbury*, p. 643
8. Interview with Kay Evans, BBC Radio 4, *The Listener*, 20.11.1975
9. QV, *Letters 1886-1901*, Vol. III, pp. 343-4, QV to N, 1.3.1899 [draft]
10. Lee, S., *King Edward VII*, Vol. I, p. 692
11. McLean, R., *Royalty and Diplomacy in Europe, 1890-1914*, pp. 141-2
12. Duff, D., *Hessian Tapestry*, pp. 249-50
13. QV, *Letters 1886-1901*, Vol. III, p. 150, V to QV, 18.4.1897
14. QV, *Beloved and Darling Child*, p. 203, QV to V, 24.4.1897
15. QV, *Letters 1886-1901*, Vol. III, p. 127, QV to Bigge, 30.1.1897
16. Cecil, L., *Wilhelm II, 1900-1941*, p. 77, W to QV, 10.6.1897
17. Aronson, T., *Queen Victoria and the Bonapartes*, p. 222
18. Kurtz, H., *The Empress Eugénie*, p. 336
19. Corti, E. C. C., *Elizabeth, Empress*, p. 355
20. Marek, G. R., *The Eagles Die*, p. 365
21. QV, *Letters 1886-1901*, Vol. III, p. 145, QVJ, 17.3.1897
22. Van der Kiste, J., *Windsor and Habsburg*, p. 115, FJ to QV, 17.9.1898
23. QV, *Letters 1886-1901*, Vol. III, QVJ, p. 336, 27.1.1899
24. *Ibid.* III, pp. 375-8, W to QV, 27.5.1899
25. *Ibid.* III, p. 378, QV to W, 12.6.1899
26. von Bülow, Prince B., *Memoirs*, II, p. 305
27. QV, *Letters 1886-1901*, Vol. III, p. 421, QVJ, 21.11.1899
28. Pakula, H., *An Uncommon Woman*, p. 580, QV to V, 25.11.1899
29. Reid, M., *Ask Sir James*, p. 203
30. Aston, Sir G., *HRH The Duke of Connaught and Strathearn*, p. 223
31. Rennell, T., *Last Days of Glory*, p. 92
32. Röhl, J. C. G., *Wilhelm II: Into the Abyss...*, p. 14, E to W, 15.2.1901
33. Palmer, A., *The Kaiser*, p. 98
34. Magnus, P., p. 272, E to V, 7.2.1901
35. Seward, D., *Eugénie*, p. 288
36. Kurtz, H., p. 346
37. Lee, S., Vol. II, p. 11
38. Van der Kiste, J., *Kaiser Wilhelm II*, p. 111
39. Balfour, M., *The Kaiser and his Times, with an afterword*, p. 355

Bibliography

Books

Albert, Prince Consort, (ed.) Jagow, Dr K., *Letters of the Prince Consort, 1831-1861* (John Murray, 1938); (ed.) Bolitho, H., *The Prince Consort and his Brother: Two Hundred New Letters* (Cobden-Sanderson, 1933)

Anon., *The Empress Frederick: A Memoir* (James Nisbet, 1913)

Aronson, T., *Grandmama of Europe: The Crowned Descendants of Queen Victoria* (Cassell, 1973); *The Kaisers* (Cassell, 1971); *Queen Victoria and the Bonapartes* (Cassell, 1972)

Arthur, Sir G., *Concerning Queen Victoria and her Son* (Robert Hale, 1943)

Aston, Sir G., *HRH The Duke of Connaught and Strathearn: A Life and Intimate Study* (Harrap, 1929)

Balfour, M., *The Kaiser and his Times, with an afterword* (Penguin, 1975)

Barkeley, R., *The Empress Frederick: Daughter of Queen Victoria* (Macmillan, 1956)

Bennett, D., *Vicky: Princess Royal of Great Britain and German Empress* (Collins Harvill, 1971)

Brook-Shepherd, G., *Royal Sunset: The Dynasties of Europe and the Great War* (Weidenfeld & Nicolson, 1987); *Uncle of Europe: The Social and Diplomatic Life of Edward VII* (Cassell, 1975)

Buchanan, M., *Queen Victoria's Relations* (Cassell, 1954)

Carter, M., *The Three Emperors: Three Cousins, Three Empires and the Road to World War One* (Fig Tree, 2009)

Cassels, L., *Clash of Generations: A Habsburg Family Drama in the Nineteenth Century* (John Murray, 1973)

Cecil, A., *Queen Victoria and her Prime Ministers* (Eyre & Spottiswoode, 1953)

Cecil, L., *Wilhelm II, Prince and Emperor, 1859-1900* (University of North Carolina Press, 1989); *Wilhelm II, Emperor and Exile, 1900-1941* (University of North Carolina Press, 1996)

Clay, C., *King, Kaiser, Tsar: Three Royal Cousins who Led the World to War* (John Murray, 2006)

Connell, B., *Regina v. Palmerston: The Correspondence between Queen Victoria and her Foreign and Prime Minister, 1837-1865* (Evans Bros, 1962)

Corti, E. C. C., *The English Empress: A Study in the Relations between Queen Victoria and her Eldest Daughter, Empress Frederick of Germany* (Cassell, 1957);

The Downfall of Three Dynasties (Thornton Butterworth, 1934); *Elizabeth, Empress of Austria* (Thornton Butterworth, 1936)

Dennison, M., *The Last Princess: The Devoted Life of Queen Victoria's Youngest Daughter* (Weidenfeld & Nicolson, 2007)

Derby, Earl of, (ed.) Vincent, J., *The Derby Diaries, 1869-1878: A Selection from the Diaries of Edward Henry Stanley, 15th Earl of Derby, between September 1869 and March 1878* (Royal Historical Society, 1994)

Duff, D., *Eugénie and Napoleon III* (Collins, 1978); *Hessian Tapestry* (Frederick Muller, 1967); *The Shy Princess: The Life of Her Royal Highness Princess Beatrice, the Youngest Daughter and Constant Companion of Queen Victoria* (Evans Bros, 1958); *Victoria Travels: Journeys of Queen Victoria between 1830 and 1900, with Extracts from her Journal* (Frederick Muller, 1970)

Eyck, F., *The Prince Consort: A Political Biography* (Chatto & Windus, 1959)

Fulford, R., *The Prince Consort* (Macmillan, 1949)

Gelardi, J., *Born to Rule: Granddaughters of Victoria, Queens of Europe* (Headline, 2005)

Greville, C. C. F., (ed.) Wilson, P. W., *The Greville Diary, Including Passages Hitherto Withheld from Publication*, Vol. 1-2 (Heinemann, 1927)

Guest, I., *Napoleon III in England* (British General & Technical Press, 1952)

Haslip, J., *The Lonely Empress: A Biography of Elizabeth of Austria* (Weidenfeld & Nicolson, 1965)

Hibbert, C., *Queen Victoria: A Personal History* (HarperCollins, 2000)

Hough, R., *Louis and Victoria: The First Mountbattens* (Hutchinson, 1974)

Kohut, T. A., *Wilhelm II and the Germans: A Study in Leadership* (Oxford University Press, 1991)

Kollander, P. A., *Frederick III: Germany's Liberal Emperor* (Greenwood, 1995)

Kurtz, H., *The Empress Eugénie, 1826-1920* (Hamish Hamilton, 1964)

Lee, S., *King Edward VII*, Vols 1-2 (Macmillan, 1925-7)

Listowel, J., *A Habsburg Tragedy: Crown Prince Rudolf* (Ascent, 1978)

Longford, E., *Victoria R.I.* (Weidenfeld & Nicolson, 1964)

Lowe, C., *The Tale of a 'Times' Correspondent (Berlin, 1878-1891)* (Hutchinson, 1927)

Magnus, P., *King Edward the Seventh* (John Murray, 1964)

Mallet, M., *Life with Queen Victoria: Marie Mallet's Letters from Court* (John Murray, 1968)

Marek, G. R., *The Eagles Die: Franz Joseph, Elizabeth and their Austria* (Hart Davis, MacGibbon, 1975)

Marie Louise, Princess, *My Memories of Six Reigns* (Evans Bros, 1956)

Marie, Queen of Roumania, *The Story of My Life*, Vols 1-3 (Cassell, 1934-5)

Martin, Sir T., *The Life of HRH The Prince Consort*, Vols 1-5 (Smith, Elder, 1874-80)

Massie, R. K., *Dreadnought: Britain, Germany, and the Coming of the Great War* (Jonathan Cape, 1992); *Nicholas and Alexandra* (Victor Gollancz, 1968)

Maylunas, A., and Mironenko, S., *A Lifelong Passion: Nicolas and Alexandra, Their Own Story* (Weidenfeld & Nicolson, 1996)

McLean, R., *Royalty and Diplomacy in Europe, 1890-1914* (Cambridge University Press, 2001)

Müller, F. L., *Our Fritz: Emperor Frederick III and the Political Culture of Imperial Germany* (Harvard University Press, 2011)

Nicholas II, Tsar, (ed.) Bing, E. J., *The Secret Letters of the Last Tsar: Being The Confidential Correspondence between Nicholas II, and his Mother, Dowager Empress Maria Feodorovna* (Longmans, Green, 1938)

Noel, G., *Princess Alice, Queen Victoria's Forgotten Daughter* (Constable, 1974)

Packard, J. M., *Farewell in Splendour: The Death of Queen Victoria and her Age*

(Sutton, 2000); *Victoria's Daughters* (Sutton, 1999)

Pakula, H., *An Uncommon Woman: The Empress Frederick* (Weidenfeld & Nicolson, 1996)

Palmer, A., *The Kaiser: Warlord of the Second Reich* (Weidenfeld & Nicolson, 1978)

Ponsonby, A., *Henry Ponsonby, Queen Victoria's Private Secretary: His Life from his Letters* (Macmillan, 1942)

Pope-Hennessy, J., *Queen Mary, 1867-1953* (Allen & Unwin, 1959)

Reid, M., *Ask Sir James: Sir James Reid, Personal Physician to Queen Victoria and Physician-in-Ordinary to Three Monarchs* (Hodder & Stoughton, 1987)

Rennell, T., *Last Days of Glory: The Death of Queen Victoria* (Viking, 2000)

Ridley, J., *Bertie: A life of Edward VII* (Chatto & Windus, 2012)

Roberts, A., *Salisbury: Victorian Titan* (Weidenfeld & Nicolson, 1999)

Roberts, D., *Two Royal Lives: Gleanings from Berlin and from the Lives of Their Imperial Highnesses the Crown Prince and Princess of Germany* (T. Fisher Unwin, 1888)

Röhl, J. C. G., and Sombart, N., (ed.), *Kaiser Wilhelm II: New Interpretations* (Cambridge University Press, 1983)

Röhl, J. C. G., *The Kaiser and his Court: Wilhelm II and the Government of Germany* (Cambridge University Press, 1994); *Young Wilhelm: The Kaiser's Early Life, 1859-1888* (Cambridge University Press, 1998); *Wilhelm II: The Kaiser's Personal Monarchy, 1888-1900* (Cambridge University Press, 2004); *Wilhelm II: Into the Abyss of War and Exile, 1900-1941* (Cambridge University Press, 2014)

Röhl, J. C. G., Warren, M., and Hunt, D., *Purple Secret: Genes, 'Madness' and the Royal Houses of Europe* (Bantam, 1998)

Seward, D., *Eugénie, the Empress and her Empire* (Sutton, 2004)

Sinclair, A., *The Other Victoria: The Princess Royal and the Great Game of Europe* (Weidenfeld & Nicolson, 1981)

St Aubyn, G., *Queen Victoria: A Portrait* (Sinclair-Stevenson, 1991); *Edward VII, Prince and King* (Collins, 1979)

Stephanie of Belgium, Princess, *I was to be Empress* (Ivor Nicholson & Watson, 1937)

Van der Kiste, J., *Alfred: Queen Victoria's Second Son* (Fonthill, 2013); *Dearest Vicky, Darling Fritz: Queen Victoria's Daughter and the German Emperor* (Sutton, 2001); *Emperor Francis Joseph: Life, Death and the Fall of the Habsburg Empire* (Sutton, 2005); *Frederick III: German Emperor 1888* (Sutton, 1981) *Kaiser Wilhelm II: Germany's Last Emperor* (Sutton, 1999); *The Romanovs, 1818-1959: Tsar Alexander II of Russia and his Family* (Sutton, 1998); *Sons, Servants and Statesmen: The Men in Queen Victoria's Life* (Sutton, 2006); *Windsor and Habsburg: The British and Austrian Reigning Houses, 1848-1918* (Sutton, 1987)

Victoria, Consort of Frederick III, German Emperor, (ed.) Lee, A. G., *The Empress Frederick Writes to Sophie* (Faber, 1955); (ed.) Sir Frederick Ponsonby, *Letters of the Empress Frederick* (Macmillan, 1928)

Victoria, Queen, (ed.) Viscount Esher, *The Girlhood of Queen Victoria: A Selection from Her Majesty's Diaries Between the Years 1832 and 1840*, Vol. 1-2 (John Murray, 1912); (ed.) Benson, A. C., and & Viscount Esher, *The Letters of Queen Victoria: A Selection from Her Majesty's Correspondence between the years 1837 and 1861*, Vol. 1-3 (John Murray, 1907); (ed.) Buckle, G. E., *The Letters of Queen Victoria, 2nd Series: A Selection from Her Majesty's Correspondence and Journal between the years 1862 and 1885*, Vol. 1-3 (John Murray, 1926-8); (ed.) Buckle, G. E., *The Letters of Queen Victoria, 3rd Series: A Selection from Her Majesty's Correspondence and Journal between the years 1886 and 1901*, Vol. 1-3 (John Murray, 1930-2); (ed.) Bolitho, H., *Further Letters of Queen Victoria: From the Archives of the House of Brandenburg-Prussia* (Thornton Butterworth, 1938);

(ed.) Fulford, R., *Dearest Child: Letters between Queen Victoria and the Princess Royal, 1858-1861* (Evans Bros, 1964); (ed.) Fulford, R., *Dearest Mama: Private Correspondence of Queen Victoria and the Crown Princess of Prussia, 1861-1864* (Evans Bros, 1968); (ed.) Fulford, R., *Your Dear Letter: Private Correspondence of Queen Victoria and the Crown Princess of Prussia, 1865-1871* (Evans Bros, 1971); (ed.) Fulford, R., *Darling Child: Private Correspondence of Queen Victoria and the Crown Princess of Prussia, 1871-1878* (Evans Bros, 1976); (ed.) Fulford, R., *Beloved Mama: Private Correspondence of Queen Victoria and the German Crown Princess of Prussia, 1878-1885* (Evans Bros, 1981); (ed.) Ramm, A., *Beloved and Darling Child: Last Letters between Queen Victoria and her Eldest Daughter, 1886-1901* (Sutton, 1990); (ed.) Bentley, N., *Leaves from a Journal: A Record of the Visit of the Emperor and Empress of the French to the Queen and of the Visit of the Queen and H.R.H. The Prince Consort to the Emperor of the French 1855* (Andre Deutsch, 1961);(ed.) Hough, R., *Advice to a Grand-daughter: Letters from Queen Victoria to Princess Victoria of Hesse* (Heinemann, 1975)

Villiers, G., *A Vanished Victorian: Being the Life of George Villiers, Fourth Earl of Clarendon, 1800-1870* (Eyre & Spottiswoode, 1938)

von Bülow, Prince B., *Memoirs*, Vols 1-4 (Putnam, 1931)

von Eckardstein, Baron H., *Ten Years at the Court of St James, 1895-1905* (Thornton Butterworth, 1921)

von Holstein, F., (ed.) Rich, N., and Fisher, M. H., *The Holstein Papers: The Memoirs, Diaries and Correspondence of Friedrich von Holstein*, Vols 1-4 (Cambridge University Press, 1955-63)

von Poschinger, M., *Life of the Emperor Frederick* (Harper, 1901)

Vorres, I., *The Last Grand-Duchess: Her Imperial Highness Grand-Duchess Olga Alexandrovna* (Hutchinson, 1964)

Vovk, J. C., *Imperial Requiem: Four Royal Women and the Fall of the Age of Empires* (Bloomington, Universe, 2012)

Weintraub, S., *Albert, Uncrowned King* (John Murray, 1997); *Victoria: Biography of a Queen* (Unwin Hyman, 1987)

William II, Ex-Emperor, *My Early Life* (Methuen, 1926)

Wilson, A. N., *Victoria: A Life* (Atlantic, 2014)

Woodham-Smith, C., *Queen Victoria: Her Life and Times, Vol. 1, 1819-1861* (Hamish Hamilton, 1972)

Articles and Theses

Abrash, M., 'A Curious Royal Romance: The Queen's Son [Alfred, Duke of Edinburgh] and the Tsar's Daughter [Grand Duchess Marie Alexandrovna]' in *Slavonic & East European Review*, Vol. 47, No. 109, July 1969

Bartone, C. M., *Royal Pains: Wilhelm II, Edward VII, and Anglo-German Relations, 1888-1910* (University of Akron, August 2012). Retrieved from etd.ohiolink.edu/!etd.send_file?accession=akron1341938971&disposition=inline, accessed February 2016

Journals

Economist
Punch
The Times
The Listener

Index